SEMANTIC EXTERNALISM

Semantic externalism is the view that the meanings of referring terms, and the contents of beliefs that are expressed by those terms, are not fully determined by factors internal to the speaker but are instead bound up with the environment.

The debate about semantic externalism is one of the most important but difficult topics in philosophy of mind and language, and has consequences for our understanding of the role of social institutions and the physical environment in constituting language and the mind. In this long-needed book, Jesper Kallestrup provides an invaluable map of the problem. Beginning with a thorough introduction to the theories of descriptivism and referentialism and the work of Frege and Kripke, Kallestrup moves on to analyse Putnam's Twin Earth argument, Burge's arthritis argument and Davidson's Swampman argument. He also discusses how semantic externalism is at the heart of important topics such as indexical thoughts, epistemological scepticism, self-knowledge, and mental causation.

Including chapter summaries, a glossary of terms, and an annotated guide to further reading, *Semantic Externalism* is an ideal guide for students studying philosophy of language and philosophy of mind.

Jesper Kallestrup is Senior Lecturer in Philosophy at the University of Edinburgh, Scotland. He is the editor (with Jakob Hohwy) of *Being Reduced: New Essays on Explanation and Causation in the Special Sciences* (2008), and he has published articles in, among others, *Australasian Journal of Philosophy, Analysis, Philosophical Studies, Synthese, American Philosophical Quarterly* and *Philosophy and Phenomenological Research*.

NEW PROBLEMS OF PHILOSOPHY

Series Editor: José Luis Bermúdez

The *New Problems of Philosophy* series provides accessible and engaging surveys of the most important problems in contemporary philosophy. Each book examines a topic or theme that has either emerged on the philosophical landscape in recent years, or a longstanding problem refreshed in light of recent work in philosophy and related disciplines. Clearly explaining the nature of the problem at hand and assessing attempts to answer it, books in the series are excellent starting-points for undergraduate and graduate students wishing to study a single topic in depth. They will also be essential reading for professional philosophers. Additional features include chapter summaries, further reading and a glossary of technical terms.

Also available:

Analyticity, Cory Juhl and Eric Loomis
Fiction and Fictionalism, Mark Sainsbury
Physicalism, Daniel Stoljar
Noncognitivism in Ethics, Mark Schroeder
Moral Epistemology, Aaron Zimmerman
Embodied Cognition, Lawrence Shapiro
Consequentialism, Julia Driver
Perception, Adam Pautz
Self-Knowledge, Brie Gertler

Forthcoming:

Representational Artifacts, John Kulvicki
Imagination, Fabian Dorsch
Egalitarianism, Iwao Hirose
Emergence, Patrick McGivern
Disjunctivism, Matthew Soteriou

SEMANTIC EXTERNALISM

Jesper Kallestrup

Routledge
Taylor & Francis Group

LONDON AND NEW YORK

First published 2012
by Routledge
2 Park Square, Milton Park, Abingdon, Oxon, OX14 4RN

Simultaneously published in the USA and Canada by Routledge
711 Third Avenue, New York, NY 10017

Routledge is an imprint of the Taylor & Francis Group, an informa business

© 2012 Jesper Kallestrup

British Library Cataloguing in Publication Data
A catalogue record for this book is available from the British Library

Library of Congress Cataloging in Publication Data
Kallestrup, Jesper.
Semantic externalism / by Jesper Kallestrup.
p. cm. -- (New problems of philosophy)
Includes bibliographical references (p.) and index.
1. Semantics (Philosophy) 2. Language and languages--Philosophy.
3. Externalism (Philosophy of mind) 4. Description (Philosophy)
5. Reference (Philosophy) I. Title.
B840.K35 2011
121'.68--dc22
2011014981

ISBN: 978-0-415-44996-0 (hbk)
ISBN: 978-0-415-44997-7 (pbk)
ISBN: 978-0-203-83002-4 (ebk)

Typeset in Joanna and Scala Sans
by Taylor & Francis Books

MIX
Paper from
responsible sources
FSC® C004839
www.fsc.org

Printed and bound in Great Britain by the MPG Books Group

In memory of Iver Kallestrup

CONTENTS

Acknowledgements   ix

Introduction   1

Chapter 1 Descriptivism   10
1.1 Descriptivism expounded   10
1.2 The identity argument   15
1.3 Puzzles about belief   21
1.4 Sense, linguistic meaning and communication   26
Chapter summary   32
Annotated further reading   34

Chapter 2 Referentialism   35
2.1 Rigidity and direct reference   35
2.2 Kripke's modal argument   40
2.3 Rigidification   45
2.4 Referentialist belief ascriptions   51
Chapter summary   56
Annotated further reading   57

Chapter 3 From language to thought   58
3.1 Putnam's Twin Earth argument   58
3.2 Internalist rejoinders to the Twin Earth argument   64
3.3 Burge's arthritis argument   69
3.4 Internalist rejoinders to the arthritis argument   74
3.5 Davidson's Swampman argument   79
3.6 Externalist rejoinders to the Swampman argument   83

Chapter summary   89
Annotated further reading   91

Chapter 4 Varieties of narrow and wide content   **93**
4.1 Object-dependent thoughts   93
4.2 Indexicality and egocentric thoughts   100
4.3 Two-factor theories of content   105
4.4 Natural kind concepts revisited   112
4.5 The metaphysics of content properties   117
Chapter summary   122
Annotated further reading   124

Chapter 5 Self-knowledge   **125**
5.1 Introducing self-knowledge   125
5.2 Entitlement to self-knowledge   132
5.3 Incompatibilism   139
5.4 Slow switching   143
5.5 Reasoning   149
Chapter summary   154
Annotated further reading   156

Chapter 6 Scepticism   **157**
6.1 Scepticism about self-knowledge   157
6.2 External world scepticism   162
6.3 Putnam's proof   166
6.4 McKinsey's recipe   173
Chapter summary   183
Annotated further reading   184

Chapter 7 Mental causation   **185**
7.1 The varieties of mental causation   185
7.2 The modal argument for narrow content   190
7.3 The doppelgänger challenge   197
7.4 The explanatory value of wide content   204
Chapter summary   210
Annotated further reading   211

Glossary   **213**
Notes   **224**
Bibliography   **249**
Index   **265**

ACKNOWLEDGEMENTS

Semantic externalism has always fascinated me, not least because of the intriguing ways in which this thesis in philosophy of mind and language intersects with hotly debated topics in epistemology and metaphysics. My interest in this thesis and cognate topics began during my doctoral studies at the University of St Andrews where I learned a huge amount from Crispin Wright, Sarah Sawyer, Stephen Read and members of the Southgait Group comprising Lars Binderup, Patrick Greenough, Lars Bo Gundersen, Patrice Philie, Duncan Pritchard and Sven Rosenkranz. During a study period at the Australian National University I benefited greatly from the ideas of Frank Jackson and Philip Pettit. More recently, I am grateful to my colleagues and postgraduate students at the University of Edinburgh, especially Andy Clark, Duncan Pritchard, Evan Butts, Joey Pollock and Sam Baird for stimulating discussion. Parts of the material have been presented at various workshops and research seminars at which I received valuable comments from numerous people including Kati Farkas, Mikkel Gerken, Sandy Goldberg, Klemens Kappel, Nikolaj Jang Pedersen and Åsa Wikforss. Tim Crane kindly invited me to spend some time at the Institute of Philosophy, University of London, where a research grant from the British Academy enabled me to develop the material in this book. During my visit at the Institute of Philosophy I recall stimulating conversations with

Jonathan Berg, Tim Crane, Gabriel Segal and Catherine Wearing. I should also like to thank two anonymous referees for extremely helpful feedback on an earlier draft. Finally, but not least, Tony Bruce, Adam Johnson, Jim Thomas and Andrew Watts on the Routledge team provided tremendous support and encouragement throughout.

INTRODUCTION

To see that Jane's jumper is red and to believe that apples are wholesome are both mental states. These two states are also representational. To say that a mental state is representational is to say that it serves the function of being about something in the world, or that it takes the world to be a certain way. Perceptions and beliefs are representational states. To be in such states is to represent the world as being a certain way. The way a state represents the world as being is its representational content. In particular, being in a belief state involves being in a state that can be true or false, depending on whether the world is as the belief represents it as being. Some mental states also have phenomenal characters. To say that a perceptual experience has a phenomenal character is to say that there is something it is like for the subject who undergoes that experience. Think of the qualitative feel associated with a visual experience of a red jumper. While some philosophers take phenomenal character to be fully determined by the representational content of the perceptual experience in question, others maintain that phenomenal character cannot be exhaustively understood in terms of the representational content of that experience. That is not a dispute we shall probe into here. In fact, we shall henceforth focus on beliefs and other so-called propositional attitudes. To say that Anna believes that apples are wholesome is to say that Anna bears the attitude of belief towards the proposition that apples are wholesome. Propositions are abstract entities to which one can be belief related. They are composed of concepts and capable of being true or false. The kind of representational content that shall occupy us is propositional content. Unless explicitly stated otherwise, we shall use 'meaning' in the sense of propositional content. Some philosophers maintain that some representational content is non-conceptual. They believe that we can represent the world in ways that outstrip our conceptual resources. Anna's visual experience of shade red_{29} is phenomenally different from that of red_{31} but she has no such colour concepts. Hence, the representational content of her visual experience is more fine-grained than its propositional content. Others contend that we can fully specify the way Anna represents the world just by using concepts that she possesses, e.g. the propositional content of her experience is that that shade (demonstrating red_{29}) is thus and so. Again that is not a controversy we shall delve into in the following.

The nature of meaning, understood as propositional content, is a multifaceted, vexed issue. This book introduces and assesses what philosophers call the problem of semantic externalism. Given that most of the literature on the subject concerns the debate between semantic externalists and semantic internalists, much of the book will be taken up with examining the various arguments and positions at stake in that debate. These two camps disagree on how meaning is individuated. While those in the latter camp say that meaning is fully determined by features that are internal to the speaker, those in the former say that meaning is determined at least in part by features that are external to the speaker. Here is an example. Suppose the man fumbling for his car keys in the bush in front of you is John. While pointing at the bush you utter the sentence 'that man is drunk'. What you have said is that John is drunk. Now suppose instead that John's identical twin James is in the bush. As far as you know everything else is the same, indeed apart from the fact that the seemingly identical individuals John and James are in fact distinct, everything else is the same. While pointing at the bush you utter the same sentence. What you have said is now that James is drunk. You are internally the same in the two situations. For instance, the visual experience you have in the first situation is indistinguishable from the one you have in the second situation. The proposition you expressed by those two utterances cannot therefore be a function of what is in your head, but must rather depend on what the external world is like. The upshot is that meaning is determined at least in part by external factors possibly beyond speakers' ken. Or so semantic externalists contend. That is not terribly controversial in the case of demonstratives such as 'that' or indexical expressions such as 'I'. The mere fact that John and James are distinct individuals entails that what John expresses when he utters 'I feel elated' is different from what James expresses when he utters 'I feel elated'. Still, there also seems to be an important sense in which John and James spoke alike. After all, each of them feels elated. Similarly, there is some significant sense in which I said the same thing in the two situations, i.e. that the demonstratively identified individual is drunk. Semantic internalists intend to pinpoint the claim that meaning, or at least an aspect thereof, depends solely on what speakers are like internally, and so is insensitive to the relevant kinds of variation in the external environment. By contrast, semantic externalists are keen to stress that the meaning of natural kind terms, e.g. 'tiger' or 'water', and even social kind terms, e.g. 'carburettor' or 'sofa', are also externally individuated. The externalist strategy is, again, to let two internally identical speakers inhabit two environments identical apart from some imperceptible microphysical or sociolinguistic difference. Unbeknownst to them, their usage of these terms will thus pick out different natural or social kinds, and so what they express will be externally fixed in different ways, possibly behind their backs. But of course if what these speakers believe is determined by the propositions expressed by the sentences they use to express their beliefs, then not only is linguistic meaning externally individuated, so also are the contents of their beliefs. Semantic externalists conclude that belief content is determined externally, and therefore also the belief states themselves, provided that such states are individuated by their contents. Semantic internalists typically respond by pointing out that since the relevant environments are identical with respect to all manifest or superficial features, the best sense is made of these speakers' linguistic and physical behaviour if they are instead attributed beliefs with some common content. The contents of speakers' beliefs represent how they take the world to be, and internally identical speakers who are embedded in environments which for all they know are identical, take the world to be the same way. Importantly, semantic internalists submit that such speakers behave alike for the purposes of psychological explanation because their conceptions of how things are, are the same.

Semantic externalism gained prominence in the 1970s and 1980s, in part as a result of Saul Kripke and Hilary Putnam's revolutionary attack on the descriptive theory of reference, or simply descriptivism, in the philosophy of language. Going back to Gottlob Frege, this view says that there are sets of descriptive properties associated by competent speakers with singular and general terms which both give those terms their meaning and determine their reference. Instead these philosophers advocated the direct reference theory, or simply referentialism, according to which such terms pick out their referents directly, i.e. unmediated by any descriptive properties. On this view, the meaning of such terms is exhausted by their referents, but what determines their reference is the baptismal way in which they were initially introduced into the language and then passed on through a causal-historical chain. While descriptivism and semantic internalism, and referentialism and semantic externalism, are distinct doctrines, they nevertheless in some versions often go hand in hand. For instance, referentialism entails a version of semantic externalism. If the meaning of a referring term is given by the external object to which it refers, then such meaning is obviously externally individuated. But the converse is false. Some semantic externalists hold that the meaning of a referring term consists in a possibly descriptive way of thinking of its referent which would not exist had that term lacked a referent. To properly appreciate the case for semantic externalism as a view in philosophy of mind or thought, we need to examine the objections levelled against descriptivism as a view in philosophy of language. Similarly, in order to deepen understanding of the recent counter-revolution, led by David Lewis, Frank Jackson, David Chalmers and others, aiming to revive some brand of semantic internalism, we need to determine whether these philosophers are right that the referentialist objections can be met in a satisfactory way. The first two chapters are devoted to these issues.

Chapter 1 begins by presenting descriptivism as the view that the meaning of singular and general terms consists in descriptive content which is both what determines their reference, and is what competent speakers know when they understand them. For instance, the meaning of 'Aristotle' could be given by the definite description 'the teacher of Alexander the Great', and the meaning of 'water' could be given by 'the clear, potable liquid that fills the oceans, falls from the sky, and is called "water"'. This view has been defended by John Searle, Michael Dummett, Frank Jackson, David Lewis and others, but can be traced back to Frege and Bertrand Russell. Then Frege's case for the existence of what he called 'sense' as distinct from reference is laid out. Here sense is taken to be a mode of presentation, or a way of thinking, of the referent. This famous identity argument in its strengthened version trades on intuitions about the behaviour of referring terms in propositional attitude contexts. A propositional attitude is roughly an individual bearing an attitude towards a proposition, e.g. John believes that Mary is off work. The argument shows that sense must be what is cognitively significant to speakers: if an individual can take different cognitive attitudes towards two propositions, then they differ in sense. Finally, deploying a well-known example of Frege's, the question of whether sense might constitute a notion of linguistic meaning shared across a speech community is discussed. In this context, the role that knowledge of meaning plays in communication is examined. The pressing worry is that if sense varies hugely from speaker to speaker, then intersubjective transmission of knowledge in communication is jeopardized.

Chapter 2 starts out by introducing direct reference and rigidity, as these notions are key to understanding referentialism. Thus rigidity is the idea that a term picks out the same object at all possible worlds. A possible world is a way our world might have been. On this view, referring terms are rigid, because they are directly referential. Sentences containing referring terms thus express singular propositions, which have as their constituents the referents of those terms. Kripke's modal argument against descriptivism is then presented. This celebrated argument turns on intuitions about the behaviour of referring terms in modal contexts. The descriptvist's response is either to invoke two notions of content, or avail herself of rigidified definite descriptions. Gareth Evans defended a hybrid view according to which one aspect of content determines reference at the actual world, while another aspect of content determines reference at possible worlds. And Lewis and Jackson propose that a proper name such as 'Aristotle' be short for something like 'the actual teacher of Alexander the Great', so that 'Aristotle' refers to Aristotle even at possible worlds where someone other than Aristotle taught Alexander the Great. However, neither of these rejoinders is entirely unproblematic. Scott Soames has pointed out that speakers in a possible world perfectly resembling the actual world need have no beliefs about the actual world in order to have beliefs about Aristotle. Finally, a response due to Nathan Salmon and Scott Soames on behalf of referentialism to the belief argument from Chapter 1 is detailed. This says that singular propositional content is grasped under semantically insignificant modes of presentation.

Chapter 3 covers the transition from philosophy of language to philosophy of thought and mind. First Putnam's Twin Earth argument is presented in some detail followed by critical discussion. This argument purports to show that the meaning of natural kind terms is partially determined by underlying physical facts about the natural kinds that are picked out by those terms even if those facts are unknown to the speakers in question. The reasoning seems compelling, but some philosophers, e.g. Tim Crane, Gabriel Segal and Frank Jackson, have put forward challenging lines of discontent. Then Tyler Burge's three-way extension of Putnam's conclusion is spelled out. Firstly, if linguistic content is externally individuated, then so is mental content. Indeed if mental states themselves are partially individuated by their contents, being in a belief state with such content is also externally individuated. Secondly, mental content is not only dependent on physical facts about the external environment, it also depends on social facts about the way language is used conventionally in the speech community. Thirdly, not only is the content of natural kind terms externally individuated, so is the content of non-natural kind terms. Burge's arthritis argument is then presented, followed by critical discussion of various objections that have been levelled against this social externalist view. Here the phenomenon of semantic deference plays a pivotal role – the idea that speakers who incompletely understand an expression can nevertheless competently use that expression and have beliefs about its referent by deferring to those expert speakers who possess the relevant knowledge. Finally, Donald Davidson's Swampman example is scrutinized. This thought experiment poses a challenge not only to Davidson's own historical account of representational content but also to teleosemantics according to which the selectional histories of individuals individuate the content of their representational states. Several responses are discussed, including one which highlights a deep tension in Davidson's work on meaning and radical interpretation.

Chapter 4 begins by scrutinizing Dry Earth cases where the relevant external facts go missing. They purport to show that if content is individuated by external circumstances, then such content is also dependent for its existence on the obtaining of those circumstances. Examples of object-dependent content are given by David Kaplan's account of perceptual-demonstrative thoughts, and by Gareth Evans and John McDowell's idea of Fregean *de re* senses. Then the proposal that natural kind terms are short for rigidified definite descriptions is revisited. Given that rigidification involves an actuality operator, and that 'actually' is an indexical expression, thoughts involving the concept of water become egocentric in nature. The question is then whether the content of egocentric thoughts should be viewed as truth-conditional, or else, as David Lewis has it, consists in the self-ascription of certain properties. A natural proposal is to acknowledge the existence of two distinct components of mental content: narrow content, as internally individuated, and wide content, as externally individuated. Two such hybrid views, due to Colin McGinn and David Chalmers, are discussed in some detail. While they disagree about the semantic import of narrow content, they both assign such content the role of causally explaining behaviour. At this juncture, the semantics of natural kind concepts is revisited. In particular, Putnam and Chalmers' claim that such concepts have an indexical component is critically examined. Instead a referentialist semantics is explored. Finally, care is needed when characterizing narrow content. To be in a state with narrow content is to be in a state that supervenes on intrinsic properties, but narrow content is not intrinsic. Drawing on work by David Lewis, Frank Jackson and Robert Stalnaker, it is argued that narrow content is best seen as intra-world narrow, content that is shared by internal duplicates only within the same possible world, not across different possible worlds.

Chapter 5 is mostly devoted to the dispute between compatibilism and incompatibilism. Compatibilists claim that semantic externalism and self-knowledge are compatible, while incompatibilists deny that claim. Competent speakers are standardly credited with privileged access to the contents of their own occurrent mental states, which gives rise to a priori knowledge of these contents. But this would seem to be impossible if those contents depend for their individuation on external circumstances that such speakers have no special access to, and indeed need know nothing about. There are different ways of setting up this incompatibilist problem. Paul Boghossian argued that if a speaker is slowly but unwittingly switched back and forth between Earth and Twin Earth, she will fail to know a priori the wide contents of her occurrent thoughts, as she is unable to rule out the possibility that she is in fact having a thought with a relevantly different content. Relying on Burge's notion of self-verifying thoughts, some semantic externalists reply that a speaker can know a priori what she is thinking without having a priori knowledge whether that content is identical to, or different from, some other content that she is thinking. But Burge did not take self-verification to be what bestows warrant on second-order judgements about thoughts. Instead, speakers are a priori entitled to such judgements in virtue of the role these judgements play in critical thinking. Slow switching gives rise to another kind of problem for semantic externalism. If a competent speaker is unwittingly transported back and forth between Earth and Twin Earth, she will unawares think different wide contents when she utters sentences containing 'water'. Consequently, if she were to go through an intuitively valid argument while undergoing such transportations, occurrences of 'water' in the premises would equivocate between these distinct contents. Her reasoning would then be rendered invalid.

Chapter 6 continues to examine the epistemological implications of semantic externalism, and in particular whether this view swaps a problem about knowledge of the external world with one about knowledge of the internal world. Anthony Brueckner confronts the semantic externalist with a line of reasoning to the effect that a competent speaker's introspective belief that she is thinking that water is wet cannot constitute a priori knowledge. If this speaker knows a priori that she is thinking that water is wet, then she also knows a priori that she is not thinking that twin-water is wet. Since she does not know a priori that she is not thinking that twin-water is wet, she does not know a priori that she is thinking that water is wet. In response, some question the underlying epistemological principles, and others maintain that the content sceptical argument is self-refuting. Brueckner contends that while semantic externalism provides the basis for scepticism about self-knowledge, it offers no resources when it comes to scepticism about the external world. Putnam argued that one successfully thinks one is not a brain in a vat (BIV) only if one is not a BIV. So, if one knows a priori that one thinks that one is not a BIV, one knows a priori that one is not a BIV. Relatedly, Michael McKinsey and Paul Boghossian argue that combining a strong version of semantic externalism with self-knowledge leads to implausible a priori knowledge of ordinary contingent external world propositions. Respondents include Jessica Brown, Bill Brewer, Jim Pryor, Brian McLaughlin and Michael Tye. This last argument might be regarded as proof that anti-sceptical arguments supported by semantic externalism over-reaches by way of delivering easy knowledge of such common or garden-variety propositions.

Chapter 7 begins by emphasizing the importance of mental states causing physical states or other mental states. In particular, mental states cause their effects in virtue of their contents. Basically, what causes John to go into the pub is his desire for a beer and his belief that he can satisfy that desire by going into the pub. Had his belief or desire had a different content, John would have acted differently. But if mental content is externally individuated and causation is local, mental states with such wide content seem causally idle. John's physiological and neurological properties are causally efficacious with respect to his physical behaviour, but the features of his external environment that individuate the content of his mental states are not. This suggests that only the narrow contents of John's mental states are causally efficacious. Different ways of sharpening this challenge to semantic externalism have been proposed, most prominently by Jerry Fodor and Harold Noonan. Their arguments are presented in some detail, and the question of whether they sustain any viable notion of narrow content is assessed. In response, one might distinguish between causation and causal explanation, or between different ways of describing the effect. Thus Timothy Williamson argues that knowledge states play an irreducible role in causal explanation of behaviour, Frank Jackson and Philip Pettit argue that causal explanations can cite features that program without actually producing anything, and Fred Dretske's dual-explanandum strategy has it that the triggering physical properties of mental states are responsible for mere bodily movement, while the structuring content properties of such states are responsible for behaviour.

At the end of each chapter is an annotated list of further reading, which offers details on relevant further literature pertaining to that chapter. Additionally, each chapter is appended with a chapter summary, which allows for a swift recap of the key points in that chapter. Difficult philosophical terminology or relevant technical terms are briefly explained in the glossary of philosophical terms at the end of the book.

Semantic externalism is a vexed issue in contemporary philosophy involving a vast literature. To bring the exposition into focus, the following chapters ignore many otherwise important approaches to this intriguing debate. For instance, Fred Dretske, Michael Tye and others have argued that the contents of experiential states are equally externally individuated. As mentioned, an experiential state has phenomenal character in that there is something it is like to be in that state. We set such phenomenal externalism aside, and focus entirely on linguistic contents and the contents of propositional attitudes. Another increasingly popular branch of externalism is so-called active externalism, which maintains that the external environment plays an active role in constituting cognitive processes. Recent advocates include Andy Clark and David Chalmers. Whereas semantic externalism says that some mental contents are externally individuated, active externalism holds that the vehicles of these contents are externally located. On the face of it, semantic externalism is compatible with active internalism, and semantic internalism is compatible with active externalism. To properly assess the merits of active externalism and these intriguing compatibility claims is beyond the scope of this monograph. In order to ease exposition the chapters are also deliberately selective when it comes to particular arguments and objections. Rather than covering too much ground superficially, key territory is expounded as thoroughly as possible. While it is fair to say that a majority of professional philosophers nowadays incline towards some version of semantic externalism, the aim is throughout for the exposition to be as even-handed as possible, or at least to ensure that both sides to a given dispute are represented in the text.

1

DESCRIPTIVISM

1.1 Descriptivism expounded

Some linguistic expressions serve the purpose of referring to objects outside of language. For instance, the proper names 'David Cameron', 'West Port' and 'Edinburgh' refer to the Prime Minister, my favourite pub and the Scottish capital city, respectively.[1] As these terms purport to pick out a single object, they are *singular referring terms*. Individuals, pubs and cities are concrete, tangible objects. Other singular referring terms pick out events or even abstract objects. Think of 'Tour de France' or '1 metre'. Definite descriptions of the form 'the F' might also naturally be thought of as singular referring devices. For instance, 'the current US president' picks out Barack Obama. In contrast, the general term 'lemon' refers to all and only fruit of the kind *Citrus limon*, and the general term 'tiger' refers to all and only cats of the kind *Panthera tigris*. As these terms purport to pick out more than one object, they are *plural referring terms*. Such terms have *extensions*, which are the sets of objects to which they correctly apply. Specifically, 'lemon' and 'tiger' are *natural kind terms*, which have as their extension all and only instances or members of an underlying physical, chemical or biological kind.[2] Such kinds are more or less mind-independent demarcations that group objects together at various levels of generality. For instance, my mother is a member of the increasingly more general natural kinds *Homo sapiens*, mammal and living creature. Arguably, if an object belongs to a natural kind, then such member-ship is an essential property of that object. My mother could undergo various changes pertaining to her physical appearance or psychological profile, but she could not possibly cease to be a human being. However, to use a metaphor, not all plural referring terms carve nature at her joints in the way natural kind terms do. *Non-natural kind terms* pick out instances of artefactual kinds. Thus 'sofa' picks out long upholstered seats with a back and arms, and 'carburettor' picks out any device that blends air and fuel for an internal combustion engine. In these cases, there are no common, underlying scientific kinds, e.g. some sofas are made of metal and wool, others of oak and leather. What matters for something to count as a sofa or a carburettor is not its physical constitution, but whether it fits the job description or plays a certain functional role characteristic of sofas or carburettors.

Having distinguished these kinds of referring terms, let us now turn to their *semantics*. When it comes to referring terms, semantics has to do with those aspects of meaning that are relevant for their reference. Frege (1964/ 1893) thought that every linguistic expression possessed a reference of a kind appropriate to its category. For instance, declarative sentences refer to their truth-values, which he called 'the True' and 'the False'.[3] That is to say, such sentences are sentential names of the abstract entities the True and the False. And Frege took predicates to refer to concepts, which on his view are functions whose value, for every object as argument, is a truth-value. There is no need to follow Frege here. Some types of linguistic expressions are intuitively not referential. Predicates have extensions, e.g. all red things fall within the extension of 'being red', and sentences have truth-values, e.g. 'Ben Nevis is 1,344 metres' is true. The semantics of predicates or sentences thus pertains to those aspects of meaning that are relevant for their extension or truth-value, respectively.

If we ignore Frege's quirky terminology and instead take the most basic *semantic value* to be the truth-value of a sentence, then we can understand semantics as the theory of how the truth or falsity of a sentence is determined by the semantic values of the expressions that compose that sentence. In other words, the semantic value of an expression consists in the contribu-tion it makes to the truth or falsity of a sentence in which it occurs. The semantic value of a singular referring term is naturally identified with its reference, and the semantic value of a predicate is naturally identified with its extension.

What then does reference consist in? Reference is a unique relation between a singular or general term and one or more extralinguistic objects.

Reference is the most direct way for language to latch onto reality. Indeed the reference of a complex expression is determined by the reference of its constituents and their mode of composition. Reference is subject to the following *compositionality principle*:

(ComRef)   The truth-value of a sentence is determined by the reference (or semantic value) of its component parts and the way in which they are combined.

The last clause is important since it matters how the very same component parts are conjoined. The sentence 'Thomas hit James' may be true, while the sentence 'James hit Thomas' is false. It follows from (ComRef) that the truth-value of a sentence will remain invariant if co-referential component terms are substituted while everything else stays the same. Terms that have the same reference are interchangeable without change in truth-value. For instance, since the sentence 'Bono is the lead singer of U2' is true, and Bono also goes under the name 'Paul David Hewson', the sentence 'Paul David Hewson is the lead singer of U2' is guaranteed also to be true. Here is a *substitution principle for reference*:

(SubRef)   If the sentence 'a is F' is true and $a = b$, then the sentence 'b is F' is also true.

We can say that reference is a property that a term possesses only if it can be used in certain sentences that have a truth-value. To use Frege's example, given that the positive, non-fictive sentence 'William Tell shot an apple off his son's head' lacks a truth-value, the term 'William Tell' lacks a reference. Of course predicates can also be used in sentences that have a truth-value, e.g. 'is red' as in the false sentence 'Buckingham Palace is red'. If we wish to depart from Frege's framework when it comes to predicates, the fact that a term can be used in a sentence that has a truth-value should not be sufficient for it to count as possessing a reference.

What then is the meaning of a referring term? By 'meaning' we mean the *semantic content* of a term, i.e. that aspect of its overarching meaning which is relevant for determining the referent, if any, of that term. Meaning is what determines reference. Some aspects of this broader notion of meaning are semantically irrelevant in this way. The name 'Bono' might give rise to attitudes of artistic approval which are absent in the case of 'Paul David Hewson'. One historically influential view is *descriptivism*, which has been defended in various

versions by Russell (1994/1905), Strawson (1950), Searle (1958), Dummett (1978: Ch. 9), Kroon (1987), Lewis (1972, 1984, 1997), Jackson
(1998a, 2004) and others; indeed its roots can be traced back to Frege
(1994a/1892). The idea is that the meaning of a referring term is
descriptive in nature. More precisely, the meaning of a referring term 'a' is
given by a set of definite descriptions: 'the F', 'the G', 'the H', etc. For
instance, the meaning of 'Aristotle' is something like: the famous philosopher
of antiquity, the teacher of Alexander the Great, the author of Nicomachean
Ethics, etc. According to descriptivism, the descriptive content of a referring
term 'a' plays two distinct roles: it is what a competent speaker S knows
when she understands 'a', and it is what determines the reference of 'a'.
Descriptivism is both a theory of meaning and a theory of reference. On the face of
it, this view seems to blur the distinction between the first-order question
of what the meaning and reference of a term is from the second-order
question of what makes it the case that a term has the meaning and reference
that it does. To use Stalnaker's terminology (1997: 535–38), the first-order
question is answered by a descriptive semantics, and the second-order question
is answered by a foundational semantics. In taking descriptive content to be the
meaning of a referring term and also to be what makes that term have
the reference it has, it looks as if the question 'what is the semantics for
the term?' is conflated with the question 'what makes it the case that that term
in our language has this semantics?' However, descriptivists such as Jackson
(1998a) by no means reject that distinction. They only insist that descriptive
content can play a role in answering both questions.

Let's begin with the theory of meaning. When S understands the proper
name 'Aristotle', she knows its meaning. That name is synonymous with
the descriptions 'the famous philosopher of antiquity', 'the teacher of
Alexander the Great', 'the author of Nicomachean Ethics', etc., and so those are
what S knows in virtue of understanding the name. That is to say,
S understands the name 'Aristotle' if and only if S knows that Aristotle was
the famous philosopher of antiquity who taught Alexander the Great and
wrote Nicomachean Ethics. And the kind of knowledge S has is a priori –
knowledge that is independent of any empirical evidence. If S is competent
with 'Aristotle', then she knows a priori that, say, Aristotle taught Alexander
the Great. The speaker S could not grasp the meaning of 'Aristotle' while it
is an open question for S whether Aristotle taught Alexander the Great. For
what makes the name have the meaning it has is the fact that competent
speakers mentally associate these descriptions with it. And if grasping the
meaning of 'Aristotle' involves associating the description 'the teacher of

Alexander the Great' with that name, understanding the name suffices for knowing that Aristotle is the teacher of Alexander the Great. In short, following descriptivism, meaning is fully determined by competent speakers' mental associations. On this view, meaning is firmly in the mind of competent speakers.

But descriptivism is also a theory of reference in that descriptive content is what determines reference: a particular object is the referent of a referring term if and only if that object satisfies all the associated descriptions. These individually necessary and jointly sufficient descriptions express descriptive properties, e.g. 'the famous philosopher of antiquity' expresses the property of being the famous philosopher of antiquity.[4] So, put differently, what determines whether an object is the referent of a term is whether that object instantiates all those descriptive properties, e.g. what determines whether someone is the referent of 'Aristotle' is whether he was the famous philosopher of antiquity, taught Alexander the Great, authored Nicomachean Ethics, etc. Assuming a definite description 'the F' is an expression that refers to a unique object, if no object at all is F, or if two or more objects are F, then 'the F' fails to refer. This poses a problem about uniqueness for descriptivism. As Plato was also a famous philosopher of antiquity, there is no single famous philosopher of antiquity. But on this view 'Aristotle' refers to an object just in case it uniquely satisfies all these descriptions, including 'the famous philosopher of antiquity'. So, it looks like 'Aristotle' turns out to lack a reference. One solution is to think of the set of definite descriptions as a cluster in the sense that 'Aristotle' refers to an object just in case it satisfies most of these descriptions. That way 'Aristotle' will refer to Aristotle even if one of the associated definite descriptions fails to uniquely pick out Aristotle, or even if one such description uniquely picks out someone else. This cluster version of descriptivism was invented by Searle (1958), but has subsequently been developed by Lewis (1972, 1984) who took the cluster to comprise a disjunction of conjunctions of most of the descriptions. So, to simplify matters, suppose the three descriptions 'the F', 'the G' and 'the H' constitute the cluster assigned to the name 'a'. Then an object is the referent of 'a' just in case that object satisfies either 'the F' and 'the G', or 'the F' and 'the H', or 'the G' and 'the H'.

We have so far been using proper names as examples, but descriptivism is also a view about general terms. Take the natural kind term 'water'. On this view, the meaning of 'water' consists in descriptive content which is both what competent speakers know when they understand the term and what determines its reference. The term 'water' is synonymous with a definite description of the form: 'the clear, potable, tasteless liquid that fills the oceans and falls from the sky, etc.' In the following 'the watery stuff' will be used instead as an abbreviation, where 'watery' captures all these superficial, readily observable properties of water. So, a competent speaker S understands 'water' if and only if she knows that water is the watery stuff. As S is associating this complex description with 'water', she can know a priori that water has these watery properties. Moreover, following descriptivism, 'water' will pick out anything that satisfies 'the watery stuff', or at least anything satisfying enough of the descriptions encapsulated by that phrase. In other words, anything instantiating all or enough of the descriptive properties expressed by these descriptions will be picked out by 'water', and so count as water. For example, on Earth H_2O satisfies most if not all of these descriptions, and so H_2O is what the inhabitants on Earth refer to when they use 'water' in various sentences.

1.2 The identity argument

In Section 1.1 we presented descriptivism but adduced nothing in its support. In Sections 1.2 and 1.3 we present arguments that supposedly buttress the descriptivist outlook. Why do we need meaning over and above reference, and in particular why do we need descriptive content? Can we not just identify meaning with what we in Section 1.1 called 'semantic value'? In particular, what's wrong with Mill's view (1963/1843) that the meaning of a referring term is nothing but its reference? In Frege's famous article (1994a/1892) "On Sense and Reference", he made a crucial distinction between *sense* (German 'Sinn') and *reference* (German 'Bedeutung'). Frege thought that unless referring terms were associated with distinct senses, we could not explain what it is that a speaker S knows when she competently understands these terms. In contrast, according to *referentialism*, meaning is nothing over and above reference.[5] On this view, to know the meaning of a referring term is to know its reference. In this work (1994a/1892) Frege advanced his *identity argument*, which is targeted at referentialism. It aims to show that to know the reference of a term is to know more than is involved in knowing its sense. The identity argument is presented as a challenge to explain how true identity statements can be informative. Consider:

(1) Hesperus is Hesperus.
(2) Hesperus is Phosphorus.[6]

The propositions expressed by the sentences in (1) and (2) intuitively differ in how informative they are. Propositions, remember, are the semantic contents that sentences express. While (1) is trivial, (2) is an interesting piece of information. It is perfectly possible for a rational speaker to grasp both propositions and believe that Hesperus is Hesperus yet disbelieve that Hesperus is Phosphorus. At some point the ancient Greek astronomers disbelieved that Hesperus is Phosphorus, but they always believed that Hesperus is Hesperus. The proposition **Hesperus is Phosphorus** has a richer *informational content* than the proposition **Hesperus is Hesperus**.[7] To illustrate, some contemporary philosophers will say that the latter is an *analytic truth* and so is *a priori knowable*. To say that a proposition is analytically true is to say that it is *true in virtue of its meaning*. No empirical state of affairs makes it true. To say that a proposition is a priori knowable is to say that those who grasp that proposition can know it independently of sense experience. So, given that understanding is knowledge of meaning, understanding that proposition suffices for knowing its truth-value. That is why the ancient Greek astronomers have always believed that Hesperus is Hesperus. But when they gathered enough empirical evidence that the brightest star in the morning sky is identical to the brightest star in the evening sky, it transpired that Hesperus and Phosphorus are in fact the very same heavenly body, namely Venus. When the astronomers discovered that Hesperus is identical to Phosphorus, they acquired *a posteriori knowledge* of a *synthetic truth* − an informative truth that is not analytic. The astronomers grasped the proposition **Hesperus is Phosphorus** all along. They just lacked knowledge of its truth-value until they successfully carried out some empirical enquiry.

But if, as referentialism has it, the meaning of the terms 'Hesperus' and 'Phosphorus' flanking the identity sign in (2) consisted in their reference, then there should be no difference in the informational content between the propositions **Hesperus is Hesperus** and **Hesperus is Phosphorus**. In particular, as these propositions would be identical, the former is analytic and a priori knowable only if the latter is. Just as in the case of (1), a speaker who understood (2) would know that 'Hesperus' and 'Phosphorus' refer to the same object. Both propositions would simply be saying that this object, which is in fact Venus, is identical with itself. But since this consequence of referentialism is clearly unpalatable, the existence of sense as distinct from reference must be granted. At this juncture, some referentialists might resist the claim that (1) is analytically true and a priori knowable, maybe for independent reasons that analyticity and a priority are dubious properties of any proposition. However, these referentialists would still have to explain how (1) can be trivial in some sense in which (2) is not, i.e. how (2) can be informative in some sense in which (1) is not.

All the identity argument says is that to understand a referring term cannot consist in knowing what its reference is. More positively, Frege suggests that understanding such a term must rather consist in knowing some mode in which the speaker is presented with that referent. Frege's senses are *modes of presentation* of referents.[8] Unlike most referents of referring terms, senses are intangible entities. They are rather abstract entities, which exist eternally outside space-time. Senses are objective in being graspable, shareable and communicable by more than one speaker. Senses contrast with ideas, which are private mental images. Moreover, just as referring terms have senses, so do sentences. Frege called the sense of a sentence a *Thought*. Thoughts are not acts of thinking, but rather the objective contents of such acts. These are *representational* contents: they represent the world as being a certain way. Thoughts thus fulfil one prominent purpose of language, namely to represent how things are. Nowadays philosophers prefer talk about propositions, which is the terminology we shall mostly be adopting. So, propositions are what sentences express. More precisely, propositions are expressed by 'that'-clauses as in 'Joe believes that Jill has been laid off', and are also the primary bearers of truth-values. We can say that the sentence 'snow is white' is true but only because the proposition *that* snow is white is true.

Importantly, Frege took the sense of a sentence, i.e. a Thought, to be not only composed of the senses associated with the expressions that constitute that sentence, but also determined by these component senses and the way in which they are combined. If instead of the tendentious notion of 'sense' we talk more generally about the *propositional content* of an expression as its contribution to determining the proposition expressed by sentences containing it, then propositional content is subject to a *compositionality principle*. Consider the following:

(ComProp)   The proposition expressed by a sentence is determined by the propositional contents of the expressions that constitute that sentence and the way in which these contents are combined.

In other words, propositions are determined by their (propositional) components and their manner of composition. And this propositional structure resembles the structure of the sentence that expresses the proposition in question. For instance, the constituents of the proposition **snow is white** as expressed by the sentence 'snow is white' are the meanings of 'snow' and 'is white', and these propositional constituents **snow** and **is white** are ordered in the same way as those expressions occur in that sentence. Moreover, the proposition expressed by a sentence is determined by the condition on the truth of that sentence. So, we can take the propositional content of an expression to be fixed by the contribution it yields to determining the truth-conditions of sentences containing it. In short, truth-conditional content determines propositional content. If in a particular proposition one component is swapped for a different component, or if the order of existing propositional components is swapped around, then the result is a distinct proposition. The proposition **Superman flies** is distinct from the proposition **Tarzan flies**, because the propositional content **Superman** is distinct from the propositional content **Tarzan**. After all, 'Tarzan' and 'Superman' refer to different individuals. Similarly, the proposition **Clark Kent fancies Lois Lane** is distinct from the proposition **Lois Lane fancies Clark Kent**, because the same propositional contents are arranged differently in the two propositions. Thus (ComProp) entails the following *substitution principle for propositional content*:

(SubProp)   The proposition **a is F** is identical to the proposition **b is F** if and only if the propositional content **a** is identical to the propositional content **b**.

For Frege senses *qua* modes of presentation are supposed to play several roles reminiscent of descriptive content. The sense of referring term '*a*' is both what speaker S knows when she competently understands '*a*', and what determines the reference of '*a*'. What S has is thus knowledge that uniquely identifies the referent of '*a*'. But that is not all. The knowledge S has also constitutes the way in which S takes the referent of '*a*' to be. That is, the sense of '*a*' is the conceptual representation of its referent, which S grasps in virtue of associating it with '*a*'.[9] For Frege such representations are *cognitively significant* in a distinctive way:

(CogSig)   The proposition **a is F** and the proposition **b is F** have the same cognitive significance if and only if a rational speaker S who grasps both propositions cannot simultaneously believe that *a* is F and disbelieve that *b* is F.

Importantly, if two propositions differ in their cognitive significance, then they are distinct propositions. For Frege senses are therefore individuated in a fine-grained manner. If there is a difference in the cognitive significance between the proposition **Superman flies** and the proposition **Tarzan flies** in that a rational and competent speaker can at the same time believe that Superman flies but disbelieve that Tarzan flies, then these two propositions are distinct. And if the only difference between them is that one contains the propositional content **Superman** while the other contains the propositional content **Tarzan**, then these two contents are distinct. This follows from (SubProp).

The different propositions **Superman flies** and **Tarzan flies** illustrate that differences in reference make for differences in sense, but there can be differences in sense even when there is no difference in reference. Sense is what determines reference such that if two terms differ in reference, they also differ in sense. The names 'Superman' and 'Tarzan' illustrate that point. But two terms can differ in sense even though they have the same reference. Sense is more fine-grained than reference. The names 'Hesperus' and 'Phosphorus' illustrate that point. Understanding 'Hesperus' and 'Phosphorus' cannot consist in knowing their referents, but must rather consists in knowing modes of presentations of their referents, or ways of identifying their referents. Only then can the differences in cognitive significance or informational content between the propositions **Hesperus is Hesperus** and **Hesperus is Phosphorus** be adequately accounted for. For if the sense of 'Hesperus' differs from the sense of 'Phosphorus' despite the two names being co-referential, then these two propositions are also different. This follows from (SubProp). And if the propositions are different, then there is no mystery about how one can be analytic and a priori knowable while the other is synthetic and a posteriori knowable.

We can run the identity argument using natural kind terms instead of proper names. Consider the following two sentences:

(3)   Water is water.
(4)   Water is H_2O.

Utterances of (3) and (4) express propositions with different cognitive significance. It is perfectly possible for a rational speaker to grasp both propositions and believe that water is water yet disbelieve that water is H_2O.[10] The proposition **water is water** is analytically true and so a priori knowable, while the proposition that **water is H_2O** is synthetically true and so merely a posteriori knowable. Given (CogSig), these two propositions differ in their cognitive significance, and are therefore different propositions. The only difference between them is that one contains the propositional content **water** while the other contains the propositional content **H₂O**. It therefore follows from (SubProp) that **water** and **H₂O** are distinct. But 'water' and 'H₂O' are co-referential, so propositional content must be distinct from, and more fine-grained than, reference. The upshot is again that referentialism – the view that the meaning of 'water' and 'H₂O' is exhausted by their reference – must be false. The referentialist might again take issue with analyticity and a priority, but it remains the case that (3) and (4) differ in their informational content: (4) is certainly no triviality.

The identity argument makes the crucial assumption that if the proposition that p and the proposition that q differ in their cognitive significance or informational content then p and q are distinct propositions. As we will revisit cognitive significance in Section 1.3, let's focus on differences in informational content as sufficient for individuation of propositions. The referentialist might well challenge that assumption in which case the identity argument would not carry much conviction. The difference in informational content between the propositions **Hesperus is Hesperus** and **Hesperus is Phosphorus** is an epistemic difference, and there is no compelling reason why an epistemic difference should be due to a semantic difference. For instance, it may be that epistemic differences are due to differences in pragmatically imparted information, rather than semantically encoded information. To illustrate that distinction, consider the highway warning 'Don't drink and drive'. The intended information is that one should not first drink and then drive, but that temporal order is not semantically encoded. Where semantics deals with types of expressions, pragmatics deals with tokens of expressions i.e. specific utterances of such expressions.[11] And it may be that an utterance of (2) can impart information beyond what that sentence type encodes. The difference in informational content between 'Hesperus' and 'Phosphorus' is thus due to the fact that they contribute differently to what is uttered by sentences containing them, but this contribution is semantically irrelevant. It has no bearing on which proposition is expressed. So, while both (1) and (2) semantically express the very same proposition, utterances of them impart distinct information, which explains why (1) is trivial in a way in which (2) is not.

Note finally that even if the assumption that propositions are individuated in terms of their informational content is granted, the identity argument falls short of establishing the existence of descriptive content. In order to vindicate descriptivism some additional reason must be offered as to why senses *qua* modes of presentation should be thought of exclusively in descriptive terms. Of course once descriptive content is on-board we can explain how true identity statements can be informative. If the sense of 'Hesperus' is given by 'the brightest star in the evening sky' and the sense of 'Phosphorus' is given by 'the brightest star in the morning sky', and understanding is knowledge of these definite descriptions, then a competent speaker S can know a priori that the brightest star in the evening sky is the brightest star in the evening sky, yet S cannot know a priori that the brightest star in the evening sky is the brightest star in the morning sky. But the question was why we should accept descriptive content in the first place.

1.3 Puzzles about belief

We saw in the previous section how the identity argument relied on the assumption that propositions be individuated in terms of their informational content or cognitive significance. The problem with the identity argument was, however, that there are ways of explaining away differences in informational content or cognitive significance that have no semantic bearing on propositional content. What is needed is a case where two propositions, or parts thereof, differ in informational content or cognitive significance yet there is also a firm intuition that they differ in truth-value. For if they differ in truth-value, then these propositions must be distinct. Remember, propositions have truth-conditions: if the conditions under which one sentence is true differ from the conditions under which another sentence is true, then these two sentences express different propositions. The problem with (1) and (2), and with (3) and (4), was that they all have the same truth-value. So, we need to strengthen the identity argument in such a way that substitution of co-referring terms makes for a semantic difference, a difference in truth-value. The remedy is simple. We just embed the sentences in (1) and (2), and in (3) and (4), inside the scope of a belief operator. Consider:

(5)   The ancient astronomers believed that Hesperus is Hesperus.
(6)   The ancient astronomers believed that Hesperus is Phosphorus.

It is agreed on all sides that (5) is true. The ancient astronomers surely believed that Hesperus is identical to itself. But it seems very odd to say they believed that Hesperus is Phosphorus. Not because they were incompetent with the relevant bits of language. They thought of Hesperus as the brightest star in the evening sky, and they thought of Phosphorus as the brightest star in the morning sky, but they possessed no evidence indicating that in actual fact the brightest star in the evening sky is identical to the brightest star in the morning sky. They would in fact behave in various ways as if Hesperus and Phosphorus were distinct. For example, if asked whether Hesperus is identical to Phosphorus, they would not hesitate to answer in the negative. It thus looks as if (6) is false.

Now we can run the belief argument. Suppose that referentialism is true. The two terms 'Hesperus' and 'Phosphorus' both refer to the same planet, namely Venus. Because, on this view, the meaning of these terms is exhausted by their referents, they must have the same meaning. The only difference between the sentences in (5) and (6) is that the second occurrence of 'Hesperus' in (5) is replaced in (6) by an occurrence of 'Phosphorus'. As these two terms have the same meaning, (5) and (6) should express the same proposition. This follows from our substitution principle for propositional content (SubProp). Remember, to say that 'Hesperus' and 'Phosphorus' have the same meaning is to say that their propositional contents are identical, i.e. they yield the same contribution to any propositions that are expressed by sentences containing them. But (5) and (6) must express different propositions since they have different truth-values. So, referentialism is false: the meaning of a referring term must be distinct from its reference.

We can mount the same belief argument using the natural kind terms in (3) and (4) instead. Suppose Anna understands the term 'H_2O': she knows it picks out molecules consisting of two hydrogen atoms for every oxygen atom. Anna is also competent with 'water', but she possesses no evidence that would enable her to connect the two terms. She would, for instance, refuse to assent to the sentence 'water is H_2O' – in fact, she might dissent from that sentence. Consider:

(7)   Anna believes that water is water.
(8)   Anna believes that water is H_2O.

There is no question that (7) is true, but (8) strikes us as false. Again referentialism is in trouble. The only difference between (7) and (8) is that while (7) contains two occurrences of 'water', (8) contains one occurrence of 'water' and one occurrence of 'H_2O'. But given that meaning is reference on this view, (7) and (8) should express the same proposition, because the two terms 'water' and 'H$_2$O' are co-referential. However, that cannot be so if they differ in truth-value. It looks like meaning is something over and above reference.

Both versions of the belief argument assume that belief-ascribing sentences of the form 'S believes that a is F' express a two-place belief relation between a believer S and the proposition expressed by the sentence 'a is F' embedded inside the scope of a belief operator. Sentences ascribing beliefs specify the believed contents, and these contents are the propositions expressed by the embedded 'that'-clauses of these sentences. The propositions to which S is belief-related represent those features of reality that the belief is about. And given that propositions have truth-conditions, the contents of S's beliefs are true just in case things are the way those contents say they are. One may take issue with this assumption about the logical form of sentences attributing beliefs, but we shall not delay over alternative views here.[12] Note, however, that even if sound, the belief argument falls short of establishing descriptivism. Just as in the case of the identity argument, it is one thing to say that meaning is not reducible to reference, another thing to say that meaning is descriptive in nature. Nevertheless, the descriptivist may well be much better placed to answer the belief argument. For instance, if the descriptive contents of 'Hesperus' and 'Phosphorus' are **the brightest star in the evening sky** and **the brightest star in the morning sky**, respectively, then it will be true that the ancient astronomers believed that the brightest star in the evening sky is the brightest star in the evening sky, but false that the ancient astronomers believed that the brightest star in the evening sky is the brightest star in the morning sky. But there is more to say.

Remember our *substitution principle for reference* from Section 1.1:

(SubRef)   If the sentence 'a is F' is true and $a = b$, then the sentence 'b is F' is also true.

The idea is that co-referring terms can be substituted in *extensional contexts* without change in truth-value. A term occurs in an extensional context just in case the sentence containing it is not embedded inside the scope of an intentional operator like a belief operator. A term occurs in an *intentional context* just in case the sentence containing it is embedded inside the scope of such an operator. So, the name 'Superman' occurs in an extensional context in the sentence 'Superman flies', but in an intentional context in the sentence 'Lois Lane believes that Superman flies'. Consider now a related substitution principle pertaining to intentional contexts:

(SubRef*)   If the sentence 'S believes that a is F' is true and $a = b$, then the sentence 'S believes that b is F' is also true.

The belief argument seems to show that (SubRef*) is false. The problem for referentialism is that this view is committed to (SubRef*). For if 'S believes that a is F' reports that S is belief-related to the proposition expressed by 'a is F', and the co-referring 'a' and 'b' yields the same contribution to determining the propositions expressed by the sentences 'a is F' and 'b is F', then 'S believes that a is F' and 'S believes that b is F' express the same proposition. It follows that if one belief-ascribing sentence is true, so is the other. The descriptivist, however, will reject (SubRef*), possibly for the reason that Frege offered. Frege (1994a/1892) suggested that terms occurring in intentional contexts take indirect reference: they refer to their customary sense. As the name 'Superman' occurs in 'Lois Lane believes that Superman flies' the name refers, not to Superman himself, but to the sense of that name. That sense could be given by 'the superhero who flies around chasing criminals in his blue costume with a red cape'. The name 'Clark Kent' has a different sense as given by something like 'the shy reporter who wears glasses and works for *Daily Planet*'. This means that 'Clark Kent' in 'Lois Lane believes that Clark Kent flies' refers to a different sense. Using the compositionality principle for reference (ComRef) from Section 1.1, 'Lois Lane believes that Superman flies' can thus be true while 'Lois Lane believes that Clark Kent flies' is false. The two belief-ascribing sentences differ in truth-value, because some of their constituent terms differ in reference.[13]

One prominent response on behalf of referentialism is to show that puzzles about beliefs arise even if (SubRef*) is ignored. Kripke (1979) argued that commonsensical principles lead to contradiction without relying on (SubRef*). If that were so, belief puzzles would be a general problem and not just a concern for referentialists. Here are two such principles. The first is a *disquotation* principle linking assent with belief:

(Disquotation)   If a competent speaker S sincerely and reflectively assents to 'a is F', then S believes that a is F.

The rationale behind (Disquotation) is that to utter the sentence 'a is F' is to assert that a is F, and that to assert that a is F is to express the belief that *a* is F. The second is a *consistency principle* linking rationality with absence of logically contradictory beliefs:

(Consistency)   If a speaker S reflectively and occurrently believes that *a* is F and that *a* is not F, then S is not fully rational.

The idea is that if S is as rational as anyone gets, then S does not hold contradictory beliefs. Kripke now argues that a contradiction can be derived from (Disquotation) and (Consistency) alone. Kripke (1979: 265) asks us to imagine the following:

> Peter may learn the name 'Paderewski' with an identification of the person named as a famous pianist. Naturally, having learned this, Peter will assent to 'Paderewski had musical talent', and we can infer – using 'Paderewski', as we normally do, to name the Polish musician and statesman: Peter believes that Paderewski had musical talent. ... Later, in a different circle, Peter learns of someone called 'Paderewski' who was a Polish nationalist leader and Prime Minister. Peter is sceptical of the musical abilities of politicians. ... Using 'Paderewski' as a name for the statesman, Peter assents to 'Paderewski had no musical talent'. Should we infer, by [(Disquotation)], Peter believes that Paderewski had no musical talent, or should we not?

By letting Peter assent to 'Paderewski had musical talent' in one context of utterance and to 'Paderewski had no musical talent' in a different context of utterance, while not knowing that the two occurrences of 'Paderewski' are co-referring, we avoid using (SubRef*). Here we can follow Kaplan (1989) in taking a context of utterance to be a possible occasion of use consisting of a speaker, hearer, time and location. Here is Kripke's paradox:

(9)   Peter is fully rational.

(10)   'Paderewski' in the music-context and 'Paderewski' in the politics-context are co-referring.

(11)   Peter assents to 'Paderewski had musical talent' and Peter assents to 'Paderewski had no musical talent'.

(12)   So, given (Disquotation), Peter believes that Paderewski had musical talent and Peter believes that Paderewski had no musical talent.

(13)   So, given (Consistency), Peter has contradictory beliefs and is not fully rational.

There is a lot to say about Kripke's paradox, but we shall only briefly consider one descriptivst response.[14] In order for 'S believes that *a* is F' and 'S believes that *a* is not F' to express contradictory beliefs, the embedded sentences '*a* is F' and '*a* is not F' must express contradictory propositions. For instance, S can simultaneously believe that the bank is F and that the bank is not F without violating norms of rationality if only she believes that the money bank is F and that the riverbank is not F. In short, contradictory beliefs are not between the embedded sentences, but between the propositions expressed by them. On the descriptivist account, contradictory beliefs are between descriptive propositions – propositions made up of descriptive contents – but in this case, Peter associates the name 'Paderewski' with different descriptive contents in the two contexts: Paderewski-the-statesman and Paderewski-the-musician. Since the proposition **Paderewski-the-statesman had no musical talent** does not contradict the proposition **Paderewski-the-musician had musical talent,** Peter holds no contradictory belief. This means that (Consistency) fails to apply, and Kripke's paradox is blocked.

1.4 Sense, linguistic meaning and communication

In the previous section we looked at the belief argument purporting to establish the existence of senses *qua* modes of presentation or ways of thinking of referents. Sense is a way of thinking of something as the satisfier of some condition such that if an object happens to satisfy it then that object is the referent of the name to which that sense is associated. Frege plays with the idea of taking that condition to be descriptive, but in footnote 4 in his "On Sense and Reference", he notices a problem with this descriptivist account of sense:

> In the case of actual proper names such as 'Aristotle' opinions as to the sense may differ. It might, for instance, be taken to be the following: the pupil of Plato and the teacher of Alexander the Great. Anybody who does this will attach another sense to the sentence 'Aristotle was born in Stagira' than will a man who takes as the sense of the name: the teacher of Alexander the Great who was born in Stagira. So long as the reference remains the same, such variations of sense may be tolerated, although they are to be avoided in the theoretical structure of a demonstrative science and ought not to occur in a perfect language.

The worry is that if one speaker's (S's) understanding of a sentence involving a referring term 'a' requires S to be in possession of some way of thinking of its referent, then how can the informational content of that sentence be transmitted to a different speaker S* if S* employs some very different way of thinking of that referent? If those ways of thinking are not reflected in any mutually shared meaning of 'a', then what reason does S have for thinking that by using 'a' S refers to the same object as S* does when S* uses 'a'? All the belief argument shows is that speakers must associate some sense with 'a', but if this sense is not intersubjectively shared, then for all they can tell, they might easily be speaking past each other. Consequently, communication is in danger of breaking down. In Dummett's words (1978: 130), the argument has:

> ... a major defect: it has no tendency to show that the sense of a word is a feature of the language. It shows, at best, that each speaker, if he is to associate a reference with a word, must attach a particular sense to it; it does not show any necessity for different speakers to attach the same sense to any one word, so long as the senses, which they all attach to it determine the same reference. It therefore leaves open the possibility that the sense of a word is not part of its meaning at all, if meaning is to be something objective and shared by all speakers ...

But, Dummett continues (1978: 132):

> ... the use of language for communication ... depends upon the informational content of a sentence being constant from speaker to speaker. If language is to serve as a medium of communication, it is not sufficient that a sentence should in fact be true under the interpretation placed on it by one speaker just in case it is true under that placed on it by another; it is also necessary that both speakers should be aware of the fact.

What must be argued is that sense is needed not just in a *theory of speakers' reference*, but also in a *theory of reference for a common language*. If we could show not only that every speaker associates a sense with the terms they use for reference, but also that they associate approximately the same sense with those terms, sense would make out *linguistic meaning* as a conventional feature of their common language.

We ordinarily rely on a distinction between information that we know for sure via some empirical means and information that defines our subject matter. While the first appears in encyclopedias, the second appears in dictionaries. Linguistic meaning is information of the latter kind. Speakers grasp such meaning when they understand language as conventionally used. Unless they are expert speakers, their knowledge is typically implicit, and can take a good deal of reflection to explicate. That is why they typically consult dictionary entries where it has already been articulated by those in the know. Senses might also be listed as entries in encyclopedias if, say, Aristotle is commonly thought of as the teacher of Alexander the Great, or indeed as entries in dictionaries. But senses need not appear in print anywhere. Ways of thinking can be idiosyncratic pieces of information that nobody has bothered to write down. Suppose I think of Aristotle as my uncle's favourite philosopher.

On the face of it, senses thus seem different from linguistic meaning. Remember also that for Frege senses are eternal, changeless, abstract entities which have all their semantic properties independently of the activity of language users. Linguistic meaning, on the other hand, is conventional and determined by the contingent ways in which speakers use their language. Had they used language differently, different linguistic meaning would replace such existing meaning.

The *problem about communication* is a worry about how the senses as ways of thinking of objects, which different speakers associate with given names, must be related if communication is to be possible. Let's dwell on Frege's example in his paper "The Thought":

> Suppose ... that Herbert Garner knows that Dr Gustav Lauben was born on 6 September 1875 in N.N. and [that] this is not true of anyone else; suppose, however, that he does not know where Dr Lauben now lives nor indeed anything else about him. On the other hand, suppose that Leo Peter does not know that Dr Lauben was born on 6 September 1875 in N.N. Then as far as the proper name 'Dr Gustav Lauben' is concerned, Herbert Garner and Leo Peter do not speak the same language, although they do in fact refer to the same man with this name; for they do not know that they are doing so.

Imagine Garner utters 'Dr Lauben is wounded', in the presence of Peter. Peter assumes that by 'Dr Lauben' Garner refers to the same man Peter uses 'Dr Lauben' to refer to. Peter is right and so comes to believe that Dr Lauben is wounded. Is this a case of successful communication? There is some sense in which what Garner said when he uttered 'Dr Lauben is wounded' is what Peter apprehended. They both understood that utterance as being about Dr Lauben having the property of being wounded. It might thus seem that information has successfully been transferred from Garner to Peter. Maybe therefore preservation of reference suffices for understanding. As long as Peter gets the reference right, he will understand what Garner said, despite them having no identifying knowledge in common. Consider this proposal:

(A)   We need only get the reference right: mutual reference is necessary and sufficient for mutual understanding, hence for communication.

The worry with (A) is not the necessity claim: preservation of reference is imperative if we are to rely on others' testimony as a means of understanding what they said. It is rather that mutual reference does not suffice for securing transmission of information by means of language. It is true that as long as Garner and Peter refer to the same man, they run no risk of distorting information. The problem is that although Garner and Peter refer to the same man, they do so unwittingly. And they have no effective means by which they could come to know of their co-referential use of 'Dr Lauben', because there is no overlap in their identifying knowledge of Dr Lauben. But communication requires understanding, and understanding is a species of knowledge: to understand what someone has said is to know what was said. The purpose of communication is to facilitate transmission of knowledge and not just true beliefs.

Peter does not know what Garner has said, because he does not know who 'Dr Lauben' refers to in Garner's utterance, even though that name accidentally refers to the same man in Peter's idiolect. Garner's statement prompts Peter to form a true belief, but true belief is not knowledge. Peter has no justification to believe that he believes what Garner believes. Peter cannot rely on the wording since it is coincidental that Garner and himself use orthographically identical names of Dr Lauben. It seems that all Peter is entitled to infer from Garner's statement is that someone named 'Dr Lauben' has been wounded.

One might object that since Dr Lauben is causally responsible for both Peter's and Garner's use of 'Dr Lauben', Peter does not merely acquire a true belief, but also a true belief with the right causal history. One might even insist that Peter comes to know that Dr Lauben is wounded, because a true belief that p amounts to knowledge if caused by the fact that p.[15]

But suppose Peter knows of Dr Lauben only under his *other name* 'Gustav Hendricks'. Imagine also that Peter has no reason to think that 'Dr Lauben' and 'Gustav Hendricks' are co-referring. As it turns out, Peter forms the belief that Hendricks is wounded upon hearing Garner's assertion of 'Dr Lauben has been wounded'. According to (A), communication achieves its purpose in securing that Peter acquires a belief which resembles Garner's belief in being about the same man having the same property. But intuitively Peter lacks knowledge of what Garner said. As Peter lacks evidence that Dr Lauben is identical to Gustav Hendricks, he is lucky that his belief is about the same man, and such luck excludes knowledge. No belief that is true as a result of luck can constitute knowledge. Although Peter gets the reference right, he has not understood Garner's statement. So, perhaps (A) should be replaced by:

(B)   We need only know that we have got the reference right: knowledge of mutual reference is necessary and sufficient for mutual under-standing, hence for communication.

If Peter knows that by 'Dr Lauben' Garner refers to the man Peter uses 'Dr Lauben' to refer to, then Peter understands Garner's statement since he knows that Garner says of Dr Lauben that he is wounded. But how does Peter come to know that they are talking about the same man? Often enough we rely on the mere wording. I say 'Barack Obama is on BBC News'. You accept my assertion, and thereby come to believe that Barack Obama is on BBC News. In normal contexts, you assume I mean the current US president, and not your uncle who goes under the same name. Normally, this common identifying knowledge is contextually presupposed and never actually brought out. But if you had just told me about your uncle, it might be unclear whom I was talking about. For each of the Obamas, we possess distinct identifying knowledge, but there is also enough common ground between us to resolve the issue.

Suppose instead I say 'John was late' in a context in which we both know that I could have meant either of two men. In order for you to know what I said, you must know which one I intended. Communication succeeds only after my utterance has been disambiguated by drawing on common associated properties: 'I meant John, the German, not John, the Englishman'. You must think of the referent of my use of 'John' in such a way that you can know whom I was referring to. And it is hard to see how you could do that if we were not thinking of that referent in relevantly similar ways.

Understanding requires that speakers think of objects in similar ways. So, maybe the way to knowingly get the reference right is for there to be common identifying knowledge. This suggests:

(C)   We need to share some identifying knowledge: mutual descriptive content is both necessary and sufficient for mutual understanding, hence for communication.

Consider two putative counter-examples to (C). Take first the necessity claim. Suppose Lingers understands with Peter by the name 'Dr Lauben' the only doctor who lives in a house known to both of them, and suppose furthermore that Lingers understands with Garner by 'Dr Lauben' the unique individual born 6 September 1875. Then one might think that both Garner and Peter could communicate with Lingers, although not with each other. But if Lingers reports Garner's utterance to Peter, then Peter will come to know on the basis of testimony that Garner uses 'Dr Lauben' to refer to the same man that he uses 'Dr Lauben' to refer to. So, in this indirect way, Peter could come to understand what Garner said.

Were it not for Lingers, Peter and Garner could not successfully have exchanged information. In basic cases where two speakers purport to communicate directly, it still holds that knowledge of mutual reference goes via mutually associated descriptive properties. Peter is able to communicate with Lingers only because they share identifying knowledge of Dr Lauben. Moreover, Peter and Garner could share some identifying information by way of deferring to Lingers: with 'Dr Lauben' they could both associate the property of being the man whom Lingers uses 'Dr Lauben' to refer to. When Peter then hears Garner uttering 'Dr Lauben is wounded', Peter can infer that Garner believes that whomever Lingers uses 'Dr Lauben' to refer to is wounded.

Now take the sufficiency claim. Suppose I saw a very drunk American in the Cellar Bar last night and decided to call him 'Jack'. After I left, you saw the same guy, dubbed him 'Jack', and associated the same identifying information with the name, namely the drunk American in the Cellar Bar last night. Later on we met up and you told me what happened: 'Jack got thrown out'. This utterance prompted me to believe that Jack got thrown out. Despite shared descriptive properties and same reference, intuitively I have not understood what you said. Only by chance do we end up thinking about the same man in the same way. For all I can tell, 'Jack' in your mouth picks out the quiet Scotsman in the Cellar Bar last night. Such luck excludes knowledge of what you said. So, there are cases in which understanding requires not only that speakers think of objects in similar ways, but also know that they do. This recommends a strengthening of (C):

(D)   We need to knowingly share some identifying knowledge: known mutual descriptive content is both necessary and sufficient for mutual understanding, hence for communication.

The original proposal (C) may suffice in those cases where the context provides sufficient information for the speakers to know they are talking about the same thing, but in other cases they must know they share the same identifying information. Suppose I had named him 'Jones', and your utterance of 'Jack got thrown out' somehow caused me to believe that Jones got thrown out. I only saw one drunk in the Cellar Bar last night, and therefore assumed you were talking about him. It is clear that I lack knowledge since I do not know the man you refer to by 'Jack' is the man I refer to by 'Jones'. The only way to know that is to know that by 'Jack' and 'Jones' we associate the same identifying information: the drunk American in the Cellar Bar last night.[16]

The upshot is that if we are to communicate by means of referring terms, there must be some uniformity in the kind of descriptive properties we associate with them. In the case of general terms like 'water' or 'sofa', one can expect a community-wide consensus in associated descriptive properties, and in the case of proper names a less extensive and more speaker-relative agreement. Communication cannot take place between speakers who think about objects in radically different ways. If speakers by and large associate the same descriptive properties with the same referring terms, then they are properties of such terms as used in a common language, and not merely in each speaker's idiolect.

Chapter summary

In this chapter we reviewed the case for descriptivism – the view that singular and general referring terms have descriptive content which is both what determines their reference and what competent speakers know in virtue of understanding them. Although Frege did not explicitly advocate descriptivism, his notion of sense as a mode of presentation of the referent can be cashed out in descriptive terms, thus yielding a kind of descriptive content. Then we examined Frege's identity argument. According to referentialism, the meaning of a referring term simply consists in its reference such that two terms have the same meaning if they refer to the same object. The problem is that sentences of the form '*a* is *a*' and '*a* is *b*' differ in cognitive significance. For instance, Lois Lane believes that Superman is Superman, but intuitively she does not believe that Superman is Clark Kent. This suggests that the proposition expressed by '*a* is *a*' is different from the proposition expressed by '*a* is *b*', hence that the meaning of '*a*' is different from the meaning of '*b*'. But since '*a*' and '*b*' are co-referring, their meaning must be something over and above their reference. In response, the referentialist could deny that a difference in cognitive significance entails a difference in propositional content. After all, both '*a* is *a*' and '*a* is *b*' are true. The remedy is to prefix these sentences by a belief operator. For instance, while 'Lois Lane believes that Superman is Superman' is true, 'Lois Lane believes that Superman is Clark Kent' is intuitively false. Given that identical propositions have the same truth-values, the two belief-ascribing sentences must express distinct propositions. The only difference between these sentences is that one contains an occurrence of 'Superman' where the other contains an occurrence of 'Clark Kent'. Consequently, these two proper names differ in meaning. If this belief argument is sound, it shows that meaning cannot be exhausted by reference, but it does not establish that such meaning is descriptive in nature. Kripke famously responded by generalizing this puzzle about belief. True, referentialists are committed to the principle that co-referring terms can be substituted in belief contexts without change in truth-value. But this substitution principle should not be blamed. For equally untoward consequences regarding ascriptions of belief can be deduced by merely invoking other seemingly benign principles that govern our practice of belief ascription. The final part of the chapter was concerned with a worry about the communality of sense due to Frege and Dummett. All the belief argument demonstrates is that speakers must associate some senses with the terms they grasp, but if these senses are not shared between speakers, communication is jeopardized. That is to say, sense is called for in a theory of speakers' reference, but importantly also in a theory of reference for a common language. Various proposals were canvassed as to what the necessary and sufficient conditions for mutual understanding, and hence for successful communication, consist in. The somewhat inconclusive outcome was that in some cases sharing senses is sufficient and necessary for mutual understanding, yet in other cases speakers must also know that they share such senses if they are to correctly understand each other.

Annotated further readings

Alex Millar's *Philosophy of Language* (2007) and William Lycan's *Philosophy of Language* (2008) and are both excellent introductions to philosophy of language. They include very accessible chapters on Frege's philosophy of language and on descriptivism. A more demanding but highly recommendable discussion of meaning and reference in philosophy of language is François Recanati's (1993) *Direct Reference: From Language to Thought*. For a more detailed introduction to various aspects of Frege's philosophy see Harold Noonan's *Frege: A Critical Introduction* (2001). Richard Heck's (1995) "The Sense of Communication" is specifically on the problem about communication as it arises for Frege. Michael Dummett's writings on Frege are difficult but of very high quality. See for instance chapters 4, 5, 6, 9 and 11 in his *Frege. Philosophy of Language* (1973). *The Blackwell Guide to the Philosophy of Language* (2006), edited by Michael Dewitt and Richard Hanley, contains in chapters 10, 14 and 15 thorough treatments of the semantics of proper names, general terms and propositional attitude ascriptions. *The Oxford Handbook of Philosophy of Language*, edited by Brian McLaughlin, Ansgar Beckermann and Sven Walter, includes in chapters 13, 17, 18, 21 and 22 in-depth exposition and discussion of propositional content, the semantic–pragmatic distinction, linguistic and speaker reference, and proper names and natural kind terms. Nathan Salmon's (1986) *Frege's Puzzle* is a classic discussion of Frege's puzzle about belief.

2

REFERENTIALISM

2.1 Rigidity and direct reference

In Chapter 1 we presented Frege's argument that sense is individuated in a more fine-grained way than reference because sense has cognitive significance. Sense is a mode of presentation of the referent, and so is distinct from the referent. Two distinct terms, or two identical terms occurring in distinct contexts, can be associated with distinct senses even though they have the same reference. Descriptivism adds that modes of presentation are captured by a cluster of definite descriptions. This view has it that the reference of a singular or general term '*a*' is mediated by a set of descriptive properties such that an object is the referent of '*a*' if and only if that object has all or enough of those properties. As mentioned, descriptivism contrasts with referentialism according to which meaning is exhausted by reference, to use a slogan. On this view, the sole semantic function of a referring term is to pick out an object as the referent of that term. In this chapter referentialism is presented and an argument in its support is discussed.

There are two ways of spelling out the slogan. Negatively, referentialism is the view that a singular or general term has no descriptive content mediating its reference. What makes the name 'Aristotle' refer to the man Aristotle is not the fact that Aristotle instantiates various descriptive properties associated with that name such as being the teacher of Alexander the

Great. Sentences containing 'Aristotle' do not express descriptive propositions, nor does understanding 'Aristotle' involve knowing a cluster of definite descriptions expressing those properties. Positively, referentialism says
that a singular or general term '*a*' refers *directly* to its referent such that the
meaning or propositional content of '*a*' – its contribution to determining
the proposition expressed by sentences containing '*a*' – consists in its
referent. What the name 'Aristotle' contributes to determining the proposition expressed by the sentence 'Aristotle was a philosopher' is simply the
man Aristotle himself. That is to say, such a sentence expresses the *singular*
proposition **Aristotle was a philosopher**, which is the ordered pair consisting
of Aristotle himself and the property of being a philosopher. The propositional content of 'Aristotle' is singular in virtue of that proposition containing Aristotle as a constituent. Consequently, to understand 'Aristotle'
is to know of Aristotle that the name 'Aristotle' refers to him. Such
knowledge requires that one is appropriately epistemically hooked up with
Aristotle, e.g. is acquainted with Aristotle or otherwise stands in some
causal-historical relation to him.[1]

Just like descriptivism, referentialism is both a theory of meaning and a
theory of reference, but unlike descriptivism, referentialism draws a sharp
distinction between the first-order question of what the meaning and
reference of a term is from the second-order question of what makes it the
case that a term has the meaning and reference that it has. To say that
the meaning of a referring term is nothing over and above its reference is
to answer the first-order question. As regards the second-order question,
referentialists typically invoke some causal-historical account. At some point
in time the name 'Aristotle' was introduced into language by some ceremonial act of baptism, e.g. let 'Aristotle' refer to the baby boy in the blue cradle.
Those present at that time picked up the name, and then passed it on
through generations via some causal chain of communication. This causal-
historical link is not the meaning or reference of 'Aristotle', but rather
determines its meaning and reference. The link explains how the name
came to have the reference and meaning it actually has.[2]

Note that, as in the example of 'Aristotle', referentialists typically allow
for definite descriptions to play the role of *fixing the reference* of a term.
Speakers can conveniently introduce a name into their language by stipulating
that it is to refer to whoever satisfies a certain definite description. But
referentialists are adamant that descriptions can fix the reference without
giving the meaning of a term.[3] Once the term is up and running in the language,
the reference-fixing description ceases to play the reference-determining

role. All the reference-determining work is then done by the causal-historical link. In particular, competently understanding the term need not involve any knowledge of that description. All such understanding takes is knowledge of whom or what the term refers to.

Now, if understanding the name 'Aristotle' consists in knowledge of whom it refers to, one might wonder how a competent speaker S can know who that name refers to without knowing that it refers to, say, the teacher of Alexander the Great. To know who 'Aristotle' refers to is to know of Aristotle that 'Aristotle' refers to him. In general, to know of an object that it has a certain property is to have *de re* knowledge, and there can arguably be no bare *de re* knowledge. Every piece of de re knowledge rests on some piece of de dicto knowledge − knowledge that the object is F. For instance, if S knows of Edinburgh that it is beautiful, then she knows that the Scottish capital city, or David Hume's place of birth, etc., is beautiful. So, when S knows of Aristotle that 'Aristotle' refers to him, S's knowledge can always be further characterized by citing that piece of de dicto knowledge on which S's de re knowledge rests, e.g. her knowledge that 'Aristotle' refers to whoever was the teacher of Alexander the Great.[4] Then it looks like understanding 'Aristotle' consists in knowingly associating some definite description with that name.

In response, the referentialist will insist that even if true, all the foregoing shows is that S must know that 'Aristotle' refers to whoever satisfies some descriptive condition. That falls short of showing that what S knows constitutes even in part the propositional content of 'Aristotle', i.e. that the content of S's knowledge has any semantic import. Moreover, the referentialist might simply deny that de re knowledge always relies on de dicto knowledge. Knowing of Aristotle that 'Aristotle' refers to him might rather consist in having certain abilities to recognize (pictures of) Aristotle, or abilities to discriminate between (pictures of) him and relevant alternatives.

The notion of *direct reference* should be distinguished from the related but different notion of *rigid designation*. As mentioned, the notion of direct reference entails the notion of singular propositional content: a term '*a*' is directly referential if and only if sentences containing '*a*' express non-descriptive, singular propositions. In short, the propositional content of a directly referential term is singular. The notion of rigid designation, however, does not entail the notion of singular propositional content. Let me explain. To say that a singular or general term '*a*' is a *rigid designator*, or just rigid, is to say that '*a*' refers to the same object in all possible worlds.[5] Here a *possible world* can be thought of as a way things might have been. Nomologically possible worlds – worlds consistent with the laws of nature – are often distinguished from metaphysically possible worlds – worlds that may include violations of those laws. When a rigid designator is said to refer to the same object in all possible worlds, the domain of worlds is that of metaphysically possible worlds. Thus Kripke (1980: 48ff.) convincingly argued that as a matter of fact ordinary proper names and natural kind terms are rigid in just that way. For instance, 'Aristotle' is rigid, because that name refers to Aristotle in all possible worlds, and 'water' is rigid, because that natural kind term refers to H_2O in all possible worlds.[6]

In contrast, most definite descriptions are non-rigid. In the actual world 'the teacher of Alexander the Great' refers to Aristotle, but in some other possible world that description refers to Plato, because in that world Plato taught Alexander the Great. But de facto rigid descriptions like 'the smallest even prime', and essential descriptions like 'the individual with α', where α abbreviates a particular individual's genetic make-up or biological origin, are also rigid. The former happens to pick out the number 2 in all possible worlds, and the latter happens to pick out in all possible worlds whoever actually has α. For if Aristotle has α, then he necessarily has α.[7] Or consider so-called *descriptive names*. Dummett (1981: 562ff.) and Evans (1979: 179–82) suggested that descriptive names have their reference essentially fixed by certain definite descriptions such that these names have descriptive content while still rigid. Consider the following stipulation:

(Stipulation)   Let 'Julius' refer to whoever uniquely invented the zip fastener.

In (Stipulation) the name 'Julius' is not shorthand for 'the inventor of the zip fastener', because the former is a rigid designator while the latter is non-rigid. Given that Whitcomb L. Judson actually invented the zip, 'Julius' refers to him in all possible worlds. But while 'the inventor of the zip fastener' picks out Whitcomb L. Judson in the actual world, that description picks out Alexander G. Bell in a possible world in which Bell invented the zip. Nevertheless, it is essential that someone who understands 'Julius' know that 'Julius' has been introduced as a name for the inventor of the zip whoever that was.

Now we can see why the notion of rigidity does not entail the notion of singular propositional content. The sentence 'the smallest even prime is a natural number' expresses a descriptive proposition, rather than a singular proposition containing the number 2 and the property of being a natural number. Nevertheless, the subject term is a rigid designator. Rigidity is a weaker notion than that of direct reference. If a term is directly referential, it is also rigid, but a term can be rigid without being directly referential. On the one hand, directly referential terms are tagged onto their referents: their propositional content consists in the objects to which they refer. As such terms are entirely devoid of descriptive content, there is no space for them to pick out different objects in different possible worlds. They are rigid *de jure* in so far as semantic rules secure their rigidity. On the other hand, some rigid terms have descriptive content as part of their propositional content, and so will pick out an object in virtue of that object instantiating certain descriptive properties. Those de facto rigid descriptions or descriptive names are therefore not directly referential.[8]

In order to decide whether any given referring term is rigid, Kripke (1980: 48–49, 83–92) proposed an intuitive test for rigidity, which we may dub the 'Gödel–Schmidt test':

A referring term '*a*' is rigid if and only if it is false that someone other than *a* might have been *a*.

Take the proper name 'Gödel', and ask whether someone other than Gödel might have been Gödel. That seems false, indeed it seems false even if we imagine a possible world in which Schmidt discovered the incompleteness of arithmetic. In that world there is no inclination to say that Schmidt is Gödel. Rather, it is a possible world where Gödel failed to discover what he discovered in the actual world. 'Gödel' passes the test and so is rigid. Now take the definite description 'the discoverer of the incompleteness theorem', and ask whether someone other than the discoverer of the incompleteness theorem might have discovered the incompleteness theorem. That seems true. Gödel did discover that theorem, but there is a possible world in which Schmidt made that discovery, and in that world, 'the discoverer of the incompleteness theorem' refers to Schmidt. That description fails the test and so is non-rigid.

Bear in mind that sentences of the form 'the F might not have been the F' are ambiguous. To use one of Lewis' examples (1980), 'the winner might not have been the winner' is true if understood as:

(1)   The winner, possibly s/he is not the winner,

where 'the winner' takes *wide scope* with respect to the modal operator 'possibly'. If Alex is the winner in the actual world, then (1) says that there is a possible world in which Alex lost, and that is uncontroversially true. But 'the winner might not have been the winner' is false if understood as:

(2)   Possibly, the winner is not the winner,

where 'the winner' takes *narrow scope* with respect to the modal operator 'possibly'. What (2) says is that there is a possible world in which the winner in that world lost, and that is uncontroversially false. The point is now that in order for the Gödel–Schmidt test to work the terms in question must be given wide-scope readings – otherwise the Gödel–Schmidt test will fail to deliver the intuitively correct classifications. For example, 'the discoverer of the incompleteness theorem' would be rendered rigid. Even so, the Gödel–Schmidt test is by no means a knock-down argument that ordinary proper names are rigid. A staunch descriptivist could maintain that someone other than Gödel might have been Gödel on the grounds that the name 'Gödel' is simply shorthand for 'the discoverer of the incompleteness of arithmetic'. However, most ordinary speakers would surely regard such a descriptivist as having rather deviant linguistic intuitions. Note finally that for some terms applying the Gödel–Schmidt test may deliver no determinate answer. For instance, one may think that since 'Jack the Ripper' was used by the police to refer to whoever was the murdered of several prostitutes in 1890s London, it is not clear whether that name is rigid. In fairness, it should be noted that Kripke (1980: 79) regarded that name as rigid. Or take 'the Man with the Yellow Hat' which picks out Ted Shackleford, who is a character in H. A. Rey's children books *Curious George*. It is by no means obvious that the definite description 'the Man with the Yellow Hat' is non-rigid.

2.2 Kripke's modal argument

With the advent of rigid designation, and subsequently increasing recognition that ordinary proper names and natural kind terms are rigid, descriptivism began to wane in popularity. In *Naming and Necessity* Kripke advanced a number of arguments against descriptivism which provoked a revolution in philosophy of language. Here we shall only consider the *modal argument* which purports to show that because ordinary proper names are rigid, they cannot have descriptive contents as given by sets of definite descriptions.[9] Descriptivism, remember, about 'Aristotle' says that referring with that name goes by way of associated descriptive properties, which are captured by definite descriptions such that 'Aristotle' refers to whoever uniquely instantiates those properties. To simplify matters, suppose the name 'Aristotle' is simply shorthand for the definite description 'the teacher of Alexander the Great'. That is a fairly unadorned version of descriptivism, but it will do for now. It follows that 'Aristotle' refers to an individual if and only if that individual taught Alexander the Great. We saw in Section 1.3 how this view offers a prima facie attractive way of handling problems about substitution of co-referential terms in intentional contexts. What the modal argument highlights is that descriptivism is faced with such substitution problems in *modal contexts*, i.e. sentences containing modal vocabulary such as 'necessarily' and 'possibly'. It runs as follows:

(3)   If 'Aristotle' and 'the teacher of Alexander the Great' had the same propositional content, then 'Aristotle might not have been the teacher of Alexander the Great' would be false, since semantically equivalent to 'Aristotle might not have been Aristotle', which is false.

(4)   'Aristotle might not have been the teacher of Alexander the Great' is true.

(5)   So, 'Aristotle' and 'the teacher of Alexander the Great' differ in propositional content.

Note first that nothing hangs on the particular example. We could equally well mount the modal argument using natural kind terms instead of proper names. Thus descriptivism about 'water' says that its reference goes via a set of associated descriptive properties captured by the definite description 'the watery stuff' such that 'water' refers to the stuff instantiating those properties. Being watery, remember, means having all the superficial, readily observable characteristics of water: clear, potable, odourless, falls from the sky, fills the oceans, etc. Suppose therefore that 'water' is simply shorthand for 'the watery stuff'. Now consider:

(6)   If 'water' and 'the watery stuff' had the same propositional content, then 'water might not have been the watery stuff' would be false, since semantically equivalent to 'water might not have been water', which is false.

(7)   'Water might not have been the watery stuff' is true.

(8)   So, 'water' and 'the watery stuff' differ in propositional content.

Are these modal arguments compelling? Well, they have the form *modus tollens* (if p then q and not-q; therefore not-p) and so are clearly valid. The question then arises whether the premises are true. Let's begin with premises (4) and (7). Premise (4) seems uncontroversial. Surely, there are possible worlds in which someone other than Aristotle taught Alexander the Great. Similarly, (7) strikes one as true. 'Water' rigidly refers to H_2O, and surely there are possible worlds in which H_2O lacks all those watery features, e.g. filling the oceans, running out of taps, quenching thirst.[10] Maybe some of these worlds are nomologically impossible. That would be so if among the watery properties we counted compressibility, electrical conductivity, etc. But as mentioned, 'water' refers to H_2O in all metaphysically possible worlds, and if deviant laws of nature govern such worlds, then H_2O may lack even such microphysical or chemical properties.[11]

Nevertheless, the descriptivist might object that if 'Aristotle' is shorthand for 'the teacher of Alexander the Great', then the sentence occurring in both (3) and (4) 'Aristotle might not have been the teacher of Alexander the Great' is semantically equivalent to the sentence:

(9)   'The teacher of Alexander the Great might not have been the teacher of Alexander the Great.'

Likewise, if 'water' is shorthand for 'the watery stuff', then the sentence occurring in both (6) and (7) 'water might not have been the watery stuff' is semantically equivalent to:

(10)   'The watery stuff might not have been the watery stuff.'

We saw in Section 2.1 that sentences of the form 'the F might not have been the F' are true only if 'the F' takes wide scope with respect to the modal operator 'might not have been'. One might then claim that both premises cannot be true simultaneously.

Let's take the Aristotle-version (3)–(5) first. The sentence in (9) shares that form, and so is true only on such a wide-scope reading. Given that the sentence occurring in (4) 'Aristotle might not have been the teacher of Alexander the Great' is semantically equivalent to the sentence in (9), (4) is true only on such a wide-scope reading. But then given that the sentences in (3) are also semantically equivalent to the sentence in (9), they should be interpreted in the same way. Otherwise the modal argument would commit an *operator-shift fallacy*. This means that the sentences in (3) are also true. Consequently, (3) is rendered false: 'Aristotle' and 'the teacher of Alexander the Great' could have the same propositional content while 'Aristotle might not have been the teacher of Alexander the Great' is true.

Now, let's turn to the 'water'-version (6)–(8). The sentence in (10) is true only if 'the watery stuff' takes wide scope with respect to the modal operator 'might not have been'. Given that the sentence occurring in (7) 'water might not have been the watery stuff' is semantically equivalent to the sentence in (10), (7) is true only on such a wide-scope reading. But the sentences that occur in (6) are also semantically equivalent to the sentence in (10), and should therefore be uniformly interpreted. Or else the modal argument would illicitly shift the modal operator from one premise to the next. This means that the sentences in (6) are also true. Accordingly, (6) is rendered false: it does not follow that if 'water' and 'the watery stuff' have the same propositional content, then 'water might not have been the watery stuff' is false.

On this background, the descriptivist might follow Dummett (1973: 110–51) in attempting to account for rigidity in terms of scope conventions, the idea being that proper names and natural kind terms are shorthand for wide-scope definite descriptions. But whether speakers' linguistic intuitions about rigidity can be understood in this way is doubtful. While sentences of the form 'the F might not have been the F' are true on wide-scope readings, sentences of the form 'a might not have been a' seem false even on such readings, where 'a' is a proper name or natural kind term. We shall not enter into the details here except to flag other cases where intuitions about rigidity cannot easily be accommodated by analyses in terms of scope differences. Take two non-modal sentences:

(11)   Aristotle is the teacher of Alexander the Great.
(12)   The teacher of Alexander the Great is the teacher of Alexander the Great.

Both (11) and (12) are true in the actual world, but they differ in truth-value in some possible worlds. In a possible world where Plato taught Alexander the Great, (11) is false, but (12) is true. Sentence (11) is possibly false, but (12) is necessarily true. The problem is now that since (11) and (12) contain no modal vocabulary, any manoeuvre involving scope would seem to have been blocked.[12]

Let's instead ponder on the first premise, which needs some unpacking. The conditional in (3) assumes that 'Aristotle' and 'the teacher of Alexander the Great' have the same propositional content only if they are intersubstitutable in modal contexts without change in truth-value. At first blush, that looks like a plausible assumption. Consider the following *modal substitution principle*:

(ModSub)   If the sentence 'possibly, *a* is not F' is true, and '*a*' and '*b*' have the same propositional content, then the sentence 'possibly, *b* is not F' is also true.

The rationale behind (ModSub) is that propositional content determines reference, not just in the actual world, but also in all possible worlds. So, if two referring terms have the same propositional content, then they refer to the same object in all possible worlds, and if they refer to the same object in all possible worlds, then they can be substituted in any modal sentence without changing the truth-value of that sentence.[13]

Nevertheless, one might balk at the idea that every kind of propositional content determines reference at all possible worlds. The modal argument is blocked if 'Aristotle' and 'the teacher of Alexander the Great', and 'water' and 'the watery stuff', are co-propositional despite not being co-referential at all possible worlds. Thus propositional content could be bifurcated into a component determining reference in the actual world, and a component determining reference at all possible worlds.[14] Let's revisit our descriptive name 'Julius' from Section 2.1, and dwell on the following two sentences:

(13)   Julius invented the zip.
(14)   The inventor of the zip invented the zip.

On the one hand, there is some robust sense in which (13) and (14) express the same proposition. Being competent with 'Julius' consists in knowing that the name is stipulated to pick out whoever invented the zip in the actual world. What competent speaker S asserts when she asserts (13) is therefore just what S asserts when she asserts (14). The speaker makes the same assertion about what the actual world is like. Because the way S takes the actual world to be is the same, she cannot understandingly believe (13) but not (14). On the other hand, due to the rigidity of 'Julius' and non-rigidity of 'the inventor of the zip', (13) and (14) differ in truth-value at some possible worlds. Whitcomb L. Judson invented the zip in the actual world, but suppose Alexander G. Bell invented the zip in some possible world. Both (13) and (14) are true at the actual world, but (13) is false and (14) is true at that possible world. And we have seen that differences in truth-value make for differences in propositional content. On this background, Evans (1979) and Dummett (1991: 47–48) distinguished between *content* and *proposition*, and *assertoric content* and *ingredient sense*, respectively.[15] For them, the (assertoric) content of a sentence is what is said by an utterance of that sentence, and it is also the object of belief. The proposition associated with a sentence or its ingredient sense, however, is what that sentence contributes to determining the (assertoric) content of more complex, especially modal sentences of which it is a part. So, while (13) and (14) coincide in (assertoric) content, they differ in ingredient sense/propositions. In the case of Dummett, for instance, assertions of (13) and (14) express the same contents, yet (13) and (14) embed differently inside the scope of a modal operator, as witnessed by the fact that (13) is contingent and (14) is necessary. Whether such hybrid theories of content are viable is a vexed issue to which we return in Chapters 4 and 7. A key question will be whether (assertoric) content is genuinely semantic or merely cognitively significant in serving to explain behaviour. Suffice it to say that even if the distinction between these two kinds of content holds in the case of sentences containing the descriptive name 'Julius', it is by no means obvious that the distinction is equally applicable when it comes to sentences containing ordinary proper names and natural kind terms.

2.3 Rigidification

Consider again the 'Aristotle'-version (3)–(5) of the modal argument. This argument is targeted at the simple-minded descriptivist view that 'Aristotle' is shorthand for 'the teacher of Alexander the Great', but just as in the case of 'water', any descriptivist would be inclined to invoke additional definite descriptions such as 'the famous philosopher of antiquity'. Indeed the descriptivist may insist that the set of descriptions be thought of as a *cluster* such that 'Aristotle' refers to an object just in case that object satisfies the majority of these descriptions. That way 'Aristotle' could still refer to Aristotle if it turns out that he fails to satisfy some of these descriptions. So far these descriptions have been stated in purely general, qualitative terms, but the descriptivist can avail herself of other kinds of descriptions. Here is a reason why so-called *other-dependent descriptions* should be included. On the one hand, descriptivism says that what a competent speaker S knows when she understands 'Aristotle' is a set of definite descriptions. On the other hand, what determines the reference of 'Aristotle' is precisely that very set of descriptions. Putting the theory of meaning and the theory of reference together, what S knows when she understands 'Aristotle' is what determines the reference of that name. That is to say, when S grasps the meaning of 'Aristotle', S has uniquely identifying knowledge of the referent of 'Aristotle'. The problem is that possession of such uniquely identifying knowledge seems overly demanding. In many contexts S could easily be said to be competent with 'Aristotle' even though S all by herself is unable to uniquely identify its referent. In such cases S's competence consists in part in her ability to pass the buck on by associating an other-dependent description, e.g. 'the individual that the experts from whom S has borrowed the term use "Aristotle" to refer to'. By deferring to the expert speakers in her speech community who do have sufficient identifying knowledge, S manages to use 'Aristotle' to pick out Aristotle.

This phenomenon of *semantic deference* is ubiquitous in natural language. Maybe not so much in the case of certain natural kind terms such as 'water'. In spelling out 'the watery stuff' the pertinent descriptions known by ordinary competent speakers were assumed to be purely superficial or qualitative: 'the clear, potable, odourless liquid that falls from the sky and fills the oceans, etc.' Knowing those properties does seem to constitute unique identifying knowledge of the referent of 'water' – assuming they are instantiated only by H_2O. Even so, Kroon (2004: 284) gives the example of children brought up during a severe drought in Eritrea. They have only ever seen trickles of water inside a well too deep and dark to allow them to retrieve water or detect its usual phenomenal features. Nevertheless, as they are told by aid workers who are teaching them English that the stuff is water they are able to use 'water' to refer to water. Or consider other natural kind terms. Putnam (1996: xvi) gives the example of knowing the meaning of 'elm' in virtue of knowing that elms are deciduous trees common in North America and Europe. Yet Putnam confesses that he is unable to distinguish elm tress from beech trees, and so lack unique identifying knowledge of the referent of 'elm'. Again the descriptivist's counter is that Putnam does know deferentially how beech trees differ from elm tress in that only the latter are called 'elm tress' by the experts in his speech community. The lesson is that when most ordinary speakers use names or natural kind terms, they rely on experts associating properties with these terms that do secure unique references. There is a chain of borrowings that bottoms out in the experts' associated properties. These are specialist properties distinct from the stereotypical ones that the ordinary speakers associate with the relevant terms.[16]

Obviously other-dependent descriptions are to no avail in responding to the modal argument. To see why, one need only appreciate the existence of possible worlds in which Aristotle is not the individual whom the experts use 'Aristotle' to refer to. The rigidity of 'Aristotle' ensures that 'Aristotle' refers to Aristotle even in such worlds. Consider instead our essential description 'the individual with α', where α is taken to abbreviate Aristotle's genetic make-up or biological origin. Assuming Aristotle has that make-up or origin necessarily, there is no possible world in which Aristotle is not the individual with α.[17] This essential description will therefore be rigid. In general, if two terms are both rigid, then an identity statement containing them will be necessarily true if true at all. If 'Aristotle is the individual with α' is true, then that statement is necessarily true. So, were the descriptivist to swap 'the teacher of Alexander the Great' with this essential description, premise (4) in the modal argument would be false. That is to say:

(15)   'Aristotle might not have been the individual with α'

is false. If invoked in a descriptivist theory of reference, essential descriptions thus have the advantage of ensuring that 'Aristotle' picks out Aristotle in all possible worlds. The downside is that such descriptions should not be allowed to play any role in a theory of meaning. The reason is that ordinary speakers competent with 'Aristotle' simply have no knowledge of any such essential descriptions. Worse, in the case of Aristotle presumably not even expert speakers possess such knowledge.

Similarly, in the case of 'water', the descriptivist could appeal to an essential description such as 'the stuff that is composed of two hydrogen atoms for every oxygen atom'. That would trivially guarantee that 'water' picks out H_2O in all possible worlds, and so a corresponding version of premise (7) in the modal argument would be false:

(16)   'Water might not have been the stuff that is composed of two hydrogen atoms for every oxygen atom.'

Again the drawback is that ordinary competent speakers cannot be expected to know such essential descriptions. A speaker can be perfectly competent with 'water' without knowing anything about the underlying chemistry of water. Indeed back in 1750 before Lavoisier discovered oxygen and hydrogen, not even the experts knew the relevant chemical facts. It surely sounds counter-intuitive to say that speakers were incompetent or even less than fully competent with 'water' until those facts were known. The general point is that knowledge of meaning should comprise the kind of information that can be found in dictionaries rather than encyclopedias.

Fortunately for descriptivists there are ways of *rigidifying* a definite description – turning a non-rigid description into a rigid one – that does not invoke essential descriptions. They typically appeal to certain indexical expressions as such rigidification devices. Take 'actually'. Sometimes that expression serves to place emphasis or dispel confusion as in 'actually it was Scholes, not Rooney, who was sent off'. Set those cases aside. We are interested in a distinctive logical use of 'actually' in natural language. One such logical use is to clarify matters of relative scope involving modal operators. Remember Lewis' example 'the winner might not have been the winner', which is true if 'the winner' takes wide scope with respect to the modal operator, but false if 'the winner' takes narrow scope with respect to that operator. Instead of using scope conventions to disambiguate between these two readings, introducing 'actually' yields the true reading:

(17)   The actual winner might not have been the winner.

What (17) says is that there are possible worlds in which the winner in the actual world lost. Suppose Michael Schumacher won the race in the actual world. He might not have been the winner of that race, because there is a possible world in which Lewis Hamilton won that race. 'Actual' is an indexical expression which rigidly refers to the world of the context of utterance. The rigidified definite description 'the actual F' refers to an object in some possible world just in case 'the F' refers to that object in the actual world. Whether 'actual' occurs inside or outside the scope of a modal operator, it always refers back to the actual world. Indexical expressions are *context sensitive* in that they have different referents in different contexts of utterance. When Anna uses the personal pronoun 'I', she refers to Anna, and when Thomas uses 'I' he refers to Thomas. One might then wonder how such expressions can also be rigid, and so have the same referents in all possible worlds. Here we need to distinguish contexts of utterance from *circumstances of evaluation*.[18] Contexts of utterance consist of the speaker, hearer, time and place at which the indexical expressions in question are uttered. They map such utterances onto the propositional contents expressed by those expressions, and so are needed to determine what propositional content is expressed. Circumstances of evaluation are indices consisting of contextual features that need not go together in any possible context. They map propositional contents onto referents or truth-values, and so are needed to evaluate the truth-value of the propositions expressed. Consider the sentence:

(18)   'I feel elated.'

The indexical expression 'I' refers to the speaker of the context of utterance, but is also rigid in that it refers to the same individual at all circumstances of evaluation or possible worlds. The truth of (18) depends on who the speaker is and on whether s/he feels elated. The truth-value of an utterance of (18) is thus *doubly dependent* on features of the context of utterance and on features of the circumstance of evaluation. If Anna is the speaker, then (18) expresses the proposition **Anna feels elated**. If instead Thomas is the speaker, then (18) expresses the proposition **Thomas feels elated**. 'I' is thus directly referential in that its propositional content in a context of utterance is its reference in that context. Suppose Anna feels elated in the actual world but not in some possible world W. Then that proposition is true at the actual world but false at W. Given that Anna is the speaker in the actual world, an utterance of (18) is false at W, because Anna does not feel elated in W. Once we know who the speaker is, 'I' picks out the same individual at all circumstances of evaluation or possible worlds.[19]

The same is roughly true of the indexical expression 'actual'. Consider the sentence:

(19)   'The actual winner lost.'

If (19) is uttered in the actual world, then (19) expresses the proposition **the winner in the actual world lost**. If instead (19) is uttered in some possible world W, then (19) expresses the proposition **the winner in W lost**. Suppose Schumacher won the race in the actual world but lost in W. Hamilton won the race in W. Then the proposition **the winner in the actual world lost** is false at the actual world but true at W. Given that (19) is uttered in the actual world, an utterance of (19) is true at W, because the winner in the actual world, i.e. Schumacher, did not win in W. Hamilton did. Once we know which world the sentence is uttered in, we use 'the actual winner' to talk about the same individual in all possible worlds.

Let's now revisit the modal argument, which attacked the claim that the propositional content of proper names and natural kind terms are given by definite descriptions. Given that proper names and natural kind terms are rigid while the relevant definite descriptions are non-rigid, they will differ in reference at some possible worlds. Assume that propositional content determines reference at all possible worlds such that if two expressions have the same propositional content, then they also have the same reference at all possible worlds. It then follows that the propositional content of proper names and natural kind terms cannot be given by definite descriptions. The current proposal is to grant both the conclusion and premises of the modal argument. Instead descriptivism should be modified to encompass *rigidified definite descriptions*. In the case of proper names, 'Aristotle' is shorthand for 'the actual teacher of Alexander the Great', etc. In the case of natural kind terms, 'water' is shorthand for 'the actual watery stuff'. Let's call this view *rigidified descriptivism*. It is easy to see how rigidification helps with the modal argument. Take 'water'. 'Water' and 'the actual watery stuff' are both rigid designators, and so given that they have the same reference in the actual world, namely H_2O, they have the same reference in all possible worlds. It cannot therefore be shown that these two terms differ in propositional content in virtue of a difference in reference at some possible world. In short, no difference in modal properties of these terms can threaten their co-propositionality. More precisely, a corresponding version of (7) is simply false:

(20)   'Water might not have been the actual watery stuff.'

In our world – the actual world – water is the watery stuff. There is of course a possible world in which water, i.e. H_2O, is not the watery stuff, but there is no possible world in which water is not the watery stuff in the actual world. Premise (20) is a modal sentence, as it contains the phrase 'might not have been'. To assess the truth-value of that sentence, we therefore go to possible worlds in which there is water, i.e. H_2O, and then ask whether that stuff has the property of being watery-in-the-actual-world. Water has that property in all worlds, and so (20) is false.

Let's finally consider a referentialist objection to rigidified descriptivism.[20] Given that 'water' and 'the actual watery stuff' in our mouth are both rigid designators of H_2O, they can be substituted in modal contexts without change in truth-value. For instance, the sentence 'it is necessary that water is water' is true, but so is the sentence 'it is necessary that water is the actual watery stuff'. Moreover, following rigidified descriptivism, 'water' and 'the actual watery stuff' are also substitutable in intentional contexts without change in truth-value, because the descriptive content of 'water' is **the actual watery stuff**. The sentence 'Mary believes that water is H_2O' is true if and only if the sentence 'Mary believes that the actual watery stuff is H_2O' is true. For Mary to believe that water is H_2O is for her to believe that the watery stuff in the actual world is H_2O. It may sound implausible that Mary, who is an inhabitant on Earth, cannot have beliefs about water without having beliefs about the actual world – the world she inhabits. For example, Mary could well possess the concept **water** without possessing the concept **the actual world**.[21] Be that as it may. A more serious worry arises once we turn to *mixed modal and intentional contexts*. Let Perfect Earth be just like Earth in every respect except it is located in a possible world distinct from the actual world. In particular, the watery stuff on Perfect Earth has the microstructure H_2O. Suppose also that Mary has a *doppelgänger* on Perfect Earth whom we call 'perfect-Mary'. perfect-Mary is an internal duplicate of Mary, which is to say that they are molecule-for-molecule identical. Doppelgängers are individuals who share all their *intrinsic properties* – the properties they have in virtue of the way they are in themselves, independently of which properties other objects have.[22] Intuitively, just as Mary has beliefs about water, so does perfect-Mary. Now the problem arises that when we – Earthlings – say that perfect-Mary believes that water is H_2O, we say that she believes that the watery stuff in the actual world is H_2O. For if 'water' is shorthand for 'the actual watery stuff', and 'actual' is an indexical, then our utterance of 'perfect-Mary believes that water is H_2O' expresses the proposition **perfect-Mary believes that the watery stuff in the actual world is H_2O**. But surely perfect-Mary could believe that water is H_2O without having any beliefs about the actual world, and that is something we should be able to report. The problem is not so much that perfect-Mary cannot believe that water is H_2O without having beliefs about the world that she calls 'actual' – the world containing Perfect Earth – but rather that we cannot ascribe to perfect-Mary the belief that water is H_2O without ascribing to her a belief about the world that we call 'actual' – the actual world containing Earth. It is hard to see why perfect-Mary, or anyone else, would need to have beliefs about other possible worlds in order to have beliefs about water. And of course there is nothing special about the term 'water'. The same objection applies to any proper name or natural kind term which the descriptivist purports to identify with a rigidified definite description.[23]

2.4 Referentialist belief ascriptions

In Section 1.3 referentialism was confronted with the belief argument. According to referentialism, referring terms are directly referential which

means that their propositional content consists in their reference. Substituting two co-referring terms in intentional contexts should thus preserve truth-value. That is to say, referentialism sanctions the following substitution principle pertaining to such contexts:

(SubRef*)   If the sentence 'S believes that a is F' is true and $a = b$, then the sentence 'S believes that b is F' is also true.

The belief argument aims to prove (SubRef*) false. Consider again:

(21)   Anna believes that water is wholesome.
(22)   Anna believes that H_2O is wholesome.

Assume that Anna is familiar with some chemical expressions, but that she knows next to nothing about chemistry. Anna is competent with both 'water' and 'H_2O', but she possesses no evidence bearing on the identity between their referents. So, while (21) is certainly true, (22) seems false. As the only difference between (21) and (22) is the occurrence of the co-referring terms 'water' and 'H_2O', it looks as if we have a counter-example to (SubRef*). As mentioned in Section 1.3 the belief argument assumes that a belief-ascribing sentence of the form 'S believes that a is F' expresses a two-place relation of belief between S and the proposition expressed by the embedded sentence 'a is F'. The logical forms of (21) and (22) should therefore respectively amount to:

(23)   Belief [Anna; **water is wholesome**].
(24)   Belief [Anna; **H_2O is wholesome**].

The problem for referentialism is that all propositional content about individuals and natural kinds is singular, and the two singular propositions **water is wholesome** and **H_2O is wholesome** are identical. Given that water is identical to H_2O, the proposition containing water and the property of being wholesome is identical to the proposition containing H_2O and the property of being wholesome.

However, referentialists typically agree that an utterance of (22) conveys information not conveyed by an utterance of (21). Although the sole propositional content of Anna's beliefs in (21) and (22) is the same singular proposition, she cannot believe that proposition without there being some mode of presentation under which she believes it. To use Perry's distinction

(1993) between *what* an agent believes and *how* the agent believes what she believes, the singular proposition is what Anna believes but the mode of presentation captures how she believes that proposition. One way to think of modes of presentation is as *dispositions to assent to sentences*. While Anna is clearly disposed to assent to the sentence 'water is wholesome', she is not disposed to assent to the sentence 'H_2O is wholesome'. Indeed she may be disposed to dissent from that latter sentence – the reason being that she fails to realize that 'H_2O is wholesome' expresses a singular proposition that she does in fact believe. So, the logical form of (21) and (22) is better seen as a three-place relation between Anna, the singular proposition expressed by the embedded sentence, and a mode of presentation (MoP) of that proposition:

(25)   Belief [Anna; **water is wholesome** ($water_{MoP}$, being $wholesome_{MoP}$)].
(26)   Belief [Anna; **H_2O is wholesome** (H_2O_{MoP}, being $wholesome_{MoP}$)].

Following referentialism, the key point is that modes of presentation are truth-conditionally irrelevant. The difference in informational content between utterances of (21) and (22) is due to, not a difference in semantics, but in *pragmatic implicature*. The truth-conditional content of Anna's belief is the same singular proposition, and so (21) and (22) are both strictly speaking true. But that proposition is believed under different linguistic guises. That is to say, (21) and (22) specify two distinct ways of taking that single proposition. To use Perry's distinction, there is no difference in what Anna believes, but only in how she believes what she believes. The mistaken intuition that (22) is false is due to the fact that utterances of (22) generate the false pragmatic implicature that Anna is disposed to assent to 'H_2O is wholesome'. The contention is that even if competent speakers are highly sensitive to the informational content conveyed by utterances of (21) and (22), they are equally unreliable in sorting out what is semantically encoded and what is pragmatically implicated. Especially, they are inclined to think that informational content at the level of pragmatic implicature goes into determining the truth-conditions of the reported beliefs.

Importantly, when we ascribe beliefs to others we should be as faithful as possible to the way they take the world to be. We should neither use words they do not understand, nor use them in ways in which they would not use them. There is thus a maxim governing belief ascriptions to the effect that we should remain faithful to their linguistic behaviour unless there is reason to deviate. Reporting Anna's belief using the sentence 'Anna believes that H_2O is wholesome' violates that maxim. Such violations are inappropriate, but have no impact on the truth-value of what was said. The more general point is that speakers have responsibilities not to lead hearers astray beyond asserting only what is true. If I utter 'Mark didn't launch into a fight last night' knowing that Mark never misbehaves, then I speak truly but also mislead the hearer into thinking that Mark occasionally does end up in a fight. By pragmatically implicating a falsehood I fail to fulfil my communicative requirements.

We shall not here assess whether this so-called *implicature theory* offers a persuasive explanation of speakers' intuitions about (21) and (22).[24] Let's instead return to Kripke's puzzle from Section 1.3. This revenge problem supposedly shows that (SubRef*) is not to blame in the belief argument, because our very practice of reporting beliefs is incoherent. As we saw, the descriptivist will argue that the consistency principle:

(Consistency)   If a speaker S reflectively and occurrently believes that a is F and that a is not F, then S is not fully rational

fails to apply, because the two descriptivist propositions are not contradictory. The referentialist, however, might argue that (Consistency) is simply false. Given that the singular proposition **water is wholesome** contains water as an ingredient, to believe that proposition is to believe of water that it is wholesome. To say that Anna believes that water is wholesome is to ascribe a de dicto belief to her, and to say that Anna believes of water that it is wholesome is to ascribe a de re belief to her. On the referentialist view, Anna has the *de dicto* belief that water is wholesome if and only if she has the corresponding de re belief. But there is no question that Anna can simultaneously believe of water that it is wholesome and not wholesome without being reproached with inconsistency. That happens when she thinks of water under distinct modes of presentation. So, the fact that her de re beliefs have logically contradictory properties is not reflectively accessible to her – it can only be discovered by appropriate empirical means. But if to believe of water that it is wholesome is just to believe the singular proposition **water is wholesome**, then it should equally be possible to simultaneously believe that water is wholesome and that water is not wholesome without being in the least irrational.

This should come as no surprise. Singular propositions are not individuated in terms of what we in Section 1.2 called their 'cognitive significance', but rather by their objectual constituents, independently of how they are conceptualized. And rational speakers may well fail to know various logical properties, e.g. identity or distinctness, of propositions they understand when individuated in this coarse-grained manner. It is therefore not to be expected that Anna who competently entertains such propositions can come to know their logical properties just by reflection on the contents of these propositions. What the referentialist challenges is Dummett's claim (1978: 131) that:

> It is an undeniable feature of the notion of meaning – obscure as that notion is – that meaning is *transparent* in the sense that, if someone attaches a meaning to each of two words, he must know whether these meanings are the same.

The idea is that propositional content is *epistemically transparent* in the sense that if a competent speaker S fully apprehends two propositional contents with certain logical properties, then she can come to know just by reflection that they have those properties. Consider:

(Epistemic   If a competent speaker S grasps the propositional content
Transparency)   of two referring terms, and the two terms have identical/
                  distinct propositional contents, then S knows just by reflection
                  that they have identical/distinct propositional contents.

If, as referentialism has it, (Epistemic Transparency) is false, then S can at the same time consistently and thus fully rationally believe a proposition and its negation, since their contradictory nature is not reflectively accessible to her. Consequently, (Consistency) is false too.

We shall return to (Epistemic Transparency) in Sections 5.1 and 5.4, but before we close note how neatly referentialism handles perfect-Mary's belief on Perfect Earth. On this view, the propositional content of both Mary's belief on Earth and perfect-Mary's belief on Perfect Earth is the singular proposition **water is H_2O**. Moreover, Mary and perfect-Mary conceptualize the objectual ingredients of that proposition in the very same way. That is to say, the modes under which they are presented with, or the ways in which they think of, those ingredients are identical. They both think of water as the watery stuff. Importantly, the term 'water' is not shorthand for a rigidified definite description of the form 'the actual watery stuff', and so we – Earthlings – can safely attribute to perfect-Mary the belief that water is H_2O without also having to attribute to her a belief about our world – the actual world.

Chapter summary

In this chapter we reviewed the case for referentialism – the view that singular and general referring terms are directly referential in that they pick out their referents unmediated by the satisfaction of any definite descriptions. Their reference exhausts their meaning. We elaborated on the important distinction between a rigid designator and a directly referring term. A rigid designator is a term that refers to the same object in all possible worlds. Proper names and natural kind terms are rigid designators, but so are also de facto rigid definite descriptions, e.g. 'the smallest even prime', and these descriptions are not directly referential. Kripke's modal argument against descriptivism shows that the meaning of a referring term 'a' cannot be given by definite descriptions of the form 'the F', because 'a' is rigid but 'the F' is non-rigid. These expressions differ in reference at some possible worlds, and so must also differ in meaning, provided meaning is what determines reference in all possible worlds. In response, some descriptivists take issue with this last assumption. They bifurcate content into two distinct components. The assertoric content of a sentence is what is said by an utterance of that sentence, and it is also the object of belief. Its ingredient sense, however, is what that sentence contributes to determining the assertoric content of more complex sentences of which it is a part. On this hybrid view, two otherwise identical sentences containing 'a' and 'the F' may coincide in assertoric content while differ in ingredient sense. Other descriptivists appeal to rigidified definite descriptions of the form 'the actual F', which in all possible worlds refer to whoever is the F in the actual world. On this rigidified descriptivist view, the meaning of 'a' is given by a cluster of such descriptions: 'the actual F', 'the actual G', etc. Since these descriptions and 'a' are co-referential at all possible worlds, no difference in reference establishes a difference in meaning between them. The referentialist countermove is to home in on mixed modal and intentional contexts. Imagine that Perfect Earth is exactly like Earth except located in another possible world. Moreover, Mary on Earth has a doppelgänger – an internal duplicate called 'perfect-Mary' – on Perfect Earth. Intuitively, Mary will want to say that perfect-Mary believes that water is wet. The problem for rigidified descriptivism is that if 'water' is shorthand for 'the actual watery stuff', then when Mary utters 'perfect-Mary believes that water is wet', she attributes to perfect-Mary the belief that the watery stuff in the actual world is wet. But surely, perfect-Mary need have no beliefs about the actual world in order to have beliefs about water. The last part of the chapter dealt briefly with the semantics of referentialist belief attributions. The contention was that 'S believes that p' should be seen as a three-place relation between a believer S, a singular proposition, and a semantically insignificant mode of presentation of that proposition. In light of this implicature theory, we can represent a referentialist solution to Kripke's puzzle from Section 1.3. The principle of (Epistemic Transparency) says that competent speakers have reflective access to the logical properties of propositions that they grasp or believe. But singular propositions are not epistemically transparent since it is perfectly possible for such speakers to believe a proposition and its negation without thereby being in a position to know that she holds contradictory beliefs, hence without being irrational.

Annotated further reading

William Lycan's *Philosophy of Language* (2008) is an excellent introduction to philosophy of language, in which chapter 4 is devoted to rigidity, direct reference and referentialism. Another highly recommendable discussion of meaning and reference is François Recanati's (1993) *Direct Reference: From Language to Thought*. Chapters 1, 2 and 9 deal with direct reference, singular propositions and Kripke's modal argument. Needless to say, Kripke's (1980) own *Naming and Necessity* is indispensable when it comes to these topics. For very important, albeit difficult, discussion of referentialism in general and the modal argument in particular see Nathan Salmon's (1981) *Reference and Essence*, chapters 1–6, and more recently Scott Soames' (2002) *Beyond Rigidity: The Unfinished Semantic Agenda of "Naming and Necessity"*. The Blackwell Guide to the Philosophy of Language (2006), edited by Michael Dewitt and Richard Hanley, contains in chapters 10, 14 and 15 discussion of referentialism in the context of proper names, general terms and propositional attitude ascriptions. Likewise, *The Oxford Handbook of Philosophy of Language*, edited by Brian McLaughlin, Ansgar Beckermann and Sven Walter, includes in chapters 18, 20 and 21 thorough treatments of the rigidity and direct referentiality of proper names and natural kind terms. When it comes specifically to rigidification and scope distinctions, Jason Stanley's (1997) "Names and Rigid Designation" is valuable. More in-depth analyses are found in Michael Dummett's *Frege: Philosophy of Language* (1973), Appendix to chapter 5, and in Scott Soames' (2002) *Beyond Rigidity: The Unfinished Semantic Agenda of "Naming and Necessity"*, chapter 2.

3

FROM LANGUAGE
TO THOUGHT

3.1 Putnam's Twin Earth argument

In the previous two chapters we have been examining two competing views about what the meaning of a singular or general term consists in, where the meaning of a term is understood as the propositional content of a term, i.e. the contribution it yields to determine the proposition expressed by sentences containing it. While descriptivism says that the propositional content of such a term is given by a set of definite descriptions associated with that term by competent speakers, referentialism says that the propositional content of such a term is identical to its referent. In this chapter we will examine different kinds of arguments against not just descriptivism but any view on which propositional content is a matter of competent speakers' mental associations. These arguments aim to establish that propositional content depends for its individuation instead on external features of these speakers' environment. Their strategy is to show that when features of the physical, sociolinguistic or historical environment vary while everything else is kept fixed, the identity of the content in question varies as well.

In Putnam's seminal paper "The Meaning of 'Meaning'" he proposed a Twin Earth thought experiment. We are asked to envisage the following scenario. We are back in 1750 when there was no real knowledge of chemistry. Elsewhere in our galaxy there is a planet exactly like Earth in all respects except that the clear potable liquid that fills the oceans, falls from the sky as rain, etc. – in short, the watery stuff – is not composed of H_2O. This stuff is composed of a chemically different kind of stuff that has a long complicated formula abbreviated as 'XYZ'. We Earthlings call this planet 'Twin Earth'. Although XYZ is superficially like water, and is called 'water' by the twin-Earthlings, it is not water. Natural kinds arguably have *essences* which are features whose possession is necessary and sufficient for something to be an instance of those kinds.[1] In particular, manifest natural kinds such as water are individuated by their underlying microstructure. Water is what it is in virtue of its distinctive chemical composition H_2O. XYZ is no more water than FeS_2 is gold. We call FeS_2 (or iron pyrite) 'fool's gold'. Likewise, we Earthlings will need to introduce the neologism 'twin-water' for XYZ.

Imagine moreover that everyone on Earth has a doppelgänger or an internal duplicate on Twin Earth who is physically identical to us from the skin in.[2] Ignore the annoying detail that humans are composed of approximately 60 per cent water. The notion of a doppelgänger is coherent, and we could have chosen a different example, as we shall see. In particular, Mary lives on Earth, whereas her doppelgänger twin-Mary, as we Earthlings call her, who is molecule-for-molecule identical to Mary, lives on Twin Earth. Mary and twin-Mary are not only identical in their intrinsic physical properties they are also historical and functional duplicates. When Mary and twin-Mary as toddlers went to the seaside they both uttered 'look, water!' When they as adults are thirsty they both turn on the tap in order to quench their thirst. And so on. Moreover, Putnam also assumed that Mary and twin-Mary are in exactly the same experiential and psychological states. For instance, when Mary and twin-Mary drink the liquid they call 'water' they undergo the same gustatory experience, and they both believe that the watery stuff is wholesome. Putnam recognized that competent speakers associate a set of superficial descriptions with 'water', and he dubbed the kind of content they thereby express 'the stereotype'. The stereotype associated with 'water' is **the watery stuff**: it captures the cognitively significant aspect of the meaning of 'water', but it plays no role in determining the reference of 'water'. Stereotypes are not semantic contents. These doppelgängers share psychological states in virtue of having these stereotypical beliefs in common – the beliefs that the watery stuff is thus and so.

Now Putnam mounts the following Twin Earth argument. While Mary and her fellow Earthlings causally interact only with H_2O, twin-Mary and her fellow twin-Earthlings causally interact only with XYZ. This means that when Mary uses the term 'water' she refers to H_2O, but when twin-Mary uses the term 'water' she refers to XYZ.[3] We have learned from Frege in Sections 1.1 and 1.2 that meaning determines reference such that if two terms have the same meaning, then they have the same reference. Put differently, if two terms differ in reference, they also differ in meaning. The meaning of 'water' as used by Mary determines a reference that is distinct from the reference determined by the meaning of 'water' as used by twin-Mary. So, Mary and twin-Mary must mean different things when they respectively use 'water': Mary means **water**, while twin-Mary means **twin-water**. In fact, to say that Mary and twin-Mary mean the same thing has counter-intuitive consequences. For instance, if they both meant **water** by 'water', then many of twin-Mary's beliefs would count as false such as the belief she would express by 'there is water in the jug'. But Mary and twin-Mary are stipulated to be internally identical. So, what physically goes on in their heads as well as their experiential and psychological states fall short of determining what they mean by their respective use of 'water'. That term is a homonym. As Putnam famously put it (1975: 144), "cut the pie any way you like, meanings just ain't in the head". What determine meaning are rather possibly unknown features of the physical environment. As Putnam phrased it (1996: xvii), even back in 1750, the "meaning was different because the stuff was different".[4]

Talk about properties or states *determining* other properties or states is apt to mislead. This is a claim about *individuation* rather than *causation*.[5] Following Putnam, the meaning of 'water' as used by Mary is externally individuated in terms of environmental features. Individuation is about identity: what makes something what it is. In the context of the Twin Earth argument, individuation is a question about patterns of causal relationships, e.g. Mary or her fellow speakers have causally interacted with samples of water. Causation, however, is a matter of a relation between particular events or states, e.g. the presence of water in the jug caused Mary to ask for some water. Importantly, from the fact that some of Mary's beliefs about water are caused by the presence of water, it does not follow that either Mary or her fellow speakers must have had causal encounters with water if Mary is to mean **water** by 'water'. That would be to confuse causation with indivi-duation. Similarly, from the fact that some of Mary's beliefs about water are not caused by the presence of water, it does not follow that neither her nor her fellow speakers need have had any causal encounters with water for Mary to mean **water** by 'water'. That would be to confuse lack of causation with lack of individuation.

Alternatively, we can talk about *supervenience*.[6] The Twin Earth argument thus makes two claims about supervenience. The first claim is that reference supervenes on meaning: a difference in reference between two referring terms entails a difference in their meaning. That is consistent with two terms having the same reference yet differing in meaning. Think of 'Hesperus' and 'Phosphorus' from Section 1.2. The second claim is that meaning fails to supervene on internal features of competent speakers: a difference in meaning is consistent with sameness of physical, experiential and psychological properties. Two speakers could be indiscernible in so far as these properties are concerned and yet differ in respect of what they mean when they utter distinct tokens of the same type of terms. Note that meaning fails to supervene on physical, experiential and psychological properties of speakers only if these properties are themselves intrinsic or at least internally individuated. As we will see in Section 3.3, there is reason not to think that content-bearing, psychological properties are internally individuated. Here is a more succinct version of the Twin Earth argument, couched in terms of supervenience and propositions:

(1) Mary's utterance on Earth of the sentence 'water is wet' is true if and only if H_2O, i.e. water, is wet.

(2) Twin-Mary's utterance on Twin Earth of the sentence 'water is wet' is true if and only if XYZ, i.e. twin-water, is wet.

(3) A difference in the truth-condition of a sentence entails a difference in the proposition expressed by that sentence.

(4) So, Mary and twin-Mary express different propositions when they utter different tokens of the same sentence type: Mary expresses the proposition **water is wet**, and twin-Mary expresses the proposition **twin-water is wet**.

(5) But Mary and twin-Mary are internally identical.

(6) So, the propositions Mary and twin-Mary express fail to supervene on their internal features.

The first observation to make is that there is nothing special about the natural kind term 'water' as opposed to, say, 'gold', 'heat', 'lemon', 'beech' or 'tiger'. Imagine a Twin Earth being just like Earth except that the catlike animals with yellow and blackish transverse stripes have a genetic make-up that is radically different from those of the species *Panthera tigris*. Twin-Mary calls these animals 'tigers', but provided only members of that species count as tigers, we need to coin the term 'twin-tigers' to pick out these look-a-like tigers. Neither Mary nor her doppelgänger twin-Mary has any knowledge of the underlying biology or genetics of tigers. Now we can run the Twin Earth argument once more. Mary's utterance of 'tigers are native to eastern Asia' is true if and only if tigers are native to eastern Asia, but twin-Mary's utterance of the same sentence type is true if and only if twin-tigers are native to eastern Asia. A difference in truth-conditions entails a difference in propositional content. Given that Mary and twin-Mary are doppelgängers, the propositions they express fail to supervene on their internal features. In this way the Twin Earth argument can be extended to include all such natural kind terms.

Indeed we can arguably run a Twin Earth argument to the effect that the propositional content of ordinary proper names fails to supervene on internal features. Imagine a Twin Earth being just like Earth except the individual that goes under the name 'Aristotle' had a different biological origin from the individual that the Earthlings call 'Aristotle'. Despite the two individuals sharing all their qualitative, superficial properties such as being famous philosophers of antiquity, they are numerically distinct. Here we assume with Kripke (1980) that individuals have such biological essences. It follows that the truth-condition of Mary's utterance of 'Aristotle was a philosopher' will differ from the truth-condition of twin-Mary's utterance of the same type of sentence, and so the propositions they express will fail to supervene on their internal features.

The view that propositional content fails to supervene on internal features is called *semantic externalism*.[7] More positively, the view says that such content is in part determined or individuated by features external to the individuals who are in states with that content, i.e. that such content supervenes on the conjunction of internal features (intrinsic physical, experiential, psychological properties) and external features. One can think of these external features as facts about the environment, e.g. the fact that the environment contains water, or as intrinsic properties of the environment, e.g. the property of containing water, or as extrinsic properties of the individual, e.g. the property of being in an environment containing water. If, as we suggested, external individuation of propositional content is a question about patterns of causal relations, we can talk about individuals instantiating the extrinsic property of having causally interacted with water.[8] When propositional content is dependent for its individuation on such external features, it is *widely individuated*, or just *wide*. Semantic externalists are typically happy to couch their view either positively in terms of dependency on external features, or else negatively in terms of failure of supervenience on internal features.

However, strictly speaking, these two formulations are not equivalent. Suppose that changing the external features on which propositional content depends for its individuation necessarily involves changing the internal features on which such content supervenes. There might be some necessary connection between relevant facts about the physical environment and relevant facts about brain states. In that case, propositional content would depend for its individuation on external features, because a change in those features entails a corresponding change in that content. But supervenience would still hold, because a change in the external features entails a change in the internal features too. It would be impossible to show what failure of supervenience requires, namely that propositional content changes when the external features change while the internal features are held fixed.[9]

Semantic internalism is typically taken to be the negation of semantic externalism. So, it is the view that propositional content does supervene on internal features (intrinsic physical, experiential, psychological properties) – or that such content is fully determined by such internal features.[10] Propositional content is *narrowly individuated*, or just *narrow*. In the case of the Twin Earth argument, the relevant external factors pertain to the micro-constitution of individuals' physical environment. We can then call the two opposing views *natural kind externalism* and *natural kind internalism*. The latter view says that reference of natural kind terms is fully determined by features internal to the individual such as associated descriptive properties constituting their propositional content. The former view says that such reference is partially determined by external features such as causal-historical connections between the individual and instances of the natural kind in question. Since what goes for reference goes for meaning as well, the propositional content of natural kind terms is individuated in part by those environmental features, or so natural kind externalism has it.[11]

Let's finally forestall a misunderstanding of these views which Putnam's catchy slogan that 'meanings just ain't in the head' is apt to prompt. Firstly, semantic internalists need not be committed to the claim that meaning is a psychological entity in the way that, say, the bright glow that appears to float before your eyes after momentarily starring at a light bulb is. Frege, for one, was explicit that unlike such afterimages, senses are abstract entities located outside space-time. Certainly, the semantic internalist should concede that meanings ain't in the head in that sense. What, according to Putnam (1975: 138), makes Frege a semantic internalist is his view that "'grasping' these abstract entities was still an individual psychological act." So, distinguish meaning from the property of grasping or expressing meaning. What semantic internalists hold is merely that the latter property supervenes on internal features of the individuals who instantiate that property.[12]

Secondly, to endorse Putnam's slogan is not to say that meanings are external in the way that chairs and tables are spatio-temporally located. It makes no literal sense to say that meanings are subject to perceptual detection. Fortunately, the semantic externalist incurs no commitments to such a rampant view. To use Davidson's example (1987: 451–54), having sunburn depends on standing in an appropriate causal relation to the sun, but that property is one that I, or my arm if you like, instantiates. Despite being individuated by the sun, sunburns are located where my arm is located. Sunburns are neither properties of the sun nor properties of the compound object my-arm-and-the-sun.[13] Likewise, grasping or expressing the proposition **water is wet** is a property of the individual who grasps or expresses that proposition, rather than a property of the external environment or a property of the compound object individual-and-environment, even if instantiating it depends on bearing certain causal relations to that environment.

3.2 Internalist rejoinders to the Twin Earth argument

There is a vast literature on the Twin Earth argument which we cannot fully cover here. In Section 3.3 we shall explore various ways of extending the conclusion of the Twin Earth argument, but in this section we will look at some ways in which semantic internalists have responded to that argument. Here are five rejoinders.

(i) The first concern that springs to mind is that the thought experiment is somewhat incoherent, because nothing with a radically different microstructure from H_2O could be macroscopically very like water. For XYZ to have some of the merely superficial watery properties is no doubt consistent with the laws of nature. To imagine that XYZ is running out of taps involves no violation is any such laws. But it would require deviant laws of nature for something so different from H_2O to have the more scientific watery properties that H_2O has. Think of cohesion. Because of the polar nature of water, it sticks to itself. If twin-water is to exhibit the same kind of cohesive attraction as water without XYZ being a polar molecule, then different forces must operate between the XYZ molecules. But Twin Earth is supposed to be a planet in our world governed by our laws of nature. Or take biological properties. Water is supposedly essential to biological life.

So, there could be no life on Twin Earth, and in particular Mary could have no living doppelgänger on Twin Earth.

If this objection shows that Twin Earth is metaphysically impossible then that would threaten the coherency of the thought experiment. The objector must then establish either that our laws of nature are necessarily true, or else show for instance that water is metaphysically necessary for biological life. But if the claim is merely that Twin Earth is nomologically impossible, it is unclear what this objection shows even if true. The point may be that Twin Earth could not tell us anything about the actual laws that govern propositional content, but then we need an explanation of why those laws are relevantly similar to the laws of nature that govern the properties of water.[14] Moreover, the Twin Earth argument does not hang on the assumption that H_2O and XYZ must share all their more or less scientific watery properties. Suppose XYZ lacks a cohesion property that H_2O has. If Mary and twin-Mary are unaware of this difference, it would have no material effect on the argument.

(ii) It might be suggested that Mary and twin-Mary both express the purely descriptive concept **the watery stuff** when they utter distinct tokens of 'water'. In that case, both Mary and twin-Mary use 'water' to refer to H_2O and XYZ alike. Both kinds fit the bill. 'Water' picks out a *disjunctive* natural kind rather than a unique natural kind. After all, neither has any knowledge of chemistry, nor are they able to distinguish the two kinds should they be presented with instances of them.[15] From their subjective point of view, there are no detectable differences between the way Earth and Twin Earth seem to them. Moreover, the propositional content of 'water' still determines its reference, but in a less fine-grained way than is assumed by Putnam. Compare with the general term 'vitamin', which picks out distinct organic compounds such as retinol, riboflavin and ascorbic acid. Their only common feature is that they are essential for nutrition, and are required in small quantities in the diet since they cannot be synthesized by the organism. Just as 'vitamin' picks out anything that plays a certain nutritional-functional role for an organism, 'water' picks out anything watery – anything that plays the water role. Maybe the analogy is misleading, because 'vitamin' is not a natural kind term. But then consider 'cat', which applies to all members of the family *Felidae*, but also to some animals that are not members of that family such as civet cats. If Putnam's model of natural kind terms were correct, speakers ought to correct their classificatory use of 'cat'.[16]

The problem with this *common concept strategy* is not so much how Mary could possibly refer to XYZ when she uses 'water'. Bear in mind the remote, causally isolated, heavenly objects that astrophysicists successfully refer to. Nor is the worry that water is rendered a disjunctive albeit wildly heterogeneous natural kind. Think of jade which comes as jadeite and nephrite. The problem is rather that we will have to say that XYZ counts as water, and that flies in the face of scientific practice. We do call D_2O 'heavy water', but only because its physical and chemical properties are roughly similar to those of water. Heavy water is identical to water except it contains a higher proportion than normal of the isotope deuterium. Moreover, water and heavy water differ in their superficial, stereotypical properties: while heavy water is used in nuclear reactors to slow down neutrons, water is used to put out fires and fill up swimming pools. The molecular struture XYZ on Twin Earth, however, is supposed to be chemically very different from H_2O and yet share all its superficial, stereotypical properties. A final concern pertains to lack of generality. Bear in mind that we can run Twin Earth arguments on all natural kind terms and proper names. So, even if XYZ could plausibly be classified as water, no sense can be made of the idea that two individuals who occupy distinct locations are both Aristotle.

(iii) An initially promising way to improve on (ii) is to say that 'water' is shorthand for a definite description that contains a *causal* element: 'the watery stuff of our acquaintance'. Thus when Mary uses 'water' she expresses the causally constrained descriptive concept **the watery stuff of our acquaintance**. As Mary inhabits Earth, the indexical expression 'our' refers to Earthlings. In general, 'our' will pick out the contextually salient group of individuals. That is to say, when uttered by Mary 'water' picks out the watery stuff that Earthlings are acquainted with. Being acquainted with something involves standing in some causal relationship to that thing. Consequently, 'water' in Mary's mouth picks out H_2O and only H_2O, because she and other Earthlings are causally disconnected from XYZ on Twin Earth. For instance, Mary drinks H_2O, not XYZ. Likewise, when twin-Mary uses 'water', she expresses a similar causally constrained descriptive concept, but given that she inhabits Twin Earth, 'water' in her mouth will refer to the watery stuff that she and other twin-Earthlings are causally connected with. Twin-Earthlings are now the contextually salient population that is picked out by 'our' as in 'the watery stuff of our acquaintance'. And the watery stuff that twin-Earthlings are acquainted with is XYZ. For example, twin-Mary swims in XYZ, not H_2O. Consequently, if as a matter of fact having a unique natural kind as a referent is sufficient for a term to qualify as a natural kind term, then 'water' as used by both Mary and twin-Mary is a natural kind term.[17]

The first worry with this amended proposal that springs to mind is that it fails to establish the existence of narrow content. If Mary's tokens of 'water' express the concept **the watery stuff of our acquaintance** while twin-Mary's corresponding tokens express the concept **the watery stuff of their acquaintance**, then these intrinsic duplicates express distinct concepts. We shall return to this problem in Section 4.2. Another worry is that this proposal confronts a version of the Perfect Earth objection from Section 2.3. We assumed then that Perfect Earth was a planet in some non-actual possible world. Suppose instead that Perfect Earth is a remote planet in our world – the actual world – just as Putnam's Twin Earth is meant to be. On this Perfect Earth the watery stuff is H_2O, and Mary has a doppelgänger that we call 'perfect-Mary'. The problem is now that when perfect-Mary utters 'water is wet', we Earthlings would intuitively want to ascribe to her the belief that water is wet. But if the term 'water' is simply shorthand for 'the watery stuff of our acquaintance', we would thereby have to ascribe to her the belief that the watery stuff of our acquaintance is wet. True, when perfect-Mary utters 'water is wet', she refers to the watery stuff of her and her fellow perfect-Earthlings acquaintance. But when we utter the belief-ascribing sentence 'perfect-Mary believes that water is wet', we refer to the watery stuff of our acquaintance. That seems odd. Surely we should be able to report that perfect-Mary has beliefs about water without having beliefs about any other remote planet.

(iv) Mary lacks knowledge of chemistry, and in particular she knows nothing about the microstructure of water. This may suggest that she lacks the natural kind concept **water** which those in the know possess. Knowledge of the watery properties and mere causal contact with water is insufficient to make Mary's use of 'water' express that concept – she needs to acquire relevant knowledge of chemistry too. The concept we attribute to Mary when she uses 'water' should reflect the way she takes the world to be. To say that she expresses a concept that is individuated by microstructure is to attribute to her an excessively scientific conception of the world. Similarly, twin-Mary knows nothing about the microstructure of twin-water, and so she lacks the natural kind concept **twin-water**. If we are to remain faithful to the similar non-scientific way Mary and twin-Mary think of water when we attribute concepts to them, we should instead say they both possess the descriptive concept **the watery stuff**, and this concept applies equally to H_2O and XZY. The point is that before the advent of modern chemistry in the mid-eighteenth century 'water' was a pre-scientific term which picked out anything watery. Only when the microstructure of water was empirically discovered did 'water' become a natural kind term expressing a natural kind concept. The mistake is to impose scientific intuitions about concept individuation on those who possess concepts pre-scientifically.[18]

There is no question that referring terms occasionally change their meaning in the light of new scientific findings. Following the recent discovery of many celestial objects in the outer solar system similar to Pluto, the International Astronomical Union defined the term 'planet' in 2006 in such a way that Pluto had to be reclassified as a dwarf planet. However, some scientific discoveries merely make for disclosure or fine-tuning of reference. When water was first decomposed into hydrogen and oxygen by electrolysis around 1800, the microstructure of water was uncovered. Prior to that scientists presumably thought that some uniform underlying features were causally or constitutively responsible for various observable phenomena such as solvency and cohesion. They were just either agnostic or harboured erroneous beliefs about the character of those features. The point is that speakers in 1750 could use 'water' to express a natural kind concept even if water's microstructure was unknown. All they needed was an intention to use 'water' referentially in that way, as well as a conception of water as having some hidden nature responsible for its manifest watery features. To find out whether speakers had such a conception and referential intention would require investigation of their use of 'water' in various circumstances. For instance, even back then speakers would agree that 'water' would not refer to XYZ on Twin Earth if water turns out to be composed of H_2O on Earth. If such *counterfactuals* were true of speakers in 1750, then it looks like 'water' expressed a natural kind concept even before the chemical revolution.[19]

(v) The last response is to embrace the possibility of *empty reference*. In (iii) we looked at the causally constrained descriptive concept **the watery stuff of our acquaintance**. On Earth this concept happens to pick out a unique natural kind, namely H_2O, and so might therefore be considered a natural kind concept. But natural kind concepts should not merely in actual fact pick out a unique natural kind. They should also have the aim of picking out such a kind built into them. Suppose therefore that 'water' expresses the partially descriptive concept **the unique natural kind all instances of which have the watery properties**, or better **the unique natural kind most instances of which have the watery properties**. That way some instances of that kind can lack some of the watery properties without failing to be picked out by 'water'. In that case, 'water' in Mary's mouth simply fails to refer to anything, because there is no unique kind most instances of which have the watery properties. There are two natural kinds that equally satisfy the specification: H_2O and XYZ. Consequently, our beliefs that water is thus and so are all false, because these are beliefs about the non-existing unique natural kind most instances of which have the watery properties. Similar remarks apply to twin-Mary.[20]

The problem with this response is first and foremost its credibility. 'Phlogiston', as used by seventeenth- and eighteenth-century scientists, aimed to pick out a fire-like substance in flammable materials that is liberated in burning, but this term turned out to be empty. Phlogiston theory was a flawed account of oxidization. Likewise in the case of 'caloric' and 'ether'. To deem 'water' empty, however, jars with common sense and scientific evidence. Scientific theory about water is certainly not obsolete in the way it is in these other cases. Note finally that combining (iii) and (v) yields the result that 'water' expresses the partially descriptive concept **the unique natural kind most instances with which we are acquainted have the watery properties**. Thus construed 'water' as used by Earthlings aims to pick out a unique natural kind, and succeeds in doing so: it picks out H_2O on Earth, but not XYZ on Twin Earth.

3.3 Burge's arthritis argument

Putnam's Twin Earth argument aims to establish natural kind externalism: when Mary utters a sentence containing 'water', the proposition she expresses depends in part on facts about her external physical environment, regardless of whether Mary has any knowledge or even beliefs about these facts. That is to say, the semantic or propositional content of such a sentence is wide in the sense of being partially individuated by possibly unknown, external, physical facts. The scope of the Twin Earth argument is thus limited in three respects: (i) it pertains only to the natural kind term 'water', (ii) it only says that propositional content is wide, and (iii) it only considers dependency on the external physical environment.

In this section we shall look at various ways of extending Putnam's original line of reasoning. Let's begin with (i). We saw in Section 3.1 that the Twin Earth argument made no special assumptions about the natural kind term 'water' or about the natural kind water. We can mount a similar argument to the effect that the propositional content of other natural kind terms such as 'lemon' or 'tiger' is also wide. Indeed, as illustrated, it looks as if proper names are also subject to Twin Earth arguments. Note in particular that, as mentioned in Section 3.1, Putnam also assumed that Mary and twin-Mary share all their experiential and psychological states, e.g. they both believe that the watery stuff is wholesome. Here we must tread carefully in spelling out 'the watery stuff'. For if that phrase involves any natural kind terms, then their propositional content will in turn be subject to a Twin Earth argument. Thus we can imagine a Twin Earth on which what twin-Mary calls 'water' is H_2O, but what she calls 'liquid' is virtually all a slippery granular solid.[21] Consequently, the truth-conditions of their respective utterances of 'water is a liquid' differ. Mary's utterance is true if and only if water is a liquid, but twin-Mary's utterance is true if and only if water is a twin-liquid. Given that Mary and twin-Mary express distinct propositions, the propositional content of 'liquid' fails to supervene on their internal features.

What about *non-natural kind terms*? These constitute a mixed class of distinct terms, including social, artefactual, functional and phenomenal terms. For example, 'government' refers to institutions which control states through legislation, 'stapler' refers to anything that can fasten together papers with staples, and 'pain' refers to experiences with a certain phenomenal character. Some of these terms pick out artificial kinds, e.g. 'sofa' refers to upholstered, comfortable seats with backs and arms, covered in leather or textiles, and suitable for two or more people. Others pick out disjunctions of heterogeneous, natural kinds, e.g. 'jade' refers to jadeite and nephrite. Yet others pick out artificial motleys of other kinds, e.g. 'asphalt' refers to an engineered mixture of dark bituminous pitch, distilled from crude oil, with sand or gravel. What matters for many if not all of these terms is whether the referent plays a characteristic *functional role*, regardless of its underlying chemical composition or physical microstructure. For instance, 'computer' picks out any electronic device capable of performing operations on received data in accordance with a set of instructions resulting in the production of other data. What matters is the processing of information in line with the software, not the implementation of that software by a particular hardware constitution.

We shall see in a moment that there is a persuasive way of showing that even non-natural kind terms have wide contents. But let's first dwell on (ii). As mentioned, the upshot of Putnam's Twin Earth argument is that *linguistic content* – the propositional content of referring terms or sentences – is wide, but this point carries over to *mental content* – the content of *intentional* or *representational* mental states such as beliefs.[22] To say that a mental state is representational is to say that its content represents the world as being a certain way. McGinn (1977, 1989), Davidson (1987) and Burge (1979, 1982), were the first to point out the obvious implications for such mental contents. Assume that contents of representational states determine truth-conditions. In particular, assume that the content of Mary's belief that water is wet is truth-conditional: what Mary believes is true if and only if water is wet. Likewise, what twin-Mary believes is true if and only if twin-water is wet. That assumption is plausible given that propositions are the contents of beliefs and that propositions are fixed truth-conditionally. It follows that the content of Mary's belief fails to supervene on her internal features. Here is a slightly different way of making the same point. Note first that by using the sentence 'water is wet' Mary can express the content of her belief that water is wet.[23] Likewise, we can use the de dicto belief-ascribing sentence 'Mary believes that water is wet' to express her belief content. As Burge (1982) notes, only expressions that occur inside 'that'-clauses play the role of specifying mental contents. As the sentence 'water is wet' says what the content of her belief is, that content is fixed by the proposition expressed by that sentence. That is to say, the content of her belief is fixed by the content of the sentence that she uses to express that belief. This means that if the proposition expressed by the sentence 'water is wet' is individuated by external facts, then so will the content of the belief she can express by means of that sentence. In short, if linguistic content is wide, then so is mental content.

We can draw another consequence, following McGinn (1977, 1989) and Burge (1979, 1982). Talk about belief is often ambiguous between talk about the content of a belief state and talk about the state of having a belief with a content. So far we have seen that belief content is wide if linguistic content is, but we can also now show that belief states themselves are wide. The sentence 'Mary believes that water is wet' reports a propositional attitude. To say that Mary believes that water is wet is to say that Mary bears the attitude of belief towards the proposition **water is wet**, where that proposition is determined by the truth-condition of the content clause 'water is wet'. The state Mary is in depends both on the proposition and the attitude in question. The state of believing that water is wet is distinct both from the state of believing that bread is dry, and from the state of desiring that water is wet. Beliefs and other propositional attitudes are thus individuated in part by their types of attitudes and in part by the truth-conditions of their content clauses. In particular, beliefs have their contents essentially. It follows that if the content of Mary's belief is wide then so is her belief state itself. Mary is in the state of believing that water is wet, while twin-Mary is in the state of believing that twin-water is wet. These states are essentially wide.[24] In sum, with Burge's words (1988: 650), the twin Earth thought experiment's

> common strategy is to hold constant the history of the person's bodily motion, surface stimulations, and internal chemistry. Then, by varying the environment with which the person interacts while still holding constant the molecular effects on the person's body, one can show that some of the person's thoughts vary. The upshot is that which thoughts one has ... is dependent on relations one bears to one's environment.

To say that belief states are wide means that the external environment plays a role in determining their natures. As Burge (2010: 64–65) remarks, the claim is not that belief states are not in the head, or that they are relations to the environment, or that environmental objects constitute those states or their contents. Some proponents of semantic externalism commit themselves to these stronger claims, but the thesis itself does not hang on any of them. It is perfectly compatible with the commonsensical claim that belief states are located where the believer is located.

Burge also extended Putnam's conclusion in respect of (i) and (iii). First, he argued that we could run semantic externalist thought experiments on non-natural kind terms. Secondly, he argued that mental content is dependent also on facts about one's community-wide social and linguistic practice.[25] Burge (1979) asked us to imagine an English speaker Alf who has some command of 'arthritis' although not complete mastery of that term. On previous occasions, Alf has been expressing his beliefs with sentences such as 'I have arthritis in my elbow, ankles and wrists' and 'arthritis hurts and incapacitates'. When he visits his doctor about the recent discomfort in his thigh, he takes 'arthritis' to refer to the pain in his thigh, but in actual English 'arthritis' picks out ailments of the joints only. Nobody could possibly suffer from arthritis in their thigh. Now envisage instead Alf speaking a counterfactual English in which 'arthritis' is used more liberally to pick out ailments in soft tissue as well as in joints. To say that Alf speaks a counterfactual English is to say that the English he actually speaks could have been slightly different in various aspects. Alf remains internally identical yet his actual and counterfactual tokens of 'arthritis' differ in reference. Since meaning determines reference, what Alf means by 'arthritis' is not a function of his internal features, nor are the contents of his beliefs fully fixed by such features. Burge's *arthritis argument* can be cashed out as follows:

(7)   Suppose that in an actual situation Alf has many true beliefs about arthritis, but he also assent to 'I have arthritis in my thigh'.

However, since arthritis is necessarily an ailment of the joints only, he falsely believes that he has arthritis in his thigh.

(8) Now suppose there is a counterfactual situation entirely identical to the actual except that 'arthritis' applies not only to arthritis, but also to rheumatoid ailments outside the joints, including the one in Alf's thigh. In this situation Alf is also disposed to assent to 'I have arthritis in my thigh'.

(9) In (8) Alf cannot believe that he has arthritis in his thigh, indeed no de dicto belief ascription containing 'arthritis' is true of him. Instead he truly believes that he has twin-arthritis in his thigh, since this is what the sentence 'I have arthritis in my thigh' means.

The arthritis argument rests on some at least intuitively plausible assumptions. Firstly, given Alf's minimal competence with 'arthritis' and his dispositions to defer to those in the know, including the disposition to stand corrected on matters of usage, it is right to interpret (7) as a situation in which he falsely believes that he has arthritis in his thigh. Secondly, the propositional content of 'arthritis' in (7) is not identical to the propositional content of 'arthritis' in (8) since the two terms differ in their reference. Thirdly, belief states are at least partially individuated by the truth-conditions of their content clauses.

According to Burge (1979, 1982, 1986), the arthritis argument establishes a kind of *social externalism*: intentional states are individuated by facts about correct linguistic usage in one's speech community. The identity conditions for such states pertain to features of the sociolinguistic environment.[26] Alf has the same internal features, e.g. intrinsic physical properties, in the two situations, but given (ii), the contents of his beliefs are different in those situations. So, given (iii), he is in different belief states. It follows that the state of having a belief with that content does not supervene on his internal features. Where the Twin Earth argument implies differences in linguistic content expressed by doppelgängers who are embedded in distinct physical environments, the arthritis argument implies differences in belief states between internally identical, actual and counterfactual individuals who are embedded in distinct linguistic environments. Importantly, since no special assumptions are made about 'arthritis', the arthritis argument will apply right across the language. Any concept which someone could possess but understand incompletely, and so could misapply, is subject to a version of the arthritis argument, e.g. Burge (1979: 82–84, 2007a: 23) mentions such terms as 'brisket', 'mortgage', 'red', 'contract' and 'sofa'.[27]

Before we turn to some semantic internalist rejoinders, let's revisit the assumption of the Twin Earth argument that Mary and twin-Mary are not only intrinsic physical duplicates, but also share experiential and psychological states. The pertinent psychological states were those with stereotypical contents, e.g. the belief that the watery stuff is wholesome. These belief states were thus taken to be narrow in the sense of supervening on Mary's and twin-Mary's common intrinsic properties. However, if social externalism is sustainable, then even those belief states are wide. Cashing out 'the watery stuff' involves citing such terms as 'colourless', 'thirst-quenching', 'ocean-filling', and these are all subject to corresponding versions of the arthritis argument. For instance, the state of believing that some liquid is thirst-quenching depends for its individuation on the believer being a member of a speech community in which linguistic conventions ensure that the terms 'liquid' and 'thirst-quenching' have certain public meanings.[28]

3.4 Internalist rejoinders to the arthritis argument

Just as with the Twin Earth argument there is an extensive literature discussing the cogency of the arthritis argument, which we cannot do full justice to here. We shall focus on five important objections, followed by replies on behalf of the semantic externalist.

(i) The first response is to point out that maybe best sense can be made of Alf's behaviour in both the actual situation and the counterfactual situation if he is ascribed the true belief that he has a rheumatoid ailment in his thigh. After all, Alf is fundamentally mistaken about whether this painful condition can spread to parts of his body other than his joints, and so what he believes when he utters sentences containing 'arthritis' should be distinct from what an expert rheumatologist believes when she utters such sentences. Importantly, this ascription involves no unnecessary change in language, e.g. there is no need to introduce the neologism 'twin-arthritis'. Burge has not argued why this possibility can be ignored.

The problem with this proposal is not only that Alf seems to be otherwise competent with 'arthritis', but also that he sincerely assents to 'I have arthritis in my thigh'. As mentioned in Section 2.4, speakers should remain faithful to the believers' linguistic behaviour, though one should bear in mind that this maxim is defeasible. Moreover, it should be possible to have a belief with a particular content despite incomplete knowledge of the concepts that make up that content. It is possible to believe what is not fully understood, hence to possess a concept without having knowledge of how it applies in all cases. This reflects the fact that we routinely ascribe beliefs to others using terms they lack complete knowledge of. Suppose in the actual situation Alf associates with 'arthritis' the other-dependent description: 'the ailment that the experts in my speech community use "arthritis" to refer to'. This highlights the phenomenon we in Section 2.3 called *semantic deference*. Alf's disposition to defer to those experts will enable him to use 'arthritis' to refer to arthritis even though his understanding is incomplete.[29] That is to say, Alf is using 'arthritis' with the assumption that those in the know are able to get its reference exactly right. Public language exhibits what Putnam (1996: 13) fittingly called a *division of linguistic labour*: laypeople are frequently unable to say precisely how technical terms should be applied, but they defer to those experts who have authority on the exact application conditions of those terms. Such deference involves readiness to conform to the ways that experts use the terms in question.[30]

(ii) A second response due to Donnellan (1993) and Chalmers (2002) is precisely to say that best sense can be made of Alf's behaviour in both situations if he is ascribed the same belief that he has the disease which expert speakers of the community call 'arthritis' in the thigh. This means that although the content of Alf's belief is actually false, it could have been true. Since the very same belief is false in the actual situation but true in the counterfactual situation, features of Alf's sociolinguistic environment determine the truth-value but not the content of his beliefs. It is necessary that arthritis is an ailment of the joints only, but merely contingent that 'arthritis' refers to such an ailment. Another virtue of this proposal is that it gets the reference of 'arthritis' right in both situations. Alf's grasp of 'arthritis' is incomplete, but his deferential dispositions and the division of linguistic labour ensure that he successfully refers to arthritis in the actual situation. Alf uses 'arthritis' to refer to whatever uniquely has the properties that the speakers from whom he learned the word associate with it. There is thus a chain of borrowings which bottoms out in the medical experts' specialist properties. So, this proposal seems to capture the dependence of the referent of 'arthritis' on the linguistic community which the phenomenon of semantic deference involves.

The chief worry is that belief attribution becomes too intellectual. A true utterance of 'Alf believes that he has arthritis in his thigh' attributes to Alf the *metalinguistic* belief that he has the disease referred to as 'arthritis' by speakers in his linguistic community. That may of course be true of Alf, but it should be possible for someone to have a belief involving a deferential concept without thereby having a belief about using the term for that concept with semantic deference. One can be disposed to correct one's use of a term in light of expert opinion without thereby having a belief about such corrections whenever one has a belief involving the concept for that term. In particular, children are frequently ascribed beliefs involving such deferential concepts as **red** and **sofa** in cases where we would hesitate to also ascribe to them beliefs about how their language is used in their community.[31] Moreover, Tye (2009: 65–66) points out that if this meta-linguistic view is correct, a monolingual French speaker cannot believe what Alf believes when he says 'I have arthritis in my thigh'. For such a speaker lacks beliefs about how 'arthritis' is used among Alf's English speaking peers. That is counter-intuitive.

(iii) Crane (1991: 11) stresses the importance of the distinction between the conventionally assigned meaning of a word in the public language and the concept intended to be expressed by a user of that word. Let's focus on the actual situation in (7). In order for Alf to express his belief with the sentence 'I have arthritis in my thigh', he has to believe both that he has arthritis in his thigh and that that sentence correctly expresses his belief. Crane (1991: 18) argues that the second belief is false, and that suffices to explain the falsity of Alf's utterance of 'I have arthritis in my thigh'. But given that Alf's dispositions remain the same in the two situations, we should attribute the concept **twin-arthritis** to him. So, Alf has the true belief that he has twin-arthritis in his thigh, rather than the false belief that he has arthritis in his thigh. The concept **twin-arthritis**, remember, applies equally to arthritis and to the disease Alf has in his thigh. In sum, Alf expresses the concept **arthritis**, but the concept he intends to express is **twin-arthritis**, and so he says something false when he attempts to express his belief, but he nevertheless has a true belief. In the counterfactual situation in (8) Alf also has the belief that he has twin-arthritis in his thigh. The only difference between the two situations is that when he utters 'I have arthritis in my thigh', his utterance expresses his belief correctly only in the counterfactual situation. The belief contents in both cases are exactly the same.[32]

The question is why Alf in the actual situation should be taken to have a true belief involving the idiosyncratic concept **twin-arthritis** rather than a false belief involving the public concept **arthritis**. Whenever a speaker says something false, we can always reinterpret her as having a true belief involving a deviant concept. If one were to persistently deploy that reinterpretation strategy, no speaker would thus ever have any false beliefs about the world, but only about how to correctly express those beliefs in language. The mere fact that Alf's grasp of 'arthritis' is incomplete should not entail that he intends to express a concept distinct from its con-ventionally assigned meaning. Crane (1991: 21–22) is aware of this worry, and he recommends that when we attribute belief we need consider not just Alf's actual linguistic behaviour, but also whether Alf would utter 'I have arthritis in my thigh/shinbone' were he to feel the same way in his other thigh or in one of his shinbones. The truth-values of such counter-factuals are notoriously hard to assess. But Burge can agree that we should not always take speakers' utterances at face value when attributing beliefs to them, as when someone says they had orang-utans for breakfast, believing they are some kind of fruit juice.[33] Presumably, that is why Burge stipulates in (7) that Alf has many other true beliefs about arthritis. Although Alf's actual utterance underdetermines whether he makes a genuine mistake or merely possesses a non-standard concept, we as belief-attributers have collateral evidence that Alf does possess the concept **arthritis**. So, it looks like Crane will either have to say that Alf undergoes a change in the concepts he intends to express when using 'arthritis', and so undergoes a change in the contents of the beliefs that he uses 'arthritis' to express, or else that Alf has been meaning to express the concept **twin-arthritis** on those other occa-sions, and so have had beliefs involving **twin-arthritis** all along. If the latter is the case, then Burge's stipulation in (7) seems question-begging. Instead Burge should claim more cautiously that Alf's usage of 'arthritis' resembles that of other speakers, except for his application of it to his thigh.

(iv) Segal (2000: 65) says that we cannot really make sense of Alf's state of mind in the actual situation in (7). For given that 'arthritis' simply means an inflammation in the joints, what Alf really believes when he utters the sentence 'I have arthritis in my thigh' is that he has an inflam-mation of the joints in his thigh. Alf knows fine well that thighs are not joints. Maybe Alf does not fully understand 'arthritis', but it is hard to see how one can believe a proposition one does not fully grasp. Segal (2000: 73–76, 2009: 374), following Loar (1988), develops another argument resembling Kripke's paradox from Section 1.3 to show how Burge's social externalism saddles Alf with inconsistent beliefs. Prior to visiting his doctor Alf travels to France where he learns of a condition that goes under the name 'arthrite' that it is an inflammation of the joints only. According to Burge, 'arthritis' and 'arthrite' express the same socially individuated concept **arthritis**. Yet Alf fails to realize the synonymity of these terms. For instance, he is disposed to assent to 'I have arthritis in my thigh' and 'I do not have arthrite in my thigh'. Assuming that such assent indicates belief at least when sincere and reflective, it looks like Alf holds inconsistent beliefs.

Burge would no doubt insist that just as competent speakers often possess concepts incompletely, they often do not fully grasp the propositions that they believe. There is nothing inconsistent or irrational about that. Indeed Burge (1979: 83) admits that " ... if the thought experiment is to work, one must at some stage find the subject believing ... a content, despite an incomplete understanding or misapplication." For instance, when Putnam utters the sentence 'beech tress are deciduous' he expresses the proposition **beech trees are deciduous**, despite his incomplete grasp of 'beech trees'. He believes that beech trees are deciduous. The fact that Putnam is unable to distinguish beeches from elms is no reason to think that he rather expresses the disjunctive concept **either beech tress or elm tress are deciduous**, or some other non-standard concept. All it means is that Putnam uses 'beech' deferentially. Similarly, Alf expresses the belief that he has arthritis in his thigh when he utters 'I have arthritis in my thigh'. When he utters 'Je n'ai pas d'arthrite à la cuisse' he expresses the belief that he does not have arthritis in his thigh. Due to Alf's incomplete grasp of **arthritis** he cannot detect purely by reflection that he thus expresses contradictory propositions. Alf should therefore not be blamed for irrationally holding inconsistent beliefs.

(v) Segal (2000: 66–76, 124–25) argues that Alf's use of 'arthritis' in the actual situation in (7) expresses a concept that is different from the concept expressed by the experts' use of 'arthritis' in the actual situation. The experts express the same concept by the two terms 'arthritis' and 'inflammation of the joints', because they know that these two terms are synonymous. So, they believe both that Alf does not have an inflammation of the joints in his thigh, and that Alf does not have arthritis in his thigh. But Alf expresses distinct concepts by these two terms. For Alf believes that he does not have an inflammation of the joints in his thigh, but he does not believe that he does not have arthritis in his thigh. So, Alf's partial competence with 'Arthritis' and his deferential dispositions do not suffice for him to express the same concept as the experts. By using 'arthritis' in the actual situation Alf rather expresses the concept **tarthritis**, which means roughly rheumatism. By being applicable to any hereditary autoimmune disease that can cause the symptoms Alf has in his joints and thigh, this concept corresponds to the way Alf subjectively conceives of things in this respect.

Burge would undoubtedly object to the fine-grained way in which Segal appears to individuate concepts in terms of what we in Section 1.2 call their 'cognitive significance'. An ordinary, competent speaker could believe that Hesperus is Hesperus without believing that Hesperus is Phosphorus. Astronomically informed speakers believe both propositions. That should not imply that such laypeople and expert speakers express distinct concepts by 'Hesperus' and 'Phosphorus'. For instance, if they were arguing about the truth-value of 'Hesperus is Phosphorus' we would not resolve their disagreement by having them speaking past each other in virtue of expressing distinct concepts. Similarly with 'arthritis'. It is implausible to maintain that whenever someone has an incomplete understanding of a term, she expresses a concept different from those who have a complete understanding of that term. Such reinterpretation may be appropriate when the error is radical as in the orang-utan example, but otherwise not. For if Alf were to express a concept different from that expressed by his doctor, then they would not agree as to whether Alf's utterance of 'I have arthritis in my thigh' is true. But they do agree. When the doctor tells Alf that he cannot possibly have arthritis in his thigh, Alf will typically not insist that he does have arthritis in his thigh and that the doctor is wrong. Of course, as Egan (2009: 354) observes, it may be that after the doctor's correction Alf's concept changes. Prior to correction he used 'arthritis' to express the concept **tarthritis**, but now that he knows better he expresses the concept **arthritis**, thus bringing his use of that word into line with the experts' usage.

3.5 Davidson's Swampman argument

Davidson's Swampman is the following thought experiment. Imagine Davidson wandering through a swamp when suddenly he is struck by a bolt of lightning which reduces his body to its elementary particles. Simultaneously, by some freak occurrence a nearby dead tree is transformed into an intrinsic physical duplicate of Davidson. Davidson and his duplicate – Swampman – are physically identical in so far as the numerically distinct molecules out of which they are composed are of the very same types. Here are Davidson's own words (1987: 443–44):

> Suppose lightning strikes a dead tree in a swamp; I am standing nearby. My body is reduced to its elements, while entirely by coincidence (and out of different molecules) the tree is turned into my physical replica. My replica, The Swampman, moves exactly as I did; according to its nature it departs the swamp, encounters and seems to recognize my friends, and appears to return their greetings in English. It moves into my house and seems to write articles on radical interpretation. No one can tell the difference.

In this passage Davidson seems to assume that if Davidson and Swampman are intrinsic physical duplicates, they are also behavioural duplicates. For instance, when Davidson wants a beer, and believes he can satisfy that desire by going into the pub, he will, other things being equal, go into the pub. Likewise, when Swampman seems to express a desire by uttering 'I want a beer' and a belief by uttering 'the pub is where I can drink a beer', he will, other things being equal, also enter the pub. Maybe Davidson is making the assumption that behavioural properties supervene on intrinsic physical properties such that intrinsic physical duplication entails behavioural duplication. Alternatively, it could be built into the example that Davidson and Swampman are behavioural duplicates in addition to being intrinsic physical duplicates. More precisely, they are synchronic, physical and behavioural duplicates – indiscernible in those respects only at the time t at which Swampman pops into existence by cosmic coincidence. Call that 't_1'. Davidson and Swampman are precisely not historical duplicates. Unlike Davidson, Swampman is neither part of our evolutionary history nor does he have his own developmental history. He was neither selected for by some historical process of natural selection nor created on the basis of some divine or scientific blueprint. He lacks the kind of biological origin that Davidson and other humans have, indeed if the lightning strike is discounted he sustains no causal connection to Davidson. The two individuals, remember, are constituted by entirely separate molecules.

The pressing question is whether Swampman is capable of having contentful thoughts at the time t_1 of creation and for some time thereafter.[34] Obviously, after enough time has passed Swampman will acquire a causal history necessary for him to utter meaningful expressions and think thoughts. Call that 't_2'. Davidson (1987: fn. 4) is explicit that the Swampman example is not supposed to establish that accidentally or artificially created beings are permanently incapable of thinking. For instance, he (2006: 1060) is open to the possibility that perfectly designed robots made of silicon chips and the right science-fiction hardware could in time think. The issue is therefore whether Swampman has such capability during the time interval t_1–t_2. Swampman surely appears in every way as if he perceives his environment, forms beliefs on the basis of those perceptions, and then behaves in ways that satisfy his desires given those beliefs. In the absence of knowledge of what happened in the swamp, nobody would be able to detect the difference between Swampman and Davidson. That seems to suggest that Swampman is a perceptual and intentional being in much the same way Davidson is. Of course if Swampman has beliefs at all, many of them will be false. For instance, if both were to utter 'I was born in 1917' only Davidson would be right. The problem is however that Davidson believes that Swampman should be incapable of being in any intentional states at all. The above-mentioned quote from Davidson (1987: 444) continues as follows:

> But there *is* a difference. My replica can't recognize my friends; it can't recognize anything, since it never cognized anything in the first place. It can't know my friends' names (though of course it seems to), it can't remember my house. It can't mean what I do by the word 'house', for example, since the sound 'house' Swampman makes was not learned in a context that would give it the right meaning – or any meaning at all. Indeed, I don't see how my replica can be said to mean anything by the sounds it makes, nor to have any thoughts.

This passage needs unpacking. Davidson holds a historical theory of representational content according to which past causal interaction with environmental objects is constitutive of meaningful use of language and thinking contentful thoughts. More precisely, Davidson now means **house** when he utters the word 'house', because in the past he learned the meaning of that word in a context in which a teacher pointed at a house at which they were both looking while uttering the sentence 'that's a house'. In most cases the teacher has to expose the learner to different types of houses while uttering that sentence so as to stress the commonalities between semi-detached, stone-built, etc., houses. At each occasion, the learner correlates tokens of 'house' with the teachers' demonstrations, thus figuring out what the references of those tokens are in liaison with the teacher. For this to work the innate similarity responses of teacher and learner must be very similar, i.e. they must naturally respond in roughly similar ways to what they take to be similar perceptual stimuli. If the learner's natural responses to what the teacher perceived as similar stimuli were markedly different from the teacher's responses, the teacher could not train the learner to adopt new responses. This process of *triangulation* is central to Davidson's views (1982, 1987, 1991) about linguistic and representational content. In collaboration with the teacher the learner triangulates the reference of the teacher's tokens of 'house' by identifying the object that lies at the intersection of the causal paths that run from the learner and the teacher to the objects in the external world. Triangulation thereby allows a teacher to teach the learner the meaning of 'house' in such *learning situations*.[35] Once the learner has grasped the meaning of 'house' the learner is able to deploy the concept **house** in thought, and propositional attitudes can be ascribed to the learner involving that concept. But according to Davidson (1987: 450, 1991: 201, 1994: 128), triangulation is not only needed for the acquisition of a concept, it is also what individuates that concept. When the learner now utters 'house' she means **house** in virtue of having previously triangulated a house with her teacher uttering that word. What 'house' means is fixed in part by the past circumstances in which that word was learned. More precisely, what fixes the meaning of 'house' is what has typically caused utterances of 'house'. Since similarity of responses is what pins down the relevant causes, the causes that fix the meaning are features of the external world that are shared by the teacher and the learner. Still, not all words need be learned via triangulation in a learning situation. A learner could learn the meaning of 'detached house' without ever having seen a detached house. She could learn the meaning of 'house' and 'detached' in distinct learning situations, and then put the two together to form 'detached house'. So, on Davidson's view (1987: 450), ultimately "all thought and language must have a foundation in such direct historical connections". Representational content is individuated by causal-historical connections with the external world.

Davidson's historical theory of representational content thus predicts that Swampman should lack the capacity for intentional thought. Despite being an intrinsic physical duplicate of Davidson at t_1, and sharing all of his linguistic dispositions at t_1, Swampman has not learned the meaning of 'house' in a learning situation, because he has never been in a learning situation in which he could triangulate the reference of that word. As the same goes for all other words uttered by Swampman, his language is devoid of meaning during $t_1 t_2$. These consequences of the historical theory are bullets its friends will simply have to bite. But Davidson (2006: 1061) insists that philosophical intuitions about Swampman and other science-fiction scenarios are unreliable. Our intentional concepts work well in normal circumstances, but the criteria for applying them point in opposite directions when such scenarios are being envisaged.[36]

Before turning to replies to the Swampman argument let's consider a different but related set of views to which that argument also poses a challenge. These are the *teleological theories of representational content* – or just *teleosemantics* (Millikan 1989, Papineau 1993, Dretske 1988, 1995). In recent years the Swampman example has especially been discussed against the backdrop of these theories. Their common feature is an attempt to explain the content of representational states by appeal to *teleological functions*. For instance, the thought that snow is white represents that snow is white, because of the function of the innate representational mechanisms of the brain that consume or produce that representation. To determine the teleological function of a system is to figure out what it was *selected for* by natural selection. For instance, my heart has the teleological function of pumping blood because it was selected for blood-pumping by natural selection. My heart counts as a heart in virtue of its proper function – what it is supposed to do rather than what it is disposed to do. Likewise, an innate representational part of my brain such as perceptual processing was selected for processing information by natural selection. Importantly, since natural processes of selection are historical, teleosemantics accounts for representational content in historical terms. Just as in the case of Davidson's own historical account, teleosemantics predicts that Swampman is incapable of being in states with representational content during the time interval t_1–t_2. Although his brain states are physically indistinguishable from those that Davidson is in they have no such content. The reason is that neither Swampman's brain nor any other of his component parts has any teleological function. They are simply not there to do anything. Consequently, despite their behavioural and physical similarities at t_1, Swampman's utterances of 'house' have no reference, and so are meaningless. Swampman has no thoughts. According to these theories, part of what makes Davidson have any thoughts at all is that they are rooted in his external environment via causal-historical chains of communication, but since Swampman has no causal pedigree he is utterly incapable of expressing or entertaining thoughts during t_1–t_2.

Note finally that both teleosemantics and Davidson's historical account of representational content underwrite a form of semantic externalism. If narrow content states are those that supervene on intrinsic physical properties of individuals, then Davidson and Swampman would share such states at t_1 if there were any. But Davidson and friends of teleosemantics profess that content supervenes in part on the evolutionary or at least causal history of individuals. While we have seen in Sections 3.1 and 3.3 that Putnam and Burge advocate natural kind externalism and social externalism respectively, we can say that Davidson and the teleosemanticists subscribe to distinct forms of *historical* (or *diachronic*) *externalism*. The Swampman argument can then be viewed as a challenge to any form of historical externalism.[37]

3.6 Externalist rejoinders to the Swampman argument

Having rehearsed the Swampman argument in Section 3.5, let's now probe into three externalist responses, one on behalf of Davidson and then more briefly two on behalf of teleosemantics.

(i) Lepore and Ludwig (2007) observe an interesting tension in Davidson's philosophy between the intuition that underlies the Swampman example and his views about *radical interpretation* (1967, 1973, 1994). Let's briefly rehearse the latter. Davidson aimed to construct a theory of meaning for an object language L_O by giving necessary and sufficient conditions for the truth of every sentence s in L_O. The theorems of that theory consist of T-sentences of the form: s is true in L if and only if p, where p is a sentence in the metalanguage L_M. By means of these T-sentences the theory will thus explicate what every sentence in L_O means, e.g. 'græs er grønt' is true in Danish if and only if grass is green. Such a truth-theory can then count as a theory of meaning for L_O. The radical interpreter is someone who builds such a theory of meaning for L_O without any prior knowledge of its meaning or its speakers. The way for the radical interpreter to proceed is to assign truth-conditions to the sentences of L_O by systematically correlating those sentences that are held true by the foreign speaker S with features of the external environment that the radical interpreter and S have in common. Here the assumption is that the radical interpreter can identify S's basic attitude of holding a sentence true. The pertinent observable features are the conditions under which those sentences are true, e.g. grass being green. Importantly, the truth-theory that the interpreter constructs by finding such systematic correlations must be charitable. That is to say, the radical interpreter aims to maximize agreement between herself and S. This *principle of charity*, as Davidson calls it (1967, 1973), allows the interpreter to assume from the outset that S's beliefs are mostly in agreement with her own beliefs. Since the interpreter takes her own beliefs to be mostly true, she can safely assume that so are S's beliefs. Davidson (1982, 1994) later thinks the principle of charity allows the interpreter to take the truth-conditions of S's utterance of s to be the conditions under which the interpreter recognizes that S regularly assents to s. The meaning of s is thus what typically causes S to assent to s or to hold s true, at least when s pertains to perceptual matters. Since these must be circumstances that the radical interpreter can recognize, the meaning of s consists in shared features of their external environment. That is, external causes determine meaning but only in a social setting. On Davidson's view (1973, 1994), S could not mean anything by s that was not accessible to the radical interpreter. All meaning is in principle subject to radical interpretation.[38]

The problem is now that, as Lepore and Ludwig (2007) and N. Goldberg (2008) have observed, a theory of meaning as embedded in a theory of radical understanding treats *meaning as an ahistorical phenomenon*. All a radical interpreter needs in order to determine the meaning of S's utterance of s is to correlate that utterance with those current features of the external environment that prompt that utterance. The evidence that is required for the radical interpreter to determine the meaning of s only comprises facts about S's external environment and S's dispositions to response to changes in that environment that are available at the time of interpretation. The radical interpreter need not know anything about how S learned the meaning of the expressions that compose s, or any other facts about S's causal history. Radical interpretation thus underwrites a form of *ahistorical* (or *synchronic*) *externalism*: only current features of the external environment and S's dispositions to respond to environmental changes determine what s means. And herein lies the problem for Davidson for according to his historical externalism, *meaning is a historical phenomenon*. As Lepore and Ludwig (2007: 337–39) put it, the radical interpreter would be able to determine the meaning of Davidson's utterances, but since Davidson and Swampman are physical and behavioural duplicates, the radical interpreter should also be able to determine the meaning of Swampman's utterances. But the radical interpreter cannot do that, because Swampman's utterances have no meaning, at least during the time interval t_1–t_2. Swampman, remember, fails to express anything meaningful precisely because he has no track record of causal interaction with his external environment. Unlike Davidson, Swampman has never learned the meaning of any words in a learning situation.

Against the backdrop of this tension in Davidson's work between Swampman and radical interpretation, Lepore and Ludwig take the intuition that is supposed to buttress the Swampman argument to be unconvincing. They believe that most people who were not already in the grip of historical externalism would suppose that Swampman means by his words roughly what Davidson means, or at least that Swampman is capable of having contentful thoughts. But even if the Swampman intuition is conceded, the conclusion of the argument does not follow from its premises. That is to say, the Swampman argument is a non sequitur. Lepore and Ludwig show that the considerations that Davidson brings to bear fail to support that conclusion. Firstly, Swampman has no memories prior to his creation, e.g. he cannot remember his twentieth birthday, because he did not have any. One can remember that p only if p is true. Secondly, Swampman cannot recognize Davidson's friends when he first meets them after his creation. One can recognize someone only if one has encountered them before, but Swampman has not met or seen any of these friends before. Thirdly, Swampman cannot speak a public language, e.g. he does not master

English if that requires having been immersed in an English-speaking community. Importantly, all three points are consistent with Swampman's utterances being in general meaningful and with S having contentful thoughts.[39] So, Lepore and Ludwig (2007: 288, 388) claim that the conclusion that Swampman is incapable of meaning anything by the sounds it makes or have any thoughts at all does not follow from Swampman's inability to recognize people he has not yet encountered, remember events from the past and speak English. In sum, by giving up on Swampman and its attendant historical externalism, Lepore and Ludwig thereby hope to restore consistency in Davidson's philosophy.

In response N. Goldberg (2008: 374) advises against viewing Swampman as a minor glitch on Davidson's behalf. The reason Swampman should not be demoted to a fanciful and expendable thought experiment is that, as we saw in Section 3.5, Swampman is illustrative of Davidson's other views about the acquisition and individuation of concepts in learning situations. According to these views, if a learner had never been in a past situation in which she could triangulate the referent of a word in cooperation with a teacher, she could not now use that word to mean anything. This applies to any learner, Davidson and Swampman included. The tension in Davidson's philosophy between historical externalist and ahistorical externalist elements is therefore more far-reaching than Swampman.

(ii) The second externalist response is due to Dretske (1996) who asks us to imagine the following scenario. After lightening strikes an automobile junkyard twin-Terkel − an almost intrinsic physical duplicate of Dretske's 1981 Toyota Terkel − randomly appears. Twin-Terkel has all and only the identifying features that Terkel has, e.g. a dented bumper and a small rusty scratch on the rare fender. The only difference between them is that while Terkel's gas gauge works perfectly fine, the pointer on the gauge in twin-Terkel is unresponsive to the amount of petrol in the tank. All that is common ground. The question is whether twin-Terkel's gauge is broken. If the gauge is not working, then there must be something that it is supposed to do. A broken gauge is one that fails to do what it was designed to do. But twin-Terkel's gauge was not designed to do anything, in fact it is not even a copy or reproduction of something that was designed. It lacks a teleological function. For instance, 'F' does not refer to a full tank. Because this symbol does not represent anything, the gauge would not be misrepresenting if it indicated 'F' when the tank was empty. If twin-Terkel's gauge has no such function it cannot be working correctly and so it cannot be broken or working incorrectly either. One might say that any gas gauge is by definition designed to register the amount of petrol whether it does so or not. But then the question is whether twin-Terkel has a petrol gauge (or a bumper or a fender) at all. In contrast, Terkel's petrol gauge was designed to do what the corresponding part of twin-Terkel fails to do. We know what its symbols refer to, and we know that it would be broken if it indicated 'F' when the tank was empty. In that case Terkel's gauge would misrepresent the amount of petrol in the tank.

Dretske's lesson is now the following. Given that twin-Terkel is physically and functionally indistinguishable from Terkel (apart from the petrol gauge), we are intuitively inclined to say that twin-Terkel's gauge represents the tank as being so-and-so because we do not hesitate in attributing such representational states to Terkel's gauge.[40] That inclination, however, is misleading. By analogy, given that Davidson and Swampman are physically and functionally indistinguishable, we are intuitively tempted to say that Swampman represents that so-and-so because we know that Davidson does. That temptation should also be resisted. On Dretske's view, representation requires a historically grounded ability to indicate. A symbol 'X' means X when 'X' as part of a system in a certain environment has acquired the function of indicating Xs, where 'X' acquires such an indicator function only by actually having indicated Xs in the past. Since both twin-Terkel and Swampman miraculously materialized (in a junkyard and a swamp) neither has acquired such an ability or function in the past. To use Dretske's locution (1996: 79), all is dark in the representational minds of twin-Terkel and Swampman.

(iii) The third and last externalist objection is due to Millikan (1996). She points out that species are historical entities: what species an individual belongs to depends on its historical relations to other individuals. Davidson and Millikan are both members of the kind Homo sapiens in virtue of having descended from other members of that kind. Homo sapiens and other species are real kinds which can figure in scientific generalizations, but these kinds differ from water and other Putnam-style natural kinds. What makes something water is its underlying microstructure H_2O which physically necessitates its manifest, watery properties. What accounts for instances of water being alike is their shared inner constitution. However, Davidson and Millikan have different genes although they are taken from the same gene pool. And the genes they have in common are not what make them both human. What accounts for the unity of H. sapiens are relations between ancestors and descendents. Such phylogenetic facts play a role in explaining how humans evolve as well as define the identity of that species. Now take

Swampman. At the time of creation t_1 Swampman and Davidson are physical duplicates. This means that they belong to the same real kind, but only if understood in terms of sameness of inner, physical constitution. That constitution physically necessitates the same appearance. We can thus say that Swampman and Davidson belong to the same Putnam-style natural kind: Davidson physical duplicate. Millikan and Davidson also belong to the same real kind, namely H. *sapiens*. Their ontogenetic developments are similar in that both are human offspring, underwent childhood and ado-lescence, etc. But it does not follow that Swampman and Millikan belong to the same real kind, because the relation of belonging to the same real kind is not transitive.[41] Swampman and Millikan do not both belong to either of the real kinds H. *sapiens* and Davidson physical duplicate. While Millikan is not a physical duplicate of Davidson, Swampman is not a human. What prevents Swampman from belonging to the real kind H. *sapiens* is his lack of the right developmental history: he was randomly created in a swamp rather than born to parents in a maternity ward. *Homo sapiens* and other species are essentially historical kinds whose members are united by descent.[42] Consequently, Swampman lacks most of the properties that are character-istic of humans. As Millikan (1996: 110) puts it, he has no CV, e.g. he has no parents or native language, he was never a toddler or a teenager, he is neither clever nor retarded, he never greets anyone or reaches for anything. No part of his body or brain can be said to function properly or improperly. That would make sense only if reference could be made to a historical species or social groups to which Swampman belongs. Consequently, none of his organs exist for particular purposes such as perception or thinking.

In light of the foregoing account of real kinds, Millikan (1996) claims that Swampman is in a certain sense impossible. Of course it is possible that a physical duplicate of Davidson be created by some freak accident. Although extremely unlikely that is certainly a metaphysical possibility, indeed no actual laws of nature seem to prevent that. What is metaphysically impossible is that a freak of nature should produce a physical duplicate of Davidson that is a human. Humans and other species are real kinds whose essences pertain to their evolutionary origins rather than their micro-physical constitutions. Importantly, these historical essences are a posteriori discoverable by evolutionary biology. Likewise, teleosemantics aims to empirically uncover the essences of representational real kinds, e.g. belief states, and these essences will be historical rather than microphysical. Tel-eosemantics is not primarily in the business of doing conceptual analysis. Consequently, while it is metaphysically possible that a physical duplicate of

Davidson should accidentally materialize in a swamp due to some light-ening strike, it is metaphysically impossible that an intentional duplicate of Davidson should also materialize at the same time. The intuition elicited by the thought experiment that Swampman is capable of intentionality is simply irrelevant.[43] What the experiment shows is merely that for all we know a priori or even prior to the discovery of the essences of repre-sentational real kinds, Swampman might be an intentional being in much the same way Davidson is. In that sense, that Swampman should instantiate intentional properties is an epistemic possibility. Only when the historical essence of intentionality is discovered are we in a position to pronounce on the issue of Swampman's intentionality. As it turns out, it is metaphysi-cally impossible for Swampman to instantiate such properties.

Compare with water. Suppose we know the superficial, manifest prop-erties of water but not yet its microphysical constitution. Now we reflect on Twin Earth on which there is a liquid which shares all and only those watery properties but has the radically different microphysical constitution XYZ. One might be tempted to think that XYZ should be classified as water. Any such rash judgment would however be premature. Natural kinds are individuated by their microphysical constitutions. Before we determine whether water and twin-water share such constitution we cannot tell whether these two liquids belong to the same natural kind. As microphysical constitutions are uncovered only by empirical enquiry, any such knowledge is going to be a posteriori. Consequently, any putative intuition elicited by the Twin Earth thought experiment that XYZ should be classified as water is irrelevant. What it illustrates is merely that such a classification is not ruled out a priori, indeed is consistent with what was known prior to the discovery of water's microphysical constitution. In that sense, water and twin-water belonging to the same natural kind is an epistemic possibility. That is consistent with it being metaphysically impossible that twin-water belong to the same natural kind as water. Natural kinds have their microphysical constitutions essentially. When we learned that water is H_2O we acquired a posteriori knowledge of a metaphysical necessity. As it is part of the thought experiment that XYZ is radically different from H_2O, it thus turned out to be metaphysically impossible for twin-water to belong to the same natural kind as water.[44]

Chapter summary

In this chapter we examined three prominent arguments in support of semantic externalism: the view that what a speaker means or believes when she uses certain referring terms depends on possibly unknown external features of her environment. Putnam's Twin Earth argument asks us to imagine a remote planet in the actual world which is identical to Earth in almost every respect. The only difference is that the clear, potable liquid that fills the oceans and falls from the sky, i.e. the watery stuff, has the microstructure XYZ, which is radically different from H_2O. Mary lives on Earth but she has an identical twin from the skin in on this Twin Earth. Both are ignorant of chemistry. When Mary uses 'water' she refers to H_2O, but when twin-Mary uses 'water' she refers to XYZ. The fact that Mary and twin-Mary refer to different kinds of stuff implies that they mean different things: Mary expresses the concept **water**, while twin-Mary expresses the concept **twin-water**. But Mary and twin-Mary are internally alike, so what they mean is determined behind their backs by hidden features of their physical environment. In short, linguistic content is wide. Several responses were then reviewed. Some say that Mary expresses the purely descriptive concept **the watery stuff**. In order to avoid the result that Mary's tokens of 'water' refer to XYZ, others refine that proposal so that Mary expresses the causally constrained descriptive concept **the watery stuff of our acquaintance**. Still others maintain that Mary's use of 'water' is empty since there is no unique natural kind that has all the watery properties. After critical discussion of these proposals we turned to Burge's arthritis argument, purporting to establish that mental content is wide by being dependent on features of speakers' sociolinguistic environment. We are asked to envisage two situations: an actual situation in which 'arthritis' means inflammation of the joints only, and a counterfactual situation in which 'arthritis' applies to the joints as well as rheumatoid ailments outside the joints. Alf has in both situations some true beliefs about arthritis, but he also utters the sentence 'I have arthritis in my thigh'. Burge's contention is that in the actual situation Alf expresses the false belief that he has arthritis in his thigh, but in the counterfactual situation he expresses the true, yet different belief that he has twin-arthritis in his thigh. Given that Alf is internally the same in the two situations, the contents of his beliefs are determined by features of his sociolinguistic environment. No special assumptions about 'arthritis' were made, and similar arguments could be run using terms other than natural kind terms. Again, several responses were critically assessed. Some say that we make best sense of Alf's behaviour in both the actual situation and the counterfactual situation if he is ascribed the true belief that he has a rheumatoid ailment in his thigh. Others recommend that Alf be ascribed the belief that he has the disease which expert speakers of the community call 'arthritis' but in the thigh. This reflects the fact that Alf semantically defers to those expert speakers from whom he borrowed 'arthritis' since his own grasp of that term is incomplete. Yet others maintain that Alf in both situations truly believes that he has twin-arthritis in his high. Alf's mistake in the actual situation merely consists in his false belief that the sentence 'I have arthritis in my thigh' correctly expresses that belief. We then finally considered Davidson's Swampman argument which supposedly shows that intentional states cannot depend for their individuation on the selectional histories of the individuals whose states they are. It thus presents a challenge to all historical theories of content, including Davidson's own view and tele-osemantics, according to which the content of intentional states is accounted for by appeal to teleological functions. Such content is wide in the sense of being determined by what it was selected for by natural selection. We are asked to conceive of a situation in which a lightning strike in a swamp miraculously creates an intrinsic physical duplicate of Davidson. Given that Swampman and Davidson will also be behavioural duplicates, the inclination is to attribute intentionality to Swampman in much the same way Davidson is regarded as an intentional being. Finally, three responses on behalf of historical externalism were then canvassed. Firstly, Davidson holds that certain causal connections between speaker, hearer and objects in their shared external environment must obtain if intentionality is to be attributed. However, there is a tension between Davidson's ideas about radical interpretation and learning situations in how such triangulation should be understood. Secondly, Dretske's twin-Terkel example seems to illustrate how unreliable intuitions about proper functions can be. An intrinsic physical duplicate of Dretske's Toyota Terkel has no teleological functions, because it was created by some freak of nature rather than designed by a car manufacturer. Thirdly, even if intuitions about Swampman are granted, they cannot prove teleosemantics wrong. Millikan argues that intentional states are real kinds individuated by their hidden historical essences. While it is possible for all that is known prior to the empirical discovery of these essences that Swampman is an intentional being, that is not a genuine or metaphysical possibility.

Annotated further reading

Putnam's Twin Earth argument and Burge's arthritis argument both sparked a huge debate in the philosophical literature on the nature of representational states and their contents. *The Twin Earth Chronicles*, edited by Andrew Pessin and Sanford Goldberg (1996), is a collection of articles on aspects of the Twin Earth argument. Chapters 10–15 in Nathan Salmon's (1981) *Reference and Essence* deals specifically with Putnam's theory of natural kind terms. *Reflections and Replies: Essays on the Philosophy of Tyler Burge*, edited by Martin Hahn and Bjørn Ramberg (2003), contains a number of articles discussing mostly aspects of Burge's brand of semantic externalism followed by replies by Burge. Burge (2007b) is a collection of Burge's influential articles on semantic externalism and cognate topics. Another important collection of articles is *The Externalist Challenge*, edited by Richard Schantz (2004). While part III defends semantic externalism of one stripe or another, part IV is more critical of this view. Focusing just on monographs, important recent defenses of semantic externalism include Robert Wilson's (1995) *Cartesian Psychology and Physical Minds: Individualism and the Sciences of the Mind*, Mark Rowlands' (2003) *Externalism: Putting Mind and World Back Together Again*, and Jessica Brown's (2004) *Anti-individualism and Knowledge*. All three contain very helpful introductory chapters. Important recent defenses of semantic internalism include Gabriel Segal's (2000) *A Slim Book about Narrow Content*, Katalin Farkas' (2008) *The Subject's Point of View*, and Joseph Mendola's *Anti-externalism* (2008). These monographs also provide constructive introductory material. For excellent survey articles on wide and narrow content see chapters 20 and 21 in *The Oxford Handbook of Philosophy of Mind*, edited by Brian McLaughlin, Ansgar Beckermann and Sven Walter. Chapter 3 in Burge's recent monograph *Origins of Objectivity* (2010) is devoted to clarifying the thesis he calls 'anti-individualism'. Davidson's work on meaning and representation is given a comprehensive, critical treatment by Ernest Lepore and Kirk Ludwig (2007) in their *Donald Davidson: Meaning, Truth, Language, and Reality*. Burge's (2003) "Social Anti-individualism, Objective Reference" is a critical discussion of the role of the social in Davidson's views about triangulation. Papineau's (2005) "Naturalist Theories of Meaning" is an accessible survey article on teleosemantics and other accounts of representation within a naturalist framework. For an excellent collection of recent articles by friends and foes of teleosemantics see *Teleosemantics*, edited by Graham Mcdonald and David Papineau (2006). For a range of additional arguments against historical externalism see Jerry Fodor's (1994) *The Elm and the Expert: Mentalese and Its Semantics*. Michael Huemer's (2007) "Epistemic Possibility" is of interest to those who wish to probe deeper into that notion.

4

VARIETIES OF NARROW AND WIDE CONTENT

4.1 Object-dependent thoughts

In Section 3.1 we presented the Twin Earth argument, which shows that if a natural kind concept has a reference, it is individuated externally in terms of that reference. It teaches us that having a natural kind concept is a property that fails to supervene on internal features of thinkers. But the Twin Earth argument is silent about how those concepts are individuated in circumstances where the relevant physical facts go missing. Is it possible to think thoughts about water if there is no water? By 'thoughts' is meant the contents of thoughts – what we have been calling 'propositions' – rather than the acts of thinking thoughts with those contents. Before we address that question let's backtrack a bit to consider two distinct kinds of *object-dependent thoughts*.

In Section 2.1 *singular propositions* were identified with those propositions that are expressed by sentences containing directly referential terms. Given that the propositional contents of directly referential terms consist in their reference, singular propositions are structured complexes whose constituents are the objects and properties as picked out by those terms. Singular propositions are not only individuated by the particular objects that they are about. Such propositions as conceived by the referentialist are also object-dependent. If the proper name 'Ryan Giggs' is directly referential,

then the sentence 'Ryan Giggs plays for Wales' expresses a singular proposition whose constituents are Ryan Giggs and the property of playing
(football) for Wales. Obviously, thinking that proposition depends upon
the existence of Ryan Giggs himself. If he had not existed, one could not
think that proposition. Hence, singular propositions are object-dependent.
Referentialists typically hold that speakers suffer illusions of content when
they utter sentences containing empty proper names, but this view has
the counter-intuitive consequence that distinct empty proper names should
be treated semantically alike. Assuming both 'Santa Claus' and 'Odin' are
empty proper names, then neither expresses any propositional content.
Consequently, there is no difference in the propositional content expressed
by the sentences 'Santa Claus does not exist' and 'Odin does not exist'. If
the referentialist holds that sentences containing empty proper names fail
to express even incomplete propositions, then those two sentences fail to
express any proposition at all. But then differences in propositional content
cannot feature in an explanation of how a competent speaker can consistently assent to one of these sentences while dissenting from the other.
Some alternative account is called for. For instance, in Section 2.4
the referentialist responded to the belief argument by saying that the same
singular proposition could be believed under distinct modes of presentation.
It is not obvious how this move helps with the current problem. For how
can there exist modes under which propositions are presented if there are
no propositions to be presented under those modes? This is a point to
which we shall shortly return. A more promising response is to adopt a
hybrid view. Thus, following Ludlow (2003: 404–5), 'Bill Clinton' refers
directly such that sentences containing that non-empty proper name
express singular propositions, while 'Santa Claus' is a descriptive expression
such that sentences containing that empty proper name express (partially)
descriptive propositions. On his view, whether a proper name is directly
referential or descriptive is entirely fixed by the external world, independently of facts about linguistic intentions. Ludlow's hybrid view has a reply
to the objection that referentialism cannot offer distinct semantic accounts
of distinct empty proper names. If 'Santa Claus' and 'Odin' are both empty
but express distinct (partially) descriptive contents, then so do 'Santa Claus
does not exist' and 'Odin does not exist'. Hence, we can explain how
a competent speaker can rationally assent to one of these sentences but
dissent from the other.

   Or take *perceptual demonstrative thoughts*. A demonstrative such as 'that' is an
indexical expression that requires a demonstration, typically a visual

presentation of an object in the vicinity that is singled out by pointing. Perceptual demonstrative thoughts are arguably also thoughts that one can think only if there are the right objects to have a thought about. For such thoughts are individuated by the particular objects that they are about. Suppose I utter the sentence 'that woman is German' while pointing at the pantry that I can see in front of me. Now it transpires that despite appearances there is no woman in the pantry. I suffer a perceptual hallucination. Then ask: what is the content of my thought? If propositional content is truth-conditional, it seems as if I have failed to express a complete thought. Since there is no demonstratively identified woman in the pantry, the right-hand side of the following singular truth-condition (TC) has a missing component:

(TC_1) 'That woman is German' is true if and only if ... is German.

The proposition expressed by my utterance is thus at best incomplete in that there is a gap at the place where it should have contained a woman. If there is no referent, there is nothing for my putative thought to latch on to, and so my utterance fails to express any (complete) thought. I suffer an illusion of singular content expression. But note that the sentence has its *linguistic meaning* irrespective of failure of reference. Demonstratives have what Kaplan (1989) called a *character*: a function from contexts of utterance to propositional content expressed in those contexts. In cases of reference failure we can thus fall back on the sentence 'that woman is German' being associated with the context-independent character **the demonstratively identified woman is German**. Such linguistic meaning can be apprehended even if there is no woman in the pantry. Accordingly, while there may be illusions of singular content expression, there is no illusion of associated characters.

Now consider a different kind of object-dependent thoughts. Evans (1982) and McDowell (1977, 1984, 1986) believe there are thoughts related to objects in such a way that if those objects were absent, there would be no thoughts at all. But they advocate a Fregean version of object dependence according to which such thoughts are composed of modes of presentation of objects and properties rather than the objects and properties themselves. McDowell (1984) talks about these modes of presentation as de re senses being specific to their res. Two features characterize these de re senses. On the one hand, if there is nothing for a putative de re sense to determine, then as McDowell puts it (1984: 288) there is "a gap – an absence – at, so to speak, the relevant place of mind". On the other hand, de re senses are individuated by their *cognitive significance*: if a competent speaker can believe one thought while disbelieving another, then they are distinct thoughts composed of distinct senses. Individuating senses in this fine-grained way is reminiscent of the Fregean principle (CogSig) that we discussed in Section 1.2. The de re sense associated with a term is distinct from the object referred to by that term, yet that de re sense is dependent for its existence on that object. Evans (1982: 12, 18–22, 33) also accepts Frege's distinction between sense and reference, but he takes Fregean sense to be a *way of thinking* of an object which need not amount to any descriptive content. In Sections 1.2 and 1.3 Frege's notion of sense was assimilated to the content expressed by definite descriptions, but Evans and McDowell think differently about Fregean sense. In particular, such descriptive content is object-independent. Although Evans' ways of thinking of objects are indi-viduated by their cognitive significance, there cannot, in his words (1982: 22), "be a way of thinking about something unless there is something to be thought about in that way". Thoughts are composed by Fregean senses, but they also single out particular objects to which the thinker stands in a special relation of acquaintance. As mentioned in Section 3.2, acquaintance is a causal relation. To say that I am acquainted with Edinburgh is to say that I have had some causal encounters with that place, e.g. been a regular visitor. Thoughts are object-dependent when the thinker is acquainted with objects about which she is thinking in such a way that the existence of her thoughts is contingent upon the existence of these objects. In cases of reference failure, the speaker undergoes an illusion of content expression. The only significance empty singular terms have is for a poetic or fictive use as in 'Pegasus is a horse'. To use Frege's terminology, such sentences express mock thoughts.

Remember the distinction from Section 1.1 between the first-order question in *descriptive semantics* of what the semantics for a term is, and the second-order question in *foundational semantics* of what makes a term have the semantics that it has. The Twin Earth argument and the arthritis argument are both primarily meant to address the second-order question. What Putnam should have said is that some of the features that individuate meaning 'ain't in the head'. What determine the propositional content and reference of 'water' and 'arthritis' are rather facts about speakers' external, physical or sociolinguistic environments. While the Twin Earth argument also indirectly speaks to the first-order question in denying that propositional content consists in associated definite descriptions, the arthritis argument is consistent with such a view. For instance, Burge (1979) is sympathetic to a Fregean account of propositional content yet he holds that some such content is wide. The thesis about object-dependent thoughts, however, provides primarily an answer to the first-order question: the propositional content of certain terms is object-dependent. Derivatively, this thesis speaks to the second-order question too, in that these terms have that kind of content in virtue of the speaker being acquainted with their referents.[1]

Let's now revisit the question of whether natural kind thoughts are object-dependent or better: *kind-dependent*.[2] Boghossian (1998b: 279–83) imagines that Dry Earth is a remote planet in the actual world where, despite all appearances, the lakes, rivers, taps, etc., all run bone dry. The entire community on Dry Earth mistakenly believes that there is a stuff which they call 'water' and which has all the watery properties. In short, global illusions pertaining to that stuff prevail.[3] It seems that on Dry Earth there are no conditions under which sentences containing 'water' are true. The following truth-condition has a missing component:

(TC$_2$) 'Water is wet' is true if and only if ... is wet.

This means that when *dry-Mary* — an inhabitant on Dry Earth — utters that sentence, she expresses at best an incomplete proposition. Dry-Mary is thus subject to an illusion of content expression. Unlike the demonstrative case where the illusion of content is *local* as the expression of the pertinent demonstrative thought requires being perceptually related to a particular woman in the pantry, dry-Mary suffers a *global* illusion. Someone could have expressed a thought using 'water'-sentences despite the absence of water in her local environment as long as water is abundant elsewhere. But dry-Mary is not so fortunate: she never succeeds in expressing a concept by using 'water'. For what concept could that possibly be? Boghossian (1998b: 279–83) offers two proposals: (i) her tokens of 'water' express a *compound concept* such as **the watery stuff**, or (ii) her tokens of 'water' express an *atomic concept*. An atomic concept is one that lacks conceptual constituents, and a compound concept is one that is subject to decomposition into such constituents. Suppose (i) is true. Then bear in mind that Earthly and twin-Earthly tokens of 'water' were assumed by the semantic externalist to not express such a compound concept since that would have implied that those tokens were co-referential. It was presupposed in those two non-empty cases that 'water' expresses an atomic concept, namely **water** on Earth and **twin-water** on Twin Earth. But then it is difficult to see how the same word type can express an atomic concept under conditions of successful reference and a different compound concept under conditions of unsuccessful reference. Remember that 'water' plays the same functional role on Earth, Twin Earth and Dry Earth. According to Boghossian (1998b: 281), compositionality of concepts is a function of their internal syntax, which presumably is fixed by competent speakers' semantic intentions. Whether a concept is atomic or compositional can thus be settled a priori on his view.

Korman (2007) has responded that compositionality does depend on such external features as actually having a reference. On Dry Earth, 'water'-sentences can be assigned something like descriptive truth-conditions:

(TC$_3$) 'Water is wet' is true if and only if the watery stuff is wet.

If definite descriptions make existence claims, then a dry-Earthly token of 'water is wet' expresses a false proposition, i.e. the proposition that there is exactly one watery liquid that is wet is false on Dry Earth. Now, given that competent speakers cannot know a priori whether they are on Earth or on Dry Earth, they cannot know a priori which kind of truth-conditions their tokens of that sentence have. Consequently, speakers who competently understand 'water' cannot know a priori whether they express an atomic or compositional concept.[4] Note also that those who view natural kind terms as having a descriptivist semantics when the pertinent terms are empty have a reply to the objection that referentialists must treat distinct empty natural kind terms as semantically alike. Take the empty terms 'phlogiston' and 'ether'. If these express distinct descriptive contents, then so do 'phlogiston does not exist' and 'ether does not exist'. Hence, there is no puzzle about how a competent speaker can consistently assent to one of these sentences but dissent from the other sentence.

Suppose instead that (ii) is true. One should now ask: what propositional content is expressed by such empty tokens of 'water' as uttered on Dry Earth? One can begin by ruling out the candidate that it should be the atomic concept expressed by non-empty tokens of 'water' that is expressed by empty tokens of 'water' for that would contradict the thesis that such atomic concepts are externally individuated. But, Boghossian professes (1998b: 282), if the atomic concept expressed is neither **water** nor **twin-water**, then there are arguably no other possible atomic concepts.[5]

The upshot is that even if the Twin Earth argument only licenses external individuation of concepts, the Twin Earth argument in conjunction with Boghossian's Dry Earth argument implies that natural kind concepts are kind-dependent. Let's call a version of semantic externalism that is merely supported by the Twin Earth argument or by the arthritis argument *weak semantic externalism*, and let's call a version of semantic externalism that is underpinned by the Dry Earth argument *strong semantic externalism*. While the former view is about *which* concepts are possessed in different external environments, the latter view is about *whether* concepts are possessed in said environments. Boghossian presents a strong case that weak semantic externalism entails strong semantic externalism. Note, however, that for the semantic internalist, there is nothing special about Dry Earth. On her view, Earthly, twin-Earthly and dry-Earthly tokens of 'water' all express some (causally constrained) descriptive concept. That concept is shared by all doppelgängers regardless of their external environments, and so counts as narrow content.[6]

Pace Boghossian, Burge (1982) envisaged a Dry Earth scenario in which it is possible to have **water**-thoughts without the existence of water. What he has in mind is also a case in which dry-Mary has a belief involving the concept **water** even though there exists no water at all on Dry Earth. What must be required is that there exists sufficient knowledge of chemistry among the more informed members of her community to distinguish **water** from various twin-concepts such as **twin-water**. Suppose the relevant scientific speakers have theorized that hydrogen and oxygen could bond to form H_2O. This assumes that they sustain separate causal interactions with hydrogen and oxygen so as to possess the concepts **hydrogen** and **oxygen** necessary for possessing the composite concept H_2O. Suppose also that these speakers possessed a flawed chemical analysis of the illusory stuff that is believed to be watery showing it to be composed of H_2O. Then these expert speakers qualify for possession of the concept **water**. Moreover, if dry-Mary defers to these speakers when it comes to her use of 'water', then she counts as possessing **water** despite not knowing anything about chemistry, hence not having the concept H_2O.[7] Likewise, we can imagine a situation in which only one speaker exists in an environment containing water: *lonely-Mary* is the sole inhabitant on Lonely Earth. There is no question that lonely-Mary could form the concept **water**, even though there are no other speakers in her environment. What would be required is that she had causally interacted with instances of the natural kind water and furthermore held a minimum of chemically relevant beliefs to distinguish water from other candidate twin-substances. Social relations are thus not necessary for having thoughts. What we cannot have, following Burge (1982), is a combined situation − *Mixed Earth* − in which there is someone who lacks knowledge of the chemical composition of the stuff that is believed to go under the name 'water', yet this individual has the concept **water** even though neither water nor other speakers exist in her environment. As McLaughlin and Tye (1998b: 302) remarks, that is consistent with someone having the concept **water** despite there being neither water nor other people in her environment. If someone managed single-handedly to develop a chemical theory showing the illusory watery stuff to be made of H_2O, then she counts as possessing **water**. Causal interaction with the widely separated natural kinds hydrogen and oxygen would furnish her with the concepts **hydrogen** and **oxygen** out of which she could form the concept H_2O. Indeed, despite the absence of H_2O on Dry Earth, **water** qualifies as a natural kind concept in virtue of the existence of H_2O on Earth.[8]

Although Burge (1982) did not address the question of whether **water** is an atomic concept on Dry Earth, that is plausibly what is being assumed in addition to water being a composite natural kind (H_2O). Other semantic externalists such as McLaughlin and Tye (1998b), S. Goldberg (2006b), Korman (2007) and Ball (2007) are certainly explicit that dry-Earthly tokens of 'water' can express an atomic concept. Still, Burge seems to presuppose that the acquisition conditions for the concept **water** resemble those for a composite natural kind concept, e.g. the concept H_2O. That is to say, it is required that the experts on Dry Earth have had causal encounters with the constituent natural kinds of which water is composed, and then construed a chemical theory about water deploying concepts of those constituent kinds. This raises the question of whether one could possess an atomic concept of a non-existent atomic natural kind, given what semantic externalism says about concept individuation. Take an atomic concept **x** (**oxygen**, **electron**, or what have you), and imagine a corresponding Dry Earth scenario. Assuming x constitutes an atomic natural kind, no component natural kinds would be available for the experts to causally interact with so as to build a scientific theory about x. In short, the account Burge (1982) and others offer of how one can have an atomic concept of a non-existing composite natural kind cannot easily explain how one can have an atomic concept of a non-existing atomic natural kind, given what semantic externalism says about concept individuation.

4.2 Indexicality and egocentric thoughts

The modal argument from Section 2.2 and the Twin Earth argument from Section 3.1 complement each other in their criticism of descriptivism.

A simple-minded version of this view says that speakers associate with a term individually necessary and jointly sufficient descriptive conditions for an object to be its referent. For H_2O and XYZ to be picked out by 'water', they must have every single associated watery property, and having all those watery properties suffice for them to be picked out by 'water'. The modal argument shows that these conditions are not necessary: 'water' refers to H_2O even in possible worlds where H_2O lacks the watery properties. The Twin Earth argument shows that these conditions are not sufficient: 'water' does not refer to XYZ on Twin Earth despite XYZ having all the watery properties. As we saw, in response to the modal argument descriptivists typically appeal to rigidified descriptions: 'water' is shorthand for 'the actual watery stuff', and in response to the Twin Earth argument they invoke causal descriptions: 'water' is shorthand for 'the watery stuff of our acquaintance'. In general, when faced with counterexamples, the descriptivist strategy has frequently been to incorporate the relevant properties into the set of definite descriptions which yield the propositional content of the term in question. Thus Lewis (1997) and Jackson (1998a: 212) recommend that what we learn from the arguments against descriptivism is not that the reference of a term cannot go via instantiation of descriptive properties, but rather *which* such properties mediate the reference of that term and hence articulate its propositional content.[9]

Let's first dwell on the descriptivist response to the Twin Earth argument. If, following (iii) in Section 3.2, 'water' is shorthand for 'the watery stuff of our acquaintance', then 'water' is in effect an indexical expression.[10] The reason is that 'water' will inherit the indexicality of 'our acquaintance'. The latter is an indexical expression which picks out the contextually salient community to which the speaker belongs, and in which some members have a certain causal property. That is to say, 'water' will refer to the watery stuff that the contextually salient speech community causally interacts with. So, Mary's utterances of 'water' refer to H_2O, and twin-Mary's utterances on Twin Earth of 'water' refer to XYZ. While this descriptivist proposal thus respects intuitions pertaining to 'water', e.g. that Earthly tokens of 'water' do not refer to XYZ, it is nevertheless unclear how it underwrites any form of semantic internalism. For when Mary and twin-Mary utter tokens of the same type of sentences containing 'water', their utterances have different truth-conditions:

(TC$_4$) Mary's utterance of 'water is wet' is true if and only if the watery stuff of our acquaintance is wet, while

(TC$_5$) Twin-Mary's utterance of 'water is wet' is true if and only if the
   watery stuff of their acquaintance is wet.

This truth-conditional difference stems from the indexicality of 'our
acquaintance'. True, if the descriptivist invokes causally constrained
descriptions, she need not accept that the terms which abbreviate these
descriptions express contents that are singular with respect to their referents. Instead we get a difference in truth-conditions, and so a difference in
the propositions expressed, not because of a difference in the physical
nature of the referents, but because of a difference in contextual parameters
such as the location of the speaker.[11] In this case, Mary and twin-Mary
would express different propositions even if they were embedded in identical physical environments. But then we have a propositional difference
that is not down to an internal difference, and that squares badly with
semantic internalism.

   The same point applies in the modal argument when the descriptivist
avails herself of rigidified descriptions. In Putnam's example Twin Earth is
a remote planet in the actual world, but now assume instead that Twin
Earth is a planet in a mere possible world W. Then take Mary and her
internal duplicate twin-Mary on this counterfactual Twin Earth. If 'water'
simply abbreviates 'the actual watery stuff', then their respective tokens of
'water is wet' will again differ in truth-conditions:

(TC$_6$) Mary's utterance of 'water is wet' is true if and only if the watery
   stuff in the actual world is wet.
(TC$_7$) Twin-Mary's utterance of 'water is wet' is true if and only if the
   watery stuff in W is wet.

So, the truth-conditions change with variation in which possible
worlds Mary and twin-Mary are in, and not with variation in the reference
of 'water'. Remember Perfect Earth from Section 2.3. Mary and perfect-
Mary on Perfect Earth both refer to H_2O when they use 'water', because
they are embedded in identical physical environments. But if 'water' is
shorthand for 'the actual watery stuff', then their respective tokens of
'water is wet' will nevertheless still differ in their truth-conditions. Once
more we have a propositional difference that is not due to a difference in
internal features.

Worse still, if the contents of beliefs are propositions, and if belief states are individuated by their contents, then not only will the content of Mary's belief differ from the content of twin-Mary's belief, they will be in distinct belief states solely in virtue of a difference in either their actual location or in which possible world they are in. Although that falls short of establishing the semantic externalist claim that such differences in belief states and their contents are due to differences in their external physical or sociolinguistic environment, the upshot is not one that seems congenial to semantic internalism either. For if the semantic internalist invokes indexical – causal or rigidified – descriptions in order to answer the modal argument and the Twin Earth argument, there will be cases where internal duplicates are in distinct belief states.

In response to this concern, Lewis (1979) and Jackson (2003) have argued that a difference in truth-conditions need not entail a difference in belief content when the former is due merely to shifts in contextual parameters. In effect, they challenge the semantic externalist assumption that such content is truth-conditional. To illustrate, consider Perry's example (1993: 21–23) of the philosopher Hume and the madman Heimson each believing they themselves wrote the *Treatise*. They both express their belief using 'I wrote the *Treatise*', but Hume's utterance is true if and only if Hume wrote the *Treatise*, and Heimson's utterance is true if and only if Heimson wrote the *Treatise*.[12] If propositions are determined by their truth-conditions, Hume and Heimson thus believe different propositions. Because their beliefs are about different individuals, they hold in one sense distinct de se beliefs.[13] Yet, intuitively, there is a common content to their beliefs. Heimson is mad enough to sincerely and competently accept all and only those sentences Hume accepts. Unlike Hume, Heimson is deeply confused about his own achievements, but he fully masters the linguistic rules of his language. As Lewis (1979: 525) put it, "Heimson may have got his head into perfect match with Hume's in every way that is at all relevant to what he believes". But if the sense in which they believe alike cannot be that of believing the same proposition, what is it? Lewis (1979) suggests that the shared content of their beliefs consists in both self-ascribing the property of having authored the *Treatise* at some time t. In that sense, they hold identical de se beliefs. Alternatively, we can think of the shared content as the semantically incomplete, *relativized proposition* **x wrote the Treatise at** t. Relativized propositions are functions from centred possible worlds (pairs of a world and a designated space-time point) to truth-values. So, utterances of 'I wrote the *Treatise*' are true at world W with centre $< x, t >$ if and only if W is a world where the *Treatise* was authored by *x* at t. An utterance of that sentence is true at the actual world with centre < Hume, t >, but false at the actual world with centre < Heimson, t >. The truth-values of Heimson's belief and Hume's belief differ, but the belief contents that they express by uttering that sentence are each the same function from *W* with centre < *x*, t > to truth-values.[14]

In the case of Putnam's Twin Earth, there is also a sense in which Mary and twin-Mary on this remote planet believe alike when they both utter 'water is wet'. Following Lewis, that common content consists in self-ascribing the same property of being acquainted with a unique watery stuff that is wet at t. That in effect is to say that Mary and twin-Mary both believe the same relativized proposition **the watery stuff of *x*'s acquaintance is wet at t**. Utterances of 'water is wet' are thus true at the actual world with centres < Earth, t > and < Twin Earth, t >. Not only are their respective utterances of that sentence true, the belief contents that they express by uttering that sentence are each the same function from *W* with centre < *x*, t > to truth-values. As Mary and twin-Mary are actually differently located, the truth-conditions of their respective utterances differ, but that function remains invariant.[15] Note also that when dry-Mary utters 'water is wet' on Dry Earth, she could plausibly be interpreted as believing that very same relativized proposition. The only way dry-Mary would differ from Mary and twin-Mary is that her belief would lack a truth-value due to the fact that 'water' is an empty term on Dry Earth.

Similarly when Twin Earth is taken to be a planet in another possible world *W*. If Lewis is right, then Mary and twin-Mary on this counterfactual planet believe alike in that they self-ascribe the same property of inhabiting a world in which the watery stuff is wet at t. They both believe the same relativized proposition **the watery stuff in world *x* is wet at t**. An utterance of 'water is wet' is thus true at the actual world with centre < Earth, t >, and an utterance of that sentence is true at *W* with centre < Twin Earth, t >. The belief contents that they express by uttering that sentence are each the same function from *W* with centre < *x*, t > to truth-values. As Mary and twin-Mary are counterfactually differently located, the truth-conditions of their respective utterances differ, but that function remains invariant. Note also that when perfect-Mary utters 'water is wet' on perfect-Earth, she could plausibly be interpreted as believing that very same relativized proposition, indeed perfect-Mary's belief would be true just in case Mary's and twin-Mary's beliefs are true.[16]

The moral is that differences in location make all the difference, not to what Mary and twin-Mary believe, but to the way in which we can truly report what they believe. What Mary believes when she utters 'water is wet' is just what twin-Mary believes when she utters the same sentence, but due to the hidden indexicality of 'water', we can only use that sentence to truly report Mary's belief. As Loar (1988), Lewis (1979) and Jackson (2003: 68, 2004: 326–27) stressed, we thus have to proceed very carefully when moving back and forth between the contents of beliefs and the semantics of belief-reporting sentences in cases where those sentences contain indexical elements. For belief contents are not always captured by the 'that'-clauses that are used to attribute beliefs.

4.3 Two-factor theories of content

Putnam's initial presentation of the Twin Earth argument assumed that Mary and twin-Mary are psychological duplicates: they share all stereotypical (narrow content) beliefs. Nevertheless, the semantic contents of their respective utterances of sentences containing 'water' differ. Total content is stereotypical plus reference-individuated content. So, Putnam combined semantic externalism with a form of content internalism.[17] Subsequently, several philosophers defended views according to which belief states are composite states that encompass both narrow and wide components. In this section we consider two such hybrid theories of content, due to McGinn (1982, 1989) and more recently Chalmers (2002, 2003, 2011).[18]

It was argued with Frege in Sections 1.2 and 1.3 that if identity statements are to be informative, referring terms must have sense over and above their reference. To get the epistemological profile of such statements right, these terms should have as part of their content some cognitive significance. In Section 2.2 it was then countered with Kripke that referring terms must be directly referential if certain modal statements containing them are to be true. In order to get the modal profile of such statements right, the meaning of these terms should consist in their reference. McGinn recommends that these seemingly conflicting arguments be resolved by building a two-factor theory of content, which preserves the virtues and avoids the pitfalls of both the Fregean and the Kripkean outlook. On the one hand, followers of Kripke were right to adopt singular content as what determines reference, but wrong to abandon sense altogether. On the other hand, followers of Frege were right to embrace sense as what constitutes cognitively significant content, but wrong to take sense to also be what determines reference. No single property of referring terms can play both the cognitive and the referential role: the way in which terms refer is distinct from the way in which their referents are presented in thought. Instead two components of the content of referring terms should be recognized: a *cognitive-role component* responsible for their epistemic profile and an independent *referential-role component* responsible for their modal profile.

McGinn's hybrid view pertains not just to the contents of purely extensional sentences, but also to the contents of propositional attitudes. In particular, total belief content must be recognized as a mixture of two individually necessary components of content. These components are distinct because they are subject to distinct kinds of individuation. The cognitive-role component of belief content points inward to internal representations of reality. These representations are causally responsible for the production of behaviour. This component is thus individuated in terms of being causally explainable of behaviour. The referential-role component of belief content, however, points outward to the external world. As beliefs involve relations to propositions, which are assigned truth-conditions, this component concerns the semantic relations between the internal representations and what they represent. It is thus individuated in terms of being truth-evaluable. In short, the total content of belief states decomposes into a component that is conferred by the world, saying what is represented, and a component that is conferred by us, saying how it is represented.

Let's dwell on these distinct components in some detail. The cognitive-role component is constitutive of the *causal-explanatory role of belief*. In folk psychology, behaviour is often causally explained and predicted in terms of beliefs and other contentful states. For instance, Jones entered the pub, because he desired a beer and he believed that he could satisfy that desire by going into the pub. Jones' belief and desire can feature in a causal explanation of his behaviour, because they are what caused his behaviour. For Jones' belief state to play an indispensable role in causally explaining his behaviour, it must arguably contribute to the production of that behaviour. And the aspect of that state that is causally efficacious of Jones' behaviour pertains to his internal representation – to the cognitive role of the belief. It is the aspect that internally represents the environment in such a way as to produce the behaviour of entering the pub in the light of incoming information about his environment.[19] The referential properties of Jones' state do not supervene on the cognitive role of his belief, nor do they play any causal-explanatory role. That is to say, the cognitive role is not what determines the reference of the terms that Jones uses to express his belief. Meaning determines reference, but cognitive role is not a component of an overarching notion of meaning. Cognitive role rather resides firmly in his head. It is a narrow component of content in the sense of being shared by internal duplicates inhabiting the same world. Narrow content is thus not a semantic or truth-conditional notion of content.[20] McGinn (1989: 8–9) rejects the *methodological solipsistic* view targeted by the Twin Earth argument: the view that some belief content is independent of features of both the believer's environment and world. There are no such purely solipsistic beliefs. But while McGinn (1989: 31–60) endorses Putnam's semantic externalism about the concept **water**, he also holds that artefactual concepts, concepts of perceptual appearances, sensational concepts, observational concepts and some general psychological concepts are *world-dependent* without being *environment-dependent*.[21] Basically, concepts that concern how things are as opposed to how they appear are environment-dependent, but concepts that concern merely the appearance of things are only world-dependent. Despite being situated in distinct environments, Mary and twin-Mary can be said to harbour the same beliefs about how the stuff that they call 'water' appears. No content is purely intrinsic, but some content is individuated by reference to external features without being susceptible to Twin Earth thought experiments. In the latter case, there is an existential dependency between being in states with such content and the features of the external world represented by that content even if those features obtain in a remote environment.

The referential-role component delivers reference-involving truth-conditions, which specify the objects and properties picked out by the terms that occur in the embedded clause of belief-ascribing sentences. These are the objects and properties (or property instances) to which the believer is causally connected. As belief states serve to represent aspects of the external environment, they have semantic properties, which fail to supervene on the believer's internal features. McGinn's argument for this claim rests on the *fallibility of representations*. When an object o is represented as having F, it is possible that o in fact lacks that property. In that case the representation is false, but o is still what is being represented. So, it is possible to falsely represent o as having F, only if what is represented is fixed independently of its having F. That is to say, a representation can misrepresent o as having F only if being a representation of o is independent of being a characterization of o as having F. For if that were not so, the representation would be of some other object o^* that did have F, or maybe the representation would be of no determinate object at all. Take proper names. Suppose Mary utters 'Aristotle discovered the incompleteness theorem'. Intuitively, Mary misrepresents Aristotle rather than correctly representing some deviant referent of 'Aristotle'. But suppose she mentally represents the referent of 'Aristotle' as the discoverer of the incompleteness theorem. This reflects the cognitive role which that name plays in her thought and action. Then Mary ends up with a belief that is true of Gödel. The lesson is that the reference of the name is not fixed by such representing descriptions. The naming relation is rather fixed by some causal-historical link between names and their referents. Otherwise representation by names would be necessarily infallible; or so McGinn contends.

Consider again Twin Earth. When the term 'water' occurs opaquely within the belief context 'Mary believes that water is wet', it gives us two sorts of information: the truth-conditions of the belief, and the internal representations that causally explain Mary's behaviour. That is to say, that term as it occurs in the belief-ascribing sentence makes a dual contribution to specifying the components of the content of her belief – it attributes an internal, causal-explanatory representation and it relates that representation to water in her environment. For Mary and twin-Mary the term 'water' has the same cognitive role, because they internally represent their environment in the same way. When thirsty they both reach out for a glass of what they internally represent as the watery stuff. Yet their tokens of 'water' differ in reference and hence in meaning. So, some beliefs have the same cognitive or explanatory role but differ in truth-conditions. Other beliefs have the same truth-conditions but differ in cognitive or explanatory roles. Think of 'I am thirsty for water' as uttered by Mary, and 'you are thirsty for water' as uttered by one of Mary's friends on Earth. Mary drinks water and her friend sees to it that Mary drinks water. Yet the occurrences of 'I' and 'you' are co-referential in these contexts of utterance, and so the truth-conditions of their respective utterances are identical.

Before we press on to consider another hybrid view of mental content, it should be flagged that several influential philosophers have argued persistently against the invocation of narrow content to causally explain behaviour. The claim is that narrow content is inadequate if not too obscure to play any role, or at least any irreducible role, in psychological explanation. Only wide content can do the explanatory job, or at least it can do the job equally well. Thus, by challenging the assumption that behaviour is always typed individualistically or narrowly, i.e. that doppelgängers are in exactly the same states for the purposes of psychological explanation, Peacocke, Owens, Burge and others deny that narrow content is necessary for psychological explanation. To give some examples, Peacocke (1981) argued that doppelgängers are psychologically different in so far as their distinct demonstrative beliefs cause them to act on distinct objects in their respective environments. Owens (1987) argued against the claim that cognitive psychology is bound by the principle that individuals can differ in psychological explanatory states only if there are some internal physical differences between them. On his view, there are no such states which are both individuated by their contents and supervene on internal physical features. Likewise, Burge (1989) argued that cognitive psychology individuates mental states externalistically just as such states have an externalistic character when specified in ordinary discourse. More recently, Burge (2010: 77–78) critiques the idea that semantic externalism should be true of how referents are established but not of the way referents are thought about. Content that plays cognitive and explanatory roles is in each case equally wide.[22]

Let's now turn to a more recent hybrid view of mental content due to Chalmers (2002, 2003, 2011). First we need to introduce two distinct ways of considering a possible world. Talk about possible worlds is typically about counterfactual worlds. When we *consider a possible world as counterfactual* we make a counterfactual supposition: given the way the actual world is, what if it had been such-and-such a way? But possible worlds can also be thought of as candidates for the actual world. When we *consider a possible world as actual* we make a supposition about what the actual world is like: what if the actual world is such-and-such a way? To use Stalnaker's example (2001: 146) we can ask 'what if Oswald had not killed Kennedy?' or we can ask 'what if Oswald did not kill Kennedy?' In the first case, given that Oswald did actually kill Kennedy, we want to know what would have happened had he not done so. Presumably, Kennedy would not have been killed. In the second case, we want to know what follows if Oswald is not the killer. Certainly, someone else is.[23]

Correspondingly, we can think of Twin Earth as a planet in a counterfactual world. Then we ask: given that water is H_2O, what if the watery stuff had been XYZ? Answer: due to the rigidity of 'water', our tokens of 'water' do not pick out XYZ on a counterfactual Twin Earth. Or we can think of Twin Earth as a way the actual world may be. In that case, Twin Earth could either be taken to be a distant planet in our galaxy, or else where we are located – the planet we call 'Earth'. If we Earthlings sustain no causal encounters with XYZ, then our tokens of 'water' do not pick out XYZ. Or so the Twin Earth argument purports to show. But if very surprisingly the watery stuff around here turns out to be XYZ, then our tokens of 'water' presumably do pick out XYZ. Imagine leading scientists announcing the startling discovery that what we call 'water' in our environment is in fact

XYZ. In that scenario, we should admit a pervasive error about the nature of what we refer to by 'water'.[24]

Chalmers (2002, 2006) assigns two distinct functions to a statement depending on how possible worlds are conceived. The *epistemic intension* is a function from possible worlds considered as actual to truth-values, and the *subjunctive intension* is a function from possible worlds considered as counterfactual to truth-values. Similarly, the epistemic intension of a term maps worlds considered as actual onto referents in those worlds, and the subjunctive intension of a term maps possible worlds considered as counterfactual onto referents in those worlds. More accurately, epistemic intensions are functions from *scenarios* which are roughly speaking *centred* possible worlds – worlds centred on the speaker at the time and place of her utterance – to referents or truth-values. So, some centred worlds are centred on individuals at a certain time on Earth, others on individuals at certain times on Twin Earth. This qualification is needed so as to account for Twin Earth when taken as a remote planet in our galaxy.[25]

Let's run through our well-trodden example. The epistemic intension of 'water' picks out, roughly speaking, the watery stuff at all possible worlds, while the subjunctive intension picks out H_2O at all possible worlds.[26] The epistemic intension of the statement that water is H_2O is thus true at Earth, but false at Twin Earth, and so is contingent. But the subjunctive intension of this statement is true both at Earth and at Twin Earth. So, the subjunctive intension of the statement that water is H_2O is necessary. But understanding this statement consists in knowledge of its epistemic intension, and it is not a priori knowable that the watery stuff is H_2O. Consequently, the statement that water is H_2O is necessary a posteriori.[27]

Chalmers (2002, 2003) holds that the content of a belief can be decomposed into epistemic and subjunctive intensions or contents both of which are ascribed by ordinary belief ascriptions. Subjunctive content is typically wide in terms of delivering reference-involving truth-conditions. The subjunctive content associated with Mary's token of 'water is wet' is true if and only if H_2O is wet. In contrast, the subjunctive content of twin-Mary's token of 'water is wet' is true if and only if XYZ is wet. Such content is individuated by the referents of the terms that occur in the sentence expressing it. It governs truth across all worlds considered as counterfactual. Subjunctive content is merely a posteriori knowable, because it requires empirical knowledge about which possible world is actual. Epistemic content, however, is narrow by way of being determined by internal features of the believer. Such content yields the way things are according to

Mary — it encapsulates her perspective on the world. After all, although Mary and Twin Mary refer to different liquids, it seems the way in which their conceptions present those liquids to them is the same. Epistemic content captures the way the reference of a term depends on the nature of the environment, and so is independent of the environment itself: if H_2O is the watery stuff on Earth, then 'water' picks out H_2O; if XYZ is the watery stuff on Earth, then 'water' picks out XYZ, and so on.[28] These indicative conditionals are a priori knowable by both Mary and twin-Mary. It is thus *a priori knowable* what the epistemic content is, because it can be known independently of where one is located or of which possible world is actual.[29] But note that despite being environment-independent, epistemic content can still be assigned *non-reference-involving truth-conditions*. For instance, the epistemic content associated with both Mary's and twin-Mary's tokens of 'water is wet' is true if and only if the watery stuff is wet. The right-hand side of this bi-conditional says nothing about what the referents of those tokens of 'water' are. Epistemic content is semantic as it governs truth across all possible worlds considered as actual.[30]

Note how Chalmers' two-dimensional conception of meaning resembles Kaplan's theory of indexical expressions (1989) as explained in Sections 2.3 and 4.1. On Kaplan's view, the character of an indexical expression — its linguistic meaning — is that which determines its propositional content in varying contexts of utterance. Because characters are set by linguistic conventions, they are what a competent speaker knows merely in virtue of understanding the expression in question. In contrast, because propositional content — what is said — is dependent on the context of utterance, knowledge of which propositional content is expressed requires empirical knowledge of the relevant context. Characters can be represented by a function from possible contexts of utterance to propositional content, which in turn can be represented by a function from possible circumstances of evaluations to referents. It is propositional content that is evaluated in circumstances of evaluation. While there are significant differences between Kaplan and Chalmers' theories, they both embrace two dimensions of meaning: the first dimension determines the second dimension in conjunction with a context/scenario, and the second dimension determines a referent, extension or truth-value in conjunction with a circumstance/possible world.[31]

Note finally that although Chalmers would disagree with McGinn about whether narrow content has semantic import, he would concur that only narrow content plays the causal-explanatory role of psychological states. Suppose you and I both utter 'I have a headache'. The beliefs we express each have the same epistemic, but distinct subjunctive, content. We both take an aspirin. Suppose instead you utter 'I have a headache', while I utter 'you have a headache'. The beliefs we express have distinct epistemic contents but the same subjunctive content. You take an aspirin but I do not. In short, epistemic content is what causally explains behaviour.[32]

4.4 Natural kind concepts revisited

In Sections 4.2 and 4.3 we presented two semantic internalist views which both assumed that natural kind concepts are in some sense indexical. According to Lewis (1979) and Jackson (2003), the content that intrinsic duplicates have in common consists in self-ascriptions of the same properties. For instance, when Mary and twin-Mary both utter 'water is wet' the truth-conditions of their respective utterances will differ, but they both self-ascribe the same properties of being acquainted with a unique watery stuff that is wet, and of inhabiting a world in which the watery stuff is wet. The truth-conditional difference is down to the indexicality of 'water': given that 'water' is roughly synonymous with 'the actual watery stuff of our acquaintance', the conditions under which Mary and twin-Mary's utterances of 'water'-sentences are true will vary as a result of their different locations and causal histories. Likewise, according to Chalmers (2002, 2003, 2006), the epistemic intension of a term maps (centred) worlds considered as actual onto referents in those worlds. Since epistemic intensions capture the way the reference of a term depends on the nature of the environment, these intensions are independent of the environment itself. Hence, the epistemic intension of a term constitutes its narrow content. Take 'water'. The claim is that as different possible worlds are considered as actual, or as different centres within the same world are considered, an aspect of the meaning of 'water' remains constant while its reference shifts. If H_2O is the actual watery stuff of our acquaintance, then 'water' refers to H_2O; if XYZ is the actual watery stuff of our acquaintance, then 'water' refers to XYZ, etc. Epistemic intensions, Chalmers (2002: 620) claims, are thus sort of indexical contents.

Putnam also seemed sympathetic to the claim that natural kind terms are indexical expressions or at least have a hidden indexical component. In (1975: 152) he writes that:

> ... words like 'water' have an unnoticed indexical component: 'water' is stuff that bears a certain similarity relation to the water *around here*. Water

at another time or in another place or even in another possible world has to bear the relation [same-liquid] to *our* 'water' in order to be water.

But Burge (1982) and others have vigorously criticized the attempt to assimilate Earthly occurrences of 'water' to occurrences of indexical expressions like 'here' or 'this'. Note first that when one considers whether an expression is indexical one must hold the language fixed – otherwise every expression is trivially indexical. To illustrate the point, suppose the word 'leg' is used in some remote linguistic community to refer to both legs and tails. It is certainly possible that 'leg' should be governed by very different conventions of usage. That does not show that 'leg' is an indexical expression when used by English-language speakers. More generally, failure to observe the distinction between what a word refers to given the way we actually speak and what a word would have referred to had we spoken a different language can lead to confusion. Take the children's riddle 'if a horse's tail is called a "leg", how many legs does a horse have?' The answer is four: one cannot change the number of legs a horse has just by changing the way bits of language are used. But of course if 'leg' referred to legs as well as tails, then the sentence 'a horse has five legs' would express a truth. Likewise, when settling the question of whether 'water' is an indexical expression we must consider how that natural kind term is used in English. How that term is used in different, remote or counterfactual languages is simply irrelevant.

With that caveat in hand, Burge (1982) offers two arguments which purport to show that 'water' cannot be an indexical expression. The first is that Putnam's remarks that water is stuff that bears a certain relation to the water around here, or to our water, are somewhat circular in that the indexical expressions 'around here' and 'our' are simply superfluous. As Burge (1982: 114) puts it, "water around here, or our water, is just water. Nobody else's water, and no water anywhere else, is any different. Water is simply H_2O (give or take some isotopes and impurities)". Since water is necessarily H_2O there is no need to provide for shifts in reference when different contexts are salient. Any such shifts would involve the supposition that a different language is spoken. The fact that Earthlings apply 'water' to H_2O and Twin Earthlings apply 'water' to XYZ does not show that 'water' is an indexical expression with a fixed meaning that refers to different kinds of stuff in different contexts. It shows that 'water' has a different meaning on Earth and on Twin Earth. Earthlings and Twin Earthlings therefore speak slightly different languages. That 'water' could undergo shifts in reference merely by adopting non-standard linguistic conventions is, as we have just illustrated, a general point. It says nothing about the semantics of 'water' as actually used in English.

Burge's second argument (1982) goes as follows. Suppose Mary travels to Twin Earth. Because Mary speaks English on Earth, she will continue to speak English on Twin Earth at least for a while.[33] Mary is unaware that she is no longer on Earth, and so calls XYZ 'water'. If Putnam were right that 'water' means the stuff that bears the same-liquid relation to the stuff called 'water' around here, then Mary's utterance of 'water flows in that stream' would be true. Here 'that stream' picks out the demonstratively identified stream. For the sentence 'water flows in that stream' would be semantically equivalent to the true sentence 'the stuff that bears the same-liquid relation to the stuff called "water" around here flows in that stream'. The reason the latter sentence is true as uttered on Twin Earth is that the reference of 'here' would shift. The stuff that flows in that stream does bear the same-liquid relation to the stuff that is called 'water' on Twin Earth. The stuff of the molecular structure XYZ is the stuff that flows in that stream and XYZ is the same liquid as the stuff that is called 'water' on Twin Earth. But Mary speaks English when she visits Twin Earth, and so her utterance of 'water flows in that stream' should be false. After all, there is no water on Twin Earth. In sum, 'here' shifts reference when the place of the context is shifted, but 'water' does not, so 'water' lacks the indexicality of 'here'. A similar objection applies to the claim that 'water' means whatever bears a certain similarity relation to this stuff. 'Water' as interpreted in English does not shift its reference when the speaker of the context is shifted.

Mirroring Kripke's notion of reference-fixing from Section 2.1, Putnam (1975) also suggests that indexical expressions can play a role in introducing 'water' into our language as when pointing to a class and saying 'this liquid is water'. Here we must be careful. Contrast 'water' with 'I', which Putnam (1975: 165) calls an "absolutely indexical word." Just as with demonstratives, 'I' has a linguistic meaning which determines that the referent of an utterance of 'I' in a given context is the speaker of that context, but utterances of 'I' in different contexts pick out different individuals depending on who the relevant speakers are. 'Water', on the other hand, has no context-independent, reference-determining meaning. The only kind of meaning that tokens of 'water' have in common between Mary and twin-Mary would be the associated stereotypical descriptions, but these do no reference-determining work on Putnam's view.

Burge (1982) concedes that indexical expressions can play a *reference-fixing role* of a natural kind term, but they can do so without also playing a *meaning-giving role* of such a term. One could imagine fixing the reference of 'water' by stipulating that the term is to refer to whatever bears the same-liquid relation to the stuff that is called 'water' here. If one is on Earth, then 'water' has been introduced into English as a rigid designator of H_2O. But 'water' is not thereby synonymous with 'the stuff that bears the same-liquid relation to the stuff that is called "water" here', or any other such partially indexical, definite description. Hence, the meaning of 'water' is not even in part given by the indexical expression 'here'. Moreover, the rigidity of 'water' does not hang on the rigidity of 'here'.[34] For instance, one could imagine fixing the reference of 'water' by stipulating that 'water' is to refer to the watery stuff.[35] Then 'water' is a rigid designator, but unpacking the non-rigid definite description 'the watery stuff' yields no indexical expressions. The lesson is not to lump indexicality and rigidity together: many types of expressions are rigid but not indexical.

How does the foregoing bear on the Twin Earth argument? Strictly speaking, what that argument shows is that two claims are inconsistent: (i) internal features of thinkers determine meaning, and (ii) meaning determines reference. Denying either (i) or (ii), or both, restores consistency. As we saw, Putnam recommends that (i) be rejected. If 'water' were an indexical expression in the way that, say, 'I' is, (ii) would in Putnam's view have to go. Just as Mary and twin-Mary associate the same context-independent linguistic meaning with 'I' such that Mary's tokens of 'I' refer to Mary and twin-Mary's tokens of 'I' refer to twin-Mary, they would associate with 'water' the same context-independent linguistic meaning which would then determine that Mary refers to H_2O and twin-Mary to XYZ. Given the fine-grained way in which Putnam (1975) interprets (ii), there would be a difference in reference that should entail a difference in meaning. Putnam accepts that the meaning of 'water' shifts with variations in reference. Only the stereotype is constant, but, to repeat, that aspect of meaning has no semantic import on Putnam's view.[36] The descriptivist, however, might insist that the context-independent meaning of 'water' is captured by 'the watery stuff of our acquaintance'. The claim would then be that the meaning of 'water' does determine its reference albeit in a more coarse-grained way than Putnam requires, and that meaning is determined by internal factors in that competent speakers associate this causally constrained description with 'water' as its conventional meaning. Indeed, the descriptivist will be keen to point out that this gets the reference of 'water' right with respect to Twin Earth.

If in the light of the foregoing, Lewis, Jackson and Chalmers are wrong to follow Putnam in taking natural kind terms to have indexical components, alternative semantic accounts might be worth exploring. If, moreover, descriptivism about natural kind terms is viable only if indexical components are incorporated into the semantics of such terms, then this view looks unattractive. Does referentialism fare any better? When we sketched this view in Section 2.1 we used proper names as examples. However, it is not immediately obvious how to extend referentialism about proper names to a view about natural kind terms. For instance, Mill (1963/1843) claimed that while all names *denote* objects, only general names, including natural kind terms, also *connote* properties of objects, by which he meant that objects must have certain properties in order to be denoted by such terms and these properties constitute their meaning. Ordinary proper names denote objects but have no connotation. Their meanings are nothing but their referents. But natural kind terms connote properties and denote all the objects that have those properties. Predicates denote properties of objects but have no connotation. Obviously, the referentialist would want to disagree with Mill about natural kind terms. On her view Mill is wrong to claim that natural kind terms connote meaning-constituting properties. Just as the propositional content of a proper name is the individual to which it refers, the referentialist takes the propositional content of a natural kind term to be nothing but its referent. The question is what natural kind terms refer to. Mill's claim that they refer to (or denote) all the objects instantiating the meaning-constituting properties also seems incorrect. For that is tantamount to the claim that natural kind terms refer to the objects that make up the extension of those terms, i.e. all the actual instances (or members) of the natural kinds in question. The problem is that natural kind terms are rigid designators but their extensions vary from possible world to possible world. For instance, as we saw in Section 4.1, the extension of 'water' is empty on Dry Earth, and we can imagine an entire possible world where that extension is empty. There are also possible worlds in which the members of the natural kind water are numerically distinct from those of that kind in the actual world. One way of reconciling the rigidity of natural kind terms with the possibility of such terms having empty or distinct extensions is by letting them refer to properties rather than the objects having those properties, or else to the natural kinds themselves rather than their concrete instances. So, instead of saying that 'water' refers to all the instances of the natural kind water, that natural kind term refers to the property of being water, or else that natural kind itself. On this view, natural kind terms are singular referring terms rather than plural referring terms. Importantly, by letting 'water' be a singular (rather than plural) natural kind term, rigidity is preserved. For neither the existence of the property of being water nor the existence of the natural kind water vary from possible world to possible world. This property or this natural kind can be seen as an abstract entity to which 'water' rigidly refers. What varies across possible worlds is which if any objects instantiate that property, or which if any objects are instances of that kind. These objects are non-rigidly picked out by natural kind predicates, e.g. 'is water' applies to all and only the instances of the natural kind water. In the case of 'water', 'lemon', 'tiger', etc., these properties or kinds are perfectly natural. This referentialist view is not committed to the claim that, say, 'my uncle's favourite animal' or 'vitamin' refers to gerrymandered natural kinds or disjunctive properties.

If the referentialist lets natural kind terms refer to such abstract entities as properties or natural kinds, then she will claim that the propositional contents of such terms are exhausted by these properties or natural kinds. This means that sentences in which natural kind terms occur express propositions with the properties or natural kinds that are picked out by these terms as constituents.[37] Friends of this version of referentialism are also able to counter an objection levelled against the referentialist who lets natural kind terms refer to the objects comprised in their extensions. The problem arises when two distinct natural kind terms have the same actual extension yet clearly seem to express different propositional contents. For instance, 'renate' (meaning: animal having a kidney) and 'cordate' (meaning: animal having a heart) are supposedly coextensive, but these terms clearly express different propositional contents. After all, some renates might not have been cordates, and some cordates might not have been renates. If instead the propositional content of 'renate' is given by the property of being a renate to which that term rigidly refers, and the propositional content of 'cordate' is given by the property of being a cordate to which that term rigidly refers, then the propositional contents of these terms will differ because the corresponding properties are distinct.[38]

4.5 The metaphysics of content properties

Semantic externalism can be taken to be a semantic thesis to the extent that it pertains to the character of propositional content of expressions. But it can also be viewed as a metaphysical thesis: it says that representational states such as beliefs depend for their individuation on features of the external physical, historical or sociolinguistic environment. That is to say, the identity conditions of such states concern features beyond the skin and skull of the individuals who are in them. But this view might seem initially puzzling from a metaphysical point of view. The puzzle is how there can be such individuation dependence between entities of distinct ontological categories. Did we not learn from Hume that there are no necessary connections between distinct existences? Famously, when one rolling billiard ball hits another nothing dictates that the other ball must move. Here we must tread carefully. What Hume (2000/1839–40: Bk 1, pt 3, §6) said was that:

> There is no object, which implies the existence of any other if we consider these objects in themselves.

The qualification at the end is crucial. The two existences between which there supposedly are no necessary connections must be individuated intrinsically.[39] Let us elaborate on our example from Section 3.1. Suppose my arm is sunburnt. That is contingent since I could have spent all summer in my office. But if my arm is sunburnt, the sun must have caused that condition of my arm. Nothing is a sunburn unless caused by the sun. Had I gone to a sunbed instead of the beach I could have acquired intrinsically the same tan, but that would not have been a sunburn. Unlike sunburns, tans are not identified by any particular cause – exposure to any ultraviolet radiation will suffice.[40] If we take care in specifying the condition of my skin, there is no violation of Hume's dictum. Tans and the sun are distinct existences in Hume's sense, but there are no necessary connections between them. There are necessary connections between sunburns and the sun, but these are not distinct existences in Hume's sense. Similarly in the case of Mary's state of believing that water is wet. Following semantic externalism, there is a necessary connection between that belief state and the existence of water in her environment. But these are not distinct existences in Hume's sense, because the former is individuated extrinsically in terms of the latter. Consider instead Mary's belief that the watery stuff is wet. Assuming that belief state is individuated in terms of Mary's internal features, it will count as distinct from water in Hume's sense. But there are no necessary connections between water and that state. The presence of water could well have caused Mary to be in that state, but so could the presence of twin-water had she instead been located on Twin Earth. So, the notion of a wide belief seems metaphysically unproblematic. Indeed many philosophers have thought that any state with representational content must obviously be extrinsic. Here is Stalnaker (1989: 288):

> Isn't it obvious that semantic properties, and intentional properties generally, are *relational* properties: properties defined in terms of relations between a speaker or an agent and what he or she talks or thinks about. And isn't it obvious that relations depend, in all but degenerate cases, on more than the intrinsic properties of one of the things related. This, it seems, is not just a consequence of some new and controversial theory of reference, but should follow from any account of representation that holds that we can talk and think, not just about our own inner states, but also about things and properties outside of ourselves.

Remember Frege's distinction between meaning and reference from Section 1.2. The property of using a term to refer to an external object is extrinsic in that one could not instantiate that property unless that object existed. Not surprisingly, actual reference to denizens of the external world is an external matter. But then the externality of meaning seems to follow naturally in that the property of grasping or expressing meaning cannot be intrinsic. For if reference is external and meaning determines reference, then surely meaning is external too. No extrinsic property of an object is fully determined by that object's intrinsic properties. For instance, my being taller than my sister is not determined by my height alone.

So, the key question for the semantic internalist is whether such intentional properties can be intrinsic while it is still the case that meaning determines reference in some sense. At this juncture semantic internalists often insist that intrinsicness can be understood in two crucially distinct ways, only one of which is suitable to define narrow content beliefs. Consider three kinds of properties:[41]

(i) The property of being *square* is a property that supervenes on internal structure. Necessarily, an object is square if and only if its surface is shaped by four, equally long, straight lines with right angles. Thus if an object is square then, necessarily, any internal duplicate of it will also be square. No change in relational properties could make it true that a doppelgänger of a square object was not square. Moreover, for an object to be square just is for it to have a certain set of intrinsic, geometrical properties and to understand what it is for an object to be square just is to know that it has those properties.

(ii)   The property of being *water-soluble* is also a property that supervenes on internal structure. Necessarily, an object is water-soluble if and only if under *normal conditions* it would dissolve if immersed in water. There is some internal physical state of the object, which is responsible for the behaviour such that any internal duplicate of it is normally itself water-soluble. Hence, for an object to be water-soluble is not just to be in a certain internal state in the sense that if all you know is confined to that internal state, you do not know whether it is water-soluble. You must know something about the causal connections between being in that state and behaving in a certain way on being put in water.

(iii)   The property of being a *footprint* is a property that fails to supervene on internal structure. Necessarily, something is a footprint if and only if it has a foot-shaped imprint and is caused by a foot. Intrinsic duplicates of footprints are not themselves footprints if not caused by feet – but by the way the waves happen to fall on the sand, or by using a stick. In the latter case, you might at most succeed in making a picture of a footprint intrinsically indistinguishable from a footprint. Again, if all you know is confined to the intrinsic properties of a particular imprint, you do not know whether it is a footprint. You have to know something about the causal connections between being a footprint and being caused by the impact of a foot.

Now let's compare our three properties. We may say that being square is *inter-world narrow*, where a property P of *x* is inter-world narrow if and only if in every possible world any doppelgänger of *x* has P. Being water-soluble, however, is not inter-world narrow. An object may be intrinsically similar to a soluble object and yet not dissolve when immersed in water if some anomalous environmental conditions obtain. Imagine a possible world with deviant laws of nature in which a doppelgänger of a soluble object does not dissolve if put in water. Nevertheless, the property of being water-soluble is *intra-world narrow*, where a property P of *x* is intra-world narrow if and only if in every world where *x* has P any doppelgänger of *x* has P. Within a possible world, internal duplicates are solubility duplicates, and so to find a non-soluble object internally like a soluble object, you must go to a different possible world. Intra-world narrow properties are only shared by doppelgängers across nomologically identical possible worlds, i.e. worlds governed by the same laws of nature. Lastly, being a footprint is not even intra-world narrow since there are possible worlds within which a doppelgänger of a footprint fails to be a footprint. That the waves should form what looks like a footprint is unlikely, yet consistent with the laws of nature. But note that not everything caused by the impression of a foot is a footprint. What makes an imprint in the sand a footprint is not just its aetiology, but also its foot shape, i.e. a certain internal distribution of grains of sand in the imprint. It follows that from the broad property of being a footprint, we can factor out the narrow property of being a *foot-shaped imprint*. This property is intra-world narrow: a doppelgänger in a possible world of a foot-shaped imprint x is itself a foot-shaped imprint only if x is also a foot-shaped imprint in that world. Where footprints owe their identity to particular causes, foot-shaped imprints are independent of any such (feet or waves). If your foot and my foot cause intrinsically indistinguishable imprints in the sand, then we have caused different footprints, but the same foot-shaped imprints. The property of being a foot-shaped imprint is, however, still dependent on general facts extrinsic to the sand. In a possible world where feet have abnormal shapes the imprint in the sand is not even a foot-shaped imprint. That is why we need the condition that x be a foot-shaped imprint in the world in question. To form the narrow property out of the property of being a footprint, we must qualify the imprints to include only the shapes that feet make under normal conditions.

Now distinguish between the content of an attitude and the property of having an attitude with that content. Clearly, the former is not an intrinsic property in the way being square is.[42] The representational character of content tells us that content is individuated by its truth-conditions, and truth-conditions determine mostly how the external world must be like in order for that content to be true. But if content is not intrinsic, then neither is the property of having an attitude with that content − assuming that propositional attitudes are partially individuated by their contents. If a mental property were like the property of being square, then it would be possible to explain it in terms of an individual's intrinsic properties. Someone who knew all of those intrinsic properties would also know the mental properties. But mental properties can only be understood by citing interactions with the environment. The traces made in the sand by a crawling ant of a recognizable caricature of Winston Churchill fail to depict Churchill, because the ant sustains no causal connections with Churchill. As Putnam (1981: 5) put it "thought words and mental pictures do not *intrinsically* represent what they are about".

So, the semantic internalist should not model narrow content on intrinsic properties like being square. Unlike being square, narrow content is not entirely a function of internal structure – it depends on general facts about the external world too. In possible worlds with abnormal laws of nature or deviant linguistic practices, doppelgängers of us fail to share our narrow beliefs. Narrow content is not independent of any causal interactions with the environment, like squareness is, but only of which interactions are actual and which possible. Narrow content is like being water-soluble in that the intrinsic properties, shared by doppelgängers, govern interactions with actual and possible environments. Sugar cubes that never actually get dissolved, or sugar cubes that are moved across different environments within the same possible world, do not thereby lose their solubility. Such environmental differences make for differences only in the manifestation of their solubility. What matters is that in each such environment they would dissolve if they were placed in water. Likewise, the wide content of terms determine what they actually pick out, e.g. 'water' refers to H_2O, but their narrow content determines what they pick out if the environment is so-and-so, e.g. if H_2O is the watery stuff, then 'water' refers to H_2O. Correspondingly, the wide belief that water is wet has a particular world-dependency. The property of having a belief with that content is one Mary could not have had she been on Twin Earth. This property is, like the property of being a footprint, not even intra-world narrow. In contrast, the narrow belief that the stuff that goes under the name 'water' is wet merely has a general world-dependency in much the same way being water-soluble or being a foot-shaped imprint do. This belief is shared by twin-Mary but not by any inter-world doppelgängers. We can imagine a doppelgänger of Mary's in a remote possible world, who does not share Mary's narrow belief, if in that world the linguistic practices are very different. The property of having a belief with that content is thus intra-world narrow. In brief, both narrow and wide-content beliefs hook on to the world albeit in crucially different ways[43]

Chapter summary

In this chapter we elaborated on various aspects of the distinction between narrow and wide content. The Twin Earth argument and the arthritis argument purport to demonstrate that linguistic and mental contents depend for their individuation on physical or sociolinguistic facts about the individual's external environment. But these arguments are silent about whether the individual can entertain such content in circumstances in which these facts are absent. Boghossian asks us to imagine Dry Earth – a planet just like Earth except when the inhabitants use 'water' they systematically fail to refer to anything. Despite appearances there is no stuff that has the watery properties. Boghossian's Dry Earth argument aims to show that semantic externalists are committed to the claim that Dry Earthlings express no concept by 'water', hence that the concept **water** that we Earthlings express is dependent for its existence on the existence of instances of water in our environment. That concept is kind-dependent. In response, some semantic externalists maintain that Dry Earthlings can fall back on some suitably descriptive and kind-independent concept. We then probed deeper into the view that 'water' is shorthand for 'the watery stuff of our acquaintance'. When Mary and her internal duplicate on Twin Earth utter sentences containing 'water', the truth-conditions will differ, but solely in virtue of contextual differences such as the location of the speaker. If the content of their beliefs is truth-conditional, it will thus fail to supervene on their internal features, but not in virtue of being dependent on external features of their physical environment. Lewis and Jackson have instead urged that there should be an important sense in which Mary and twin-Mary believe alike. That can be cashed out in terms of self-ascription of the same properties, e.g. being acquainted with a watery stuff that is wet. This suggests we can pinpoint two distinct aspects of mental content: a wide component which yields reference-involving truth-conditions and a narrow component which plays a cognitive role in causally explaining behaviour. We reviewed two such hybrid views due to McGinn and Chalmers. The key difference between them was that only Chalmers assigns the narrow com-ponent a reference-determining role. Crucial to his view was the dis-tinction between considering a possible world as counterfactual and considering a possible world as actual. On his view, the wide subjunctive intension of a term is a function from possible worlds considered as counterfactual to referents in those worlds, but the narrow epistemic intension of a referring term is a function from possible worlds considered as actual to referents in those worlds. We then critically examined Putnam and Chalmers' claim that natural kind concepts have indexical components. Thus Burge argued convincingly that our tokens of 'water' should not be assimilated to indexical expressions. Instead we explored a referentialist semantics of natural kind terms. The last section dwelled on the metaphysics of content properties. The proposal was that while narrow properties supervene on intrinsic properties, they are not themselves intrinsic. Having a belief with narrow content should be modelled on dispositional proper-ties. Water-solubility supervenes on intrinsic properties but is not an intrinsic property. An object is water-soluble only if it would dissolve if immersed in water. Likewise, narrow properties are not independent of any causal interactions with the environment, but only of which interactions are actual and which possible. Narrow properties are like being water-soluble in that the intrinsic properties, shared by doppelgängers, govern interactions with actual and possible environments.

Annotated further reading

Gareth Evans's (1982) *The Varieties of Reference*, chapter 1, and the articles in part II of John McDowell's (1998) *Meaning, Knowledge and Reality* are the loci classici for the notion of Fregean object-dependent thoughts. Nathan Salmon's (1986) *Frege's Puzzle* and David Kaplan's (1989) *Demonstratives* are the loci classici for the notion of object-dependent, singular propositions. For a survey article on the semantics of indexical expressions see chapter 17 in *The Blackwell Guide to the Philosophy of Language*, edited by Michael Devitt and Richard Hanley. A more demanding but highly recommendable discussion of egocentric thoughts and relativized propositions is François Recanati's (2007) *Perspectival Thought*. In particular, chapters 12–15 offer an excellent comparative study of Lewis' and Kaplan's views. Recanati's (2007) as well as his (1993) *Direct Reference: From Language to Thought*, chapters 11–12 also provide a critical exposition of various two-factor theories of content. Two-dimensional semantics has recently received much attention in the philosophical literature. Manuel Garcia-Carpintero and Josep Macia's (2006) *Two-Dimensional Semantics* contains a stellar collection of articles on aspects of this subtle framework. Martin Davies and Lloyd Humberstone's (1980) "Two Notions of Necessity" is a classic article in this respect. For two excellent critical discussions of narrow and wide content see Frances Egan's (2009) "Wide Content" and Gabriel Segal's (2009) "Narrow Content." David Braun's (2006) "Names and Natural Kind Terms" and Kathrin Koslicki's (2008) "Natural Kinds and Natural Kind Terms" are accessible survey articles on natural kind terms. Influential contributions on how best to understand the metaphysics of content-bearing mental properties are due to Robert Stalnaker, Tyler Burge, Frank Jackson and Philip Pettit. Stalnaker's papers on this topic are collected in part III in his (1999) *Context and Content*. Jackson's papers include "Mental Causation" (1996). Jackson and Pettit co-authored (1988) "Functionalism and Broad Content." "Three Theses about Dispositions" (1982) is a seminal paper on dispositions, co-written by Elisabeth Prior, Robert Pargetter and Frank Jackson. Chapter 3 in Burge's (2010) *Origins of Objectivity* contains excellent clarification on the metaphysics of wide properties.

5

SELF-KNOWLEDGE

5.1 Introducing self-knowledge

In Section 4.5 we examined the ontological implications of semantic internalism and semantic externalism. In so far as these views pertain to the propositional content of expressions, they can be seen as semantic doctrines. The dispute is over the nature of that content and what makes those expressions have that content. But since these views each say something about how mental states are individuated they can also reasonably be taken as metaphysical doctrines. The dispute is whether the identity conditions for such states include aspects of the external environment. In the next two chapters we will be occupied with the epistemological ramifications of semantic externalism, and in particular with the ways in which this view meshes with knowledge of our own mind and of the external world. In this chapter the alleged incompatibility between self-knowledge and semantic externalism will be assessed. Then in Chapter 6 we take up the issue of epistemological scepticism. Against the backdrop of semantic externalism, it transpires that scepticism about the external world is closely connected to scepticism about our internal world of mental states and their contents.

Self-knowledge is the knowledge we each enjoy of our own mental states as opposed to the knowledge we purport to have of the external world. This thesis also goes under the name 'privileged access', and we shall use both interchangeably. But self-knowledge is not merely marked out by its content; it allegedly also has a number of special epistemic features. In particular, many take it to be the thesis that a competent thinker can have a priori knowledge of her mental states: which states she is in and what their contents are. A priori knowledge is knowledge that is justificationally independent of perceptual experiences or more broadly of empirical inquiry into the external environment.[1] Historically, authority, security, immediacy and even infallibility have also been included as hallmarks of self-knowledge. Thus empiricist and rationalist philosophers have thought very differently about how best to characterize the epistemology of self-knowledge. Descartes famously held that while he could be deceived by the evil demon about the existence of his body and the external world, he could not possibly be deceived about his own existence. For to doubt that one exists requires that one thinks that one exists, and to exist on Descartes view is just to be a thing that thinks. So, it is impossible for Descartes to falsely think that he exists. Of course one might not have been thinking at least at this very moment. The claim is merely that if one is engaged in sceptical doubt, then one is thinking, and so then one must exist as a thinking thing. In short, *cogito ergo sum* – I think therefore I am. This Cartesian line of reasoning is often taken to show that one has indubitable or even infallible knowledge of one's occurrent thoughts, and that such knowledge furnishes a foundation upon which all other empirical knowledge can be based. Burge (1996) and other contemporary rationalists disagrees with much of what Descartes says about self-knowledge. But, as we shall see in Section 5.2, Burge does hold not only that judgements about certain thoughts are self-verifying, but also that the origin of some knowledge of our own mind is conceptual in kind, in contrast to perceptual knowledge of the external world which stems from perceptual experiences. Armstrong (1963) and other contemporary empiricists, however, attempt to assimilate *introspective* knowledge to perceptual knowledge of external features of reality. While introspection connotes an observational *inner sense*, i.e. looking within one's internal world, perception connotes an observational *outer sense*, i.e. attending to the external world. On this *inner sense model*, self-knowledge is ultimately based on observation of inner goings-on. Imagination, memory and reasoning might play a role in such knowledge but only in so far as one imagines, remembers or reasons about sensed states (or processes or events). For instance, when you are in pain you can come to know that you are in pain by attending to your feeling, and then form a conception of its phenomenal character, i.e. of what it is like to be in that phenomenal state. Moreover, neither introspection nor perception is a source of indubitable knowledge. Armstrong (1963) argues that since the apprehension of a mental state must be distinct from the state itself, our knowledge of our own mental states is not incorrigible. In fact, since he accepts the mind–body identity view according to which mental states are identical to states of the brain, it is logically possible that others, neurosurgeons for example, should have knowledge of our own mental states that is unmediated by observation of our sayings and doings. Still, as things actually stand, nobody has such direct knowledge. Self-knowledge is not empirically corrigible by others. Hence each of us has as a matter of fact privileged access to our own mental states.[2]

More recently, some have argued that introspection involves looking outward to what our representational states represent. When you introspect your needle-stick pain, the properties you are directly aware of are properties of your pin-pricked finger rather than properties of your pain experience. Or take propositional attitudes. Here is Evans (1982: 225) defending the transparency of belief states, i.e. the claim that introspection involves looking through those states to the external world that they represent:

> [I]n making a self-ascription of belief, one's eyes are, so to speak, or occasionally literally, directed outward – upon the world. If someone asks me 'Do you think there is going to be a third world war?', I must attend, in answering him, to precisely the same outward phenomena as I would attend to if I were answering the question 'Will there be a third world war?'

The example highlights that in some cases we do attend to aspects of the external world in order to figure out what we believe about those aspects of reality. But there might be other cases where we stubbornly hold on to a belief in light of conflicting evidence. Think of superstitious beliefs. It may also be that this method of looking outward does not reveal already existing belief states, but rather creates new such states when the evidence indicating one way or another is in. This is most likely in the case of standing beliefs such as the belief that metal expands when heated. Or it could be that this method reveals the reasons for which we believe as we do. The question 'do you think there is going to be a third world war?' is really a request for reasons why you believe one way or the other to which you might answer 'no, I don't think so, because most countries have now signed the Nuclear Non-proliferation Treaty'. To provide the requested reasons you will have to attend to the relevant outward phenomena, say by watching BBC News. But even proponents of this *transparency model* of self-knowledge hold that there are crucial differences between the way we know our own mental states and the way we know others' mental states.[3]

Any account of how the way we know our own mind differs from the way we know others' minds is bound to be controversial. Still, if focus is on what the above-mentioned – rationalist and empiricist – views of self-knowledge all try to explain, hopefully we can elaborate on those differences in a fairly theory-neutral way. All these views accept that knowledge of our own inner goings-on is accessible in a special first-person manner, whereas knowledge of others' mental life is constrained by whatever epistemic standards govern knowledge in general. We are reliable about the detection of our own mental states in a way that we are not reliable about the detection of others' mental states. This kind of epistemic security issues in an *asymmetry* in ordinary psychological discourse between first- and third-person utterances. The former are characterized by *avowals*, which are claims about, or expressions of, our own intentional or sensational states. One may distinguish between phenomenal avowals like 'I have a headache', and attitudinal avowals like 'I hope the weather stays dry'. Both have three characteristic marks:[4]

They are received as *authoritative*. If Anna understands the claim that she is in M, where M is some occurrent mental state, and Anna is sincere in making it about herself, then there is a strong prima facie case that Anna is not wrong about her being in M. Indeed if Anna's claim is of the phenomenal kind, rarely if ever would the combination of competence, sincerity and attention fail to guarantee the truth of her self-ascription. Anna could be wrong about which needle caused the pain, but she could hardly be wrong that her finger hurts – unless in making that judgement she is mistaken about the relevant concepts, or she is dishonest, or she fails to pay proper attending to her finger.[5] Not so for attitudinal avowals. There are second-order beliefs to the effect that we engage in interpretation of our first-order attitudes, and in such cases we may be mistaken about our own intentional life. Think of self-deceit. Thus Thomas may mistakenly believe that he has no repressed desires, because these are not immediately introspectible. The Freudian literature abounds with such cases. But there are also basic attitudinal cases, which involve no self-deception. These are cases of occurrent belief – beliefs that are currently being considered by the individual – rather than dispositional belief – beliefs stored in memory awaiting retrieval for deployment in practical and theoretical reasoning. If Anna sincerely, attentively and understandingly utters 'I believe that the water in the jug quenches thirst', then she has thereby provided a third person, Thomas, with a reason for thinking that Anna presently believes that the water in the jug is thirst-quenching. Of course the truth of Anna's avowal is answerable to future verbal or physical behaviour: if she refused to drink water if thirsty and presented with the jug of water, then Thomas would make better sense of Anna's overall psychology if he did not take her avowal at face value. Perhaps something similar could happen with certain phenomenal avowals. Maybe Anna subsequently discovers that on a given occasion she has mistaken an itch for a tickle without being insincere, inattentive or conceptually incompetent. The point is that the mere defeasibility of avowals provides no reason to think that the presumption in favour of their truthfulness is actually defeated. Even if both first- and third-person ascriptions are fallible, only avowals are accredited with authority. The mere fact that Thomas is sincere, focused and grasps the concepts provides no reason to think that his ascription of a mental state to Anna is true. For Thomas to have a reason to believe that Anna is sincere, attentive and understands her avowals is to have a reason to believe Anna's avowals, but Thomas' mere competence, attention and sincerity is no reason to believe his corresponding third-personal claim.

The second characteristic concerns the *non-inferential* nature of avowals. A competent speaker Anna may justifiably assert that she is in some basic mental state M without being required to adduce grounds in support of her assertion. Unlike third-person ascriptions, it would ordinarily be misplaced to demand of Anna evidence in support of her claim that she is in F. Suppose Anna sincerely, attentively and competently avows 'I have a sore throat' in the presence of Thomas who then later reports to some third person Martin: 'Anna has a sore throat'. Then suppose Martin replies 'How do you know?' Intuitively, this question is appropriate only if addressed to Thomas. Anna knows directly by introspection how things presently are with her and that is why there is no need for her to back up her self-ascriptions of basic mental states. Anna does not infer from her own verbal and physical behaviour that she is in M. Even in cases in which such evidence is available, she does not consult it. Anna does not come to know her throat is sore by observing that her tonsils are swollen and that she has difficulty in swallowing. She need only reflectively attend to her state M. Thomas has no such immediate access to Anna's basic mental states, but must rely on her sayings and doings as the basis from which he can proceed to make justified inferences about her being in such states.

The last mark is the *salience* of the objects of avowals. A basic mental state M is salient to the speaker who has it. If in normal circumstances M occurs in Anna, then Anna knows that it occurs. In similar circumstances, if

M does not occur, then it cannot seem to Anna in every way as if it does occur. Although fallible, Anna's introspective abilities are not hostage to the kind of perceptual illusions that may afflict her perceptual abilities. The reason for this is that the subject matter of self-knowledge does not exhibit the kind of appearance–reality distinction we find in the case of perception.[6] Unless she were inattentive or suffering from some cognitive malfunction, it would be very odd for a basic state like a headache or a desire for chocolate to occur in Anna without her being aware of its presence and often disposed to give expression to the thought that she is in such a state. In the normal run of things, it is hard to see in what Anna's ignorance of the truth-values of her self-ascriptions of such basic states could consist. However, in the case of non-basic states, e.g. the standing belief that Scotland is the best country in Europe to live in, omniscience is much less plausible. But it is possible for Thomas to know all relevant facts about Anna's recent behaviour yet be ignorant of features of her basic psychology. Anna's beliefs and desires are not salient to anyone but herself.

Setting disagreement over details aside, authority, non-inferentiality and salience are pretty much commonplace. But some philosophers endorse a much stronger notion of self-knowledge. The rough idea is that Anna knows a priori whether any two propositional contents towards which she has a cognitive attitude are the same or different. Here is Dummett (1978: 131):

> It is an undeniable feature of the notion of meaning – obscure as that notion is – that meaning is transparent in the sense that, if someone attaches a meaning to each of two words, he must know whether these meanings are the same.

What Dummett captures in this passage is the idea that meaning is *diaphanous* in the sense that its logical properties are fully accessible to introspection. Consider the principle we in Section 2.4 called:[7]

(Epistemic Transparency)	(i) If an attentive and competent speaker S believes that p and also believes that p*, and p and p* are the same mental contents, then S must know a priori that they are the same contents, and (ii) if S believes that p and also believes that q, and p and q are different mental contents, then S must know a priori that they are different contents.

It is a consequence of (i) that Anna must know a priori that her belief that p and her belief that p* are identical, and it is a consequence of (ii) that Anna must know a priori that her belief that p and her belief that q are different. Had meaning not been epistemically transparent in this sense, it would be possible for Anna to believe that p and to believe that p*, yet profess ignorance as to whether she believes the same or different things. But since we are inclined to think that Anna must know a priori whether she believes the same or different things, if she is fully attentive and conceptually competent, it does seem initially plausible that meaning and mental content should be epistemically transparent.

The motivation behind (Epistemic Transparency) is that for Anna to have a priori knowledge of an occurrent belief is not merely to know that she has a certain belief. It is also to know which belief that is, and that means knowing what its content is – what that belief is about. And that involves a priori knowledge of what it is to have a belief with that content, e.g. how that belief is inferentially related to other beliefs, how having it disposes Anna to behave in various ways. Having such knowledge presupposes an ability to introspectively discriminate between the content of the belief in question and other relevant belief contents. If that were not so, it would be impossible for Anna to reflectively determine the inferential and behavioural consequences of her belief. For instance, suppose Anna has introspective knowledge that she believes that only real ale is wholesome. Then Anna is thereby in a position to know that she should believe that some ale is wholesome and that bright beer is unhealthy if she were to consider these questions. Anna can also know that if she desires something wholesome and alcoholic, then other things being equal she will tend to drink real ale. This assumes an ability to discriminate between, say, that something is real ale rather than some other kind of beer.

Compare with what Evans (1982: 74–75) called:

(Russell's Principle)   In order for S to have a thought about a particular object, S must know *which object* it is about which S is thinking.

To think about an object x to the effect that it has property F involves the exercise of two separable capacities. Firstly, the capacity to think of x which could be exercised in thoughts about x to the effect that it is F or G. Secondly, the capacity to think of what it is to be F which could be exercised in thoughts about x or y to the effect that either is F. To have the capacity to think of an object thus involves a discriminating conception of the object. Here is an example. If Anna thinks that David Beckham is a footballer, then she must have two distinct capacities: the capacity to think of Beckham as exercised in the thoughts that he is a footballer, father of three sons, or Victoria Adams' husband, and the ability to think of being a footballer as exercised in the thoughts that Beckham or Ronaldo or Kaka is a footballer.

Note finally the importance of not lumping self-knowledge as captured by authority, non-inferentiality and salience together with (Epistemic Transparency). As we shall see shortly, it is clearly possible to hold that content p is salient or transparent in the weak sense that if p occurs, then Anna believes that p occurs, without it being transparent in the stronger sense that Anna is able to tell whether p is identical to, or distinct from, some other content q that Anna grasps.[8]

5.2 Entitlement to self-knowledge

In this section we will elaborate on Burge's influential account of self-knowledge, focusing on the self-verifying nature of certain thoughts and the special epistemic access we typically have to those thoughts. As we shall see in the following sections of this chapter this account offers an attractive way of reconciling semantic externalism with self-knowledge.

Let's begin by explicating some key epistemological distinctions that Burge draws. First off, Burge's notion of *warrant* (1993c, 1996, 2003b) is an epistemic genus that divides into *entitlement* and *justification*. These two sub-species have certain epistemic features in common. Both are epistemic goods or rights that have positive force in rationally supporting beliefs. Both are also defeasible (2003b: 534): a belief can be warranted either way even though its content is false. To say that a belief state is warranted implies merely it reliably indicates the truth, or to quote Burge (2003b: 532) "warrant is a good route to truth and knowledge". But these two types of warrant are also different in crucial respects. Entitlements are *epistemically externalist*. They are a type of warrant that need not be understood by or even conceptually accessible to the subject. That is to say, S can be entitled to a belief without having accessible reasons warranting the belief and without possessing the concepts needed to understand or articulate the entitlement. Justification, however, is *epistemically internalist*. That is to say, justification is warrant by *reason* that is conceptually accessible to S, and so requires that S have the conceptual repertoire necessary to grasp those reasons.[9]

Take perception as an example. Burge (2003b) claims that perceptual experiences are not propositional, i.e. such experiences have non-propositional content. For instance, children, animals and many adults undergo perceptual experiences but may lack the concepts necessary to articulate what these experiences represent. But he also claims that reasons are propositional entities. For instance, the premises in an argument are propositions, and these constitute a good reason to believe the conclusion if the argument is sound. It follows from these two claims that perceptual experiences cannot provide reasons for perceptual beliefs. As he has recently put it (2010: 435):

> Perception is not a reason. Formation of belief from perception is not reasoning. Perception does not support a belief by being a reason for it.

Moreover, justification consists in reasons in the sense that if S has justification then she has cognitive access to reasons. Hence, perceptual experiences cannot justify perceptual beliefs. But even though perceptual beliefs are not (normally) based on reasons, they are warranted in the sense that perceptual experiences entitle such beliefs. That is to say, S is entitled to rely on perception even though she is neither able to justify her relying on perception nor able to conceive such a justification. The fact that children, animals and many adults may lack abilities to justify or to explain or rationalize such justification does not rob them of warranted perceptual beliefs, because they are instead entitled to these beliefs. Here's Burge (1993c: 458–59):

> We are entitled to rely, other things equal, on perception, memory, deductive and inductive reasoning, and on ... the word of others. The unsophisticated are entitled to rely on their perceptual beliefs. Philosophers may articulate these entitlements. But being entitled does not require being able to justify reliance on these resources, or even to conceive such a justification. Justifications, in the narrow sense, involve reasons that people have and have access to. These may include self-sufficient premises or more discursive justifications. But they must be available in the cognitive repertoire of the subject.

In this passage entitlements are generalized to encompass beliefs formed on the basis of epistemic sources other than perception, such as testimony and reasoning. In a later paper (1996: 94) he adds self-knowledge to the list of sources whose deliverances we are entitled to believe. Beliefs about occurrent thoughts are not normally reason-based. Entitlements attach to such beliefs, but they do so in a way that is importantly different from entitlements to perceptual beliefs. Here is why.

On Burge's view, self-knowledge is epistemically special in a distinctive way. As explained in Section 3.3 Burge advocates social externalism according to which thoughts and other mental states are individuated at least in part by relations between the individuals who are in those states and their external (in particular sociolinguistic) environments. This is true both for S's *first-order* thought that p, and for S's *second-order* thought that she thinks that p. Each depends for its individuation on relations that S (or her fellow speakers) bears to her external environment. But S's *warrant* for her judgement that she thinks that p does not depend on empirical relations that S bears to any particular external environment. Because this warrant is not dependent on the exercise of perceptual abilities, it counts as a priori.[10] In contrast, S's warrant for her perceptual beliefs does depend on her standing in specific perceptual–experiential relations with her external environment, and so counts as a posteriori. Burge (1988: 653–54) stresses that in the act of thinking a thought involving a wide concept S must *pre-suppose* that she stands in specific environmental relations that enable her to think that thought but need have no positive epistemic attitude towards these relations.[11] If S were to reasonably doubt that she stood in such relations, then her warrant for believing that she was thinking a wide-content thought could be defeated. But absent reason for doubt, S enjoys an a priori entitlement to rely on introspective deliverances for belief formation provided that the pertinent contents are externally individuated.

The source of the warrant S has when she judges that she thinks that p is conceptual rather than empirical. Burge (1996, 1998) begins by considering cases of *cogito*-like thoughts. He (1996: 96) offers the example of judging:

(1)   I am thinking that there are physical entities,

where 'thinking' means having or engaging in thought. For (1) to be true requires merely that I have a thought whose content is that there are physical entities. And since judging that (1) involves thinking that (1), at least when conceptually aware of what is being judged, judging that (1) guar-antees its truth. This judgement thus resembles Descartes' *cogito*-thought **I am thinking** in that both are *self-verifying*. Such judgements are *infallible*: I cannot falsely judge that (1). Three points are worth making about these self-verifying judgements. Firstly, the claim that judging (1) is self-verifying is a claim about truth-conditions. It is not an epistemic claim about the a priori entitlement one can have for that judgement. That is to say, self-verification is not what accounts for the special way in which these judgements are warranted. Secondly, only judgements about one's own thoughts are self-verifying. My judgement that (1) makes it so that (1) is true, but your judgement that (1) is consistent with (1) being false. Thirdly, judgements about what one believes are not self-evident or self-verifying in the way judgements about (1) or other *cogito*-like judgements are.[12] Nevertheless, they resemble each other in crucial epistemic respects in so far as the warrant that attaches to judgements about thoughts and to judgements about beliefs is that of a priori entitlement.

Let's probe deeper into the conceptual nature of entitlements to self-knowledge. The idea is that S has an a priori entitlement to her beliefs about her own wide-content thoughts that derives from their function in *critical reasoning*. Burge takes a practice of critical reasoning for granted, and then argues that given that S's beliefs are an integral part of the overall procedures of critical reasoning that S engages in, she must be entitled to her beliefs. An example of critical reasoning is when an argument such as *modus ponens* ($p \rightarrow q$, p; therefore q) is evaluated. Here p and q are propositions or thought contents. In order to assess this argument, one must be able to recognize and assess $p \rightarrow q$ and p as reasons for q. This in turn requires an ability to think about these propositions and rational relations among them. For instance, S could figure out that the conclusion q must be true if all the premises are true. But critical reasoning also involves assessment of reasoning, and hence assessment of beliefs themselves and not merely their propositional contents. For instance, S evaluates whether it is reasonable to believe certain propositions in the light of the available evidence or whether it is reasonable to believe certain propositions, given what else is believed. Importantly, S can exercise critical reasoning on her reasoning itself in that the standards for proper reasoning that she applies to others or to abstract arguments are ones that she can also apply to her own reasoning and beliefs. She can evaluate whether with respect to a belief she holds it is reasonable to change her mind or stand fast in the light of the evidence that is available to her or what else she believes. Suppose S has just come to believe that Sven Kramer cannot skate, but S also firmly holds the beliefs that all Dutchmen skate and that Sven Kramer is a Dutchman. She can now critically assess whether that is a consistent set of beliefs and in particular whether she should uphold or abandon her recently formed belief. For this purpose she avails herself of the following *normative* principle:

(NP)   If S believes that p and S believes that if p then q, then either S
        ought not form the belief that not-q, or else S ought to abandon
        either the belief that p or the belief that if p then q (or both of these
        beliefs).

By applying this *norm of reasoning* or *rationality* S will have to abandon one of
her beliefs. Assuming S is determined to hang on to her beliefs that Sven
Kramer is Dutch and that all Dutchmen skate, S ought no longer believe
that Sven Kramer cannot skate. But in order for S to be rationally guided by
(NP) S must make judgements about what she believes and what she ought
to believe given what else she believes. She must engage in second-order
thinking about her beliefs and rational relations between them. Only then
is S in a position to realize that she must cease to hold at least one of her
beliefs if she is to restore consistency among them. If S for some bizarre
reason suddenly abandoned one of her beliefs while continuing to hold the
other beliefs, then she would act in a way that complied with (NP). But S
would not abandon that belief because of what (NP) dictates given her
other beliefs. Not violating a norm of reasoning or rationality is different
from applying that norm. When (NP) pertains to S's own beliefs she can
apply that norm only if she makes reflective judgements about her beliefs.

So far, so good. We have established that critical reasoning involves a
reflective ability to make judgements about beliefs. The next step is to argue
that critical reasoning also requires an a priori entitlement to judgements
about beliefs. Here is Burge (1996: 101–2):

> ... if one lacked entitlement to judgments about one's attitudes, there
> could be no norms of reason governing how one ought check, weigh,
> overturn, confirm reasons or reasoning. For if one lacked entitlement to
> judgments about one's attitudes, one could not be subject to rational
> norms governing how one ought to alter those attitudes given that one
> had reflected on them. If reflection provided no reason-endorsed judg-
> ments about the attitudes, the rational connection between the attitudes
> reflected upon and the reflection would be broken. So reasons could not
> apply to how the attitudes should be changed, suspended, or confirmed
> on the basis of reasoning depending on such reflection. But critical rea-
> soning just is reasoning in which norms of reason apply to how attitudes
> should be affected partly on the basis of reasoning that derives from
> judgments about one's attitudes. So one must have an epistemic entitlement
> to one's judgments about one's attitudes.

This passage needs some unpacking. To use our example, for S to engage in critical reasoning is for the norm of rationality (NP) to apply to how her beliefs should be affected by her reasoning on the basis of her reflective judgements about her beliefs. Burge's point is that unless S had an a priori entitlement to these judgements about her beliefs, she could not be subject to any such norms in so far as these norms govern how her beliefs should be affected by her reasoning from these judgements. Suppose S lacks an a priori entitlement to her reflective judgements that she believes that Sven Kramer is Dutch and that all Dutchmen skate, in fact suppose that these judgements are entirely unreasonable. In that case, it does not follow that S ought to abandon her belief that Sven Kramer cannot skate, on pain of irrationality, given her reasoning from the judgements about the other two beliefs. To say that S ought to abandon a belief is to say that she has a reason not to hold that belief. But if S has no a priori entitlement to reflective judgements about her beliefs, or if these judgements are entirely unreasonable, then there cannot be a reason for her to abandon a particular belief on the basis of reasoning from these judgements. In the absence of such entitlements, S's reflection on her beliefs and how they are rationally related could lend no reasonability to the whole reasoning process. But S typically does have such reasons. For S is involved in a practice of critical reasoning and having such reasons is part and parcel of critical reasoning when one applies it to one's own reasoning. In our example, S has reason to abandon a particular belief, given the way her reasoning from other beliefs is governed by (NR). That is possible only if S is a priori entitled to her reflective judgements that she does indeed hold these beliefs.

We have now presented an argument for the claim that in so far as S engages in critical reasoning she has an a priori entitlement to her reflective judgements about her own beliefs. To repeat, entitlement is a kind of warrant distinct from justification. If S has an undefeated warrant for a true belief then she will typically know what she believes. But since entitlement is subject to defeat, entitled beliefs may fall short of knowledge. Nevertheless, the last step in Burge's argument (1996: 102–3) is to show that S typically has a distinctive kind of knowledge of her own beliefs. The claim is that although reflective judgements about beliefs are occasionally wrong they could not be so in general if entitlements attach to such judgements. As we have seen, critical reasoning involves reflection on beliefs and assessment of whether they are related in a reasonable way. In our example, such reflection resulted in S abandoning a particular belief, thus securing a rationally coherent set of beliefs. But if judgements about beliefs based on reflection were not normally true, then such reflection could not add to the rational coherence of beliefs. If S's judgements about her own beliefs were systematically mistaken, then reflection on what she took her beliefs to be could have no bearing on whether it would be rational for her to abandon or uphold particular beliefs. Hence such reflection could not add to the reasonability of the process of critically assessing her beliefs. But given that S does engage in critical reasoning we must accept that her judgements about her beliefs are mostly true. And this means, following Burge (1996: 102–3), that S's reflection is connected to the truth of her judgements in a way that normally yields knowledge. A being who was systematically mistaken about her own beliefs, or who was right but in some accidental way that excluded knowledge, would simply not be a critical reasoner.

Let's finally ponder on a crucial respect in which self-knowledge is different from perceptual knowledge. Perceptual beliefs can be afflicted by so-called brute errors (1996, 103) – "an error that indicates no rational failure and no malfunction in the mistaken individual". Suppose S forms the belief that there is a zebra in the pen on the basis of having a visual experience as of a zebra. Without S's knowledge, the animal in the pen is a cleverly disguised mule. S's cognitive and perceptual apparatus is not to blame for her mistaken belief. The zoo authorities are. She could also make brute errors about some of her mental states, e.g. unconscious states pertaining to deep character traits or suppressed emotions. But in a range of cases involving reflectively accessible states errors must be put down to cognitive malfunction, rational deficiency or some other fault with S. As we have just seen, reflective access to belief states is constitutive of critical reasoning. Now take the empiricist, inner sense model of self-knowledge that was sketched in Section 5.1. A version of this model says that while knowledge of others' mental states is based on inferences from what they say and do, self-knowledge is non-inferential in the sense of merely being based on observation of inner goings-on. The only privilege or authority one has with respect to one's own mental states is that one is the closest observer. Importantly, just as perceptual knowledge rests on contingent, causal relations between S and her external environment, self-knowledge rests on such similar relations between S and her internal goings-on. Because these relations could fail to obtain through no fault of S's perceptual or cognitive apparatus, brute errors are possible in both cases. It follows that if the inner sense model of self-knowledge were correct across the board, brute errors would be possible even in the cases of reflectively accessible states. The upshot of Burge's argument (1996: 105–10) is that since the possibility of brute error is ruled out in such cases, this model cannot in general be correct.[13]

5.3 Incompatibilism

We have now argued on the one hand that mental contents are externally individuated, and on the other hand that we have privileged access to those contents. But self-knowledge and semantic externalism would seem to be incompatible doctrines. How could we be authoritative about the contents of our own minds if those contents depend for their individuation on external circumstances that we have no especially authoritative knowledge of, or may even lack knowledge of? How can we have privileged access to the contents of our thoughts if what makes it true that our thoughts have those contents resides in external facts to which we lack privileged access? What goes on inside us falls short of fully fixing the identity conditions of our wide-content thoughts, yet only what is mentally inside us is intro-spectively accessible. To be clear, the worry is not that we cannot know at all the contents of our thoughts if semantic externalism is true, but rather that we cannot fully know those contents just by introspective reflection if that view holds. Would we not need to consult our external physical environment in order to figure out what we are thinking?[14]

Let *incompatibilism* be the view that semantic externalism is inconsistent with self-knowledge and let *compatibilism* be the opposing view that these doctrines are consistent. Here is a first stab at mounting an incompatibilist argument:

(1) In order for S to know a priori that she thinks **water**-thoughts, i.e. thoughts containing the concept **water**, S must know a priori that she does not think **twin-water**-thoughts.

(2) For S to know a priori that she does not think **twin-water**-thoughts is for S to know a priori that she is not on Twin Earth.

(3) But S cannot know a priori that she is not on Twin Earth.

(4) So, S cannot know a priori that she thinks **water**-thoughts.

As Burge (1988: 654), Heil (1998: 138) and Boghossian (1998a: 158) argued, the problem lies with (1) which assumes an overly demanding conception of the conditions for knowledge. Compare with: in order for Anna to know that she has 20 pence in her pocket, Anna has to know that she does not have a counterfeit 20 pence in her pocket. So, by similar reasoning, Anna cannot know that she has 20 pence in her pocket. The first premise in both arguments presupposes that in order for S to know that p, S must know any proposition q whose falsity is (known to be) inconsistent with the truth of p. But in many cases, S can know that p whether or not she knows any such q as long as q is in fact true. Thus S can know introspectively that she thinks **water**-thoughts even though she cannot rule out the possibility that she thinks **twin-water**-thoughts, because she cannot rule out the possibility that she is on Twin Earth. If S's evidence is confined to perceptual experiences of manifest features of water, then all her evidence is compatible with her being on Twin Earth, hence compatible with her thinking **twin-water**-thoughts. Semantic externalism requires only that certain external conditions obtain if S is to have a certain thought, not that S knows that these conditions obtain. In general, S can know that p even though S is in no position to exclude all possibilities logically inconsistent with p. The speaker's evidence need only be incompatible with the *relevant alternatives* to what she knows, e.g. that she does not think **juice**-thoughts, or that she does not have 50 pence in her pocket.[15] The Twin Earth and counterfeit-coin scenarios are too far-fetched to be of relevance, and so can properly be ignored by S. The chief worry is not that in order for S to know a priori that she entertains a wide mental content, she must possess a priori knowledge of all its external individuating conditions, but rather how S could as much as know that content a priori in the first place given that those conditions are at best a posteriori knowable.

Before we proceed to pin down a more persuasive incompatibilist argument, let's pause to draw a distinction: *strong incompatibilism* is the view that S does not have privileged access to any of her occurrent wide-content thoughts; and *weak incompatibilism*, the view that S does not have privileged access to all of her occurrent wide-content thoughts. Only weak incompatibilism permits S having privileged access to some of these thoughts. However, either view is potentially problematic for the semantic externalist.[16] But Burge and others have shown that in some unproblematic cases occurrent wide-content thoughts are subject to privileged access. The real question centres on whether incompatibilism is true in more disputed cases. In Section 5.2, we introduced Burge's notion of a *self-verifying judgment* (1998, 1996). Let's elaborate on these judgements. Suppose:

(5)   S is thinking that water is thirst-quenching

is true. By thinking is meant entertaining the thought expressed by the embedded sentence 'water is thirst-quenching'. Suppose also that:

(6)   S judges that (5)

is true. That is, S accepts the thought expressed by (5) as true. But to do that S must engage in the thought expressed by that sentence. So, if S judges that S is currently thinking that water is thirst-quenching, then S is currently thinking that water is thirst-quenching. Judgement (5) is true if (6) is true, no matter which empirical evidence S has or lacks. The thought S entertains when she judges that (5) would not exist had it not been for the first-order thought which S thinks through thinking that second-order thought. Judgement (6) is akin to Descartes' *cogito*-thought **I am thinking** in that both are self-verifying. *Cogito*-like thoughts are self-verifying judgements about thoughts in the sense that the mere judging guarantees the truth of what is being judged. When S thinks that she is thinking that p, she is thereby thinking that p. In such episodic cases there can be no error based on a gap between the first-order thought and the second-order thought, because the first-order thought is contained as the object of the second-order thought. Judgement (6) simply inherits the content of (5) – that S is thinking that water is thirst-quenching.

Self-verifying judgements rule out a certain kind of error-possibility: that (6) should be true but (5) false. As mentioned in Section 5.2, the fact that S's judgement is self-verifying does not by itself entail that S is epistemically warranted in making that judgement or indeed that S's judgement thereby amounts to knowledge. The warrant that accrues to second-order judgements about thoughts stems from their role in critical reasoning, and this is true even for self-verifying judgements. As explained in Section 5.2, on Burge's view (1996), S is *entitled* to her second-order judgements about thoughts, including those judgements that are self-verifying, and such entitlement typically suffices for S to have knowledge of those thoughts. What is special about self-verifying judgements is that they are immune from certain kinds of error in a way other second-order judgements about thoughts are not. Because self-verifying judgements are such that one cannot drive a wedge between the first-order thought and the second-order judgement; they are immune from incompatibilist worries about certain ways in which these could come apart. For instance, if S's judgement that she is thinking a **water**-thought is self-verifying, then the possibility that her judgement is false due to her thinking instead a **twin-water**-thought could not arise. Still, it is unclear whether the existence of self-verifying judgements is sufficient to rebut all incompatibilist arguments. As Boghossian (1998a: 169–70) observed, judgements of standing mental states and occurrent mental events are not self-verifying. For example, S's judgement that she believes that Scots are friendly is not self-verifying, because S can entertain the thought **Scots are friendly** without forming a belief with that content. It is possible for S to judge that she believes that Scots are friendly when in actual fact she disbelieves that Scots are friendly.[17] Nor is S's judgement that S has a red after-image self-verifying. Also, no self-verifying thought about what S was thinking a moment ago is available to her now.[18] Yet we have privileged access to first-order thoughts that are not literally part of second-order thoughts. In fact, a vast amount of our first-order thinking is unaccompanied by second-order thinking, since not always are we self-reflectively thinking about our thoughts in the very act of thinking them. In numerous cases do we attend only subsequently to our thoughts, but we presumably still do so in a privileged way.[19] Self-verifying judgements are confined to those cases where what is judged is a constituent of that very judgement.

Davidson (1987), Heil (1998), Burge (1988, 1996), Falvey and Owens (1994) and Gibbons (1996) have made a different but closely related point about the self-referential nature of the content of occurent thoughts. Where Burge's first point is that S's mere judging that she is thinking that water is thirst-quenching guarantees the truth of what S is judging, this second point is that the content of S's thought **water is thirst-quenching** automatically carries over to her judgement that she is thinking just that. The content of the thought in (6), or at least part of that content, is self-referentially fixed by the content of the thought in (5). It is impossible that S judges that she is thinking that water is thirst-quenching when she is thinking that twin-water is thirst-quenching. The second-order thought simply contains the content of the first-order thought – **water is thirst-quenching** – as part of its subject matter. This point can embrace different kinds of propositional attitudes, and allows for one kind of fallibility. If S believes that she believes that water is thirst-quenching, then maybe she is wrong but not for the reason that she believes that twin-water is thirst-quenching. Maybe S bears some attitude other than belief or no attitude at all towards the proposition **water is thirst-quenching**. This means that whatever external individuation conditions hold for the content of S's first-order attitude will also hold for the content of her second-order attitude. The possibility of having the second-order belief is thus partially grounded in the possibility of having the first-order belief. Since S has both beliefs in the same environment, the external facts about water in virtue of which S believes that water is thirst-quenching are the same external facts in virtue of which S believes that she believes that water is thirst-quenching. So, external individuation does not all by itself give rise to additional difficulties in explaining how we can have privileged knowledge of our own minds.

5.4 Slow switching

The problem with the first incompatibilist argument from (1) to (4) is that S can know a priori that she thinks **water**-thoughts even though she cannot rule out a priori the possibility that she thinks **twin-water**-thoughts. That possibility is simply irrelevant. But suppose with Burge (1988: 659) and Boghossian (1998a: 159–60) that S were unwittingly to undergo a *series of switches* between Earth and the remote planet Twin Earth, sufficiently slow to acquire the concepts appropriate to each place. Imagine if you like a future in which space travel by the speed of light between the planets in our solar system is commonplace. How long exactly S would have to stay at each place to make for the relevant conceptual changes is unclear. As noted in Section 4.4, no immediate conceptual changes would occur upon her arrival on Twin Earth. All we know is that were S slowly enough shuttled back and forth, she would be able to sustain sufficient causal links with her environments to affect changes in her wide-content thoughts. So, suppose S is on Twin Earth at t_1 having acquired **twin-water**-thoughts, then on Earth after a switch at time t_2 long enough to affect the acquisition of **water**-thoughts, and so on. Could S tell just by introspection which thoughts she apprehends? There is no qualitative difference between thinking the two thoughts, and she has no clue as to being switched between these two – from her point of view – indistinguishable places. Of course if S thinks both the first-order thought and the second-order thought simultaneously in the same environment, then slow switching poses no additional difficulty for the semantic externalist. Since the content of the first-order thought is then contained in the second-order thought, the external individuation conditions of the former will carry over to the latter. As Burge (1996: 96) notes, no matter how S is switched around there is no way she could falsely self-ascribe the contents of her own present-tensed thoughts. But suppose S thinks the first-order thought in one environment and then later travels to a different environment in which she thinks the second-order thought. Then it certainly looks as if S's self-knowledge is jeopardized, because there is no longer any automatic content inheritance between these two thoughts. The question is then how S can introspectively discriminate between thoughts which seem identical from the inside. Since there are no introspectible clues, nothing in S's grasp of the contents of those thoughts would enable her to tell them apart. And if S cannot discriminate between these thoughts, then S lacks knowledge at t_2 of what she was thinking at t_1. For now that slow switching is a frequent occurrence, the alternative that S was thinking **water**-thoughts at t_1 becomes relevant. The fact that S is unaware of the predicament she is in does not render this alternative irrelevant. Boghossian (1998a) then claims that if S lacks knowledge at t_2 of what she was thinking at t_1, then either S has forgotten at t_2 what she knew at t_1 about what she was thinking then, or else S lacked knowledge at t_1 of what she was thinking then. The following is supposedly a platitude about memory: if S has some knowledge at t_1 and remembers at t_2 everything she knew at t_1, then S has that knowledge at t_2. But, Boghossian continues, since these wide-content thoughts are not especially difficult to remember, S never knew her thoughts in the first place. Consider the slow switching argument:

(7)   In order for S to have introspective knowledge at t_2 that she was thinking **twin-water**-thoughts at t_1, S must be able to introspectively discriminate her thinking those thoughts from all relevant alternatives.

(8)   S cannot introspectively discriminate her thinking **water**-thoughts from her thinking **twin-water**-thoughts.

(9)   If the Twin Earth switching case is actual, S thinking **water**-thoughts are relevant alternatives to her thinking **twin-water**-thoughts.

(10) So, S does not know introspectively at t_2 that she was thinking **twin-water**-thoughts at t_1.

(11) So, assuming S has forgotten nothing at t_2, S did not know introspectively at t_1 that she was thinking **twin-water**-thoughts.

One objection is to question whether S at t_2 possesses both sets of concepts. The thought experiment presupposes that S at t_2 is able to entertain both sets of thoughts, and so when on Earth at t_2 S retains the concept **twin-water** that was acquired on Twin Earth at t_1. But maybe all of S's thoughts at t_2, including the ones acquired at t_1, are **water**-thoughts. For if the contents of S's belief states are determined by the external environment, then so are also the contents of her memory states. When S travels back and forth between Earth and Twin Earth, what she remembers shifts accordingly. The claim here is not merely that the propositional content of memory states is externally individuated. Such *memory externalism* is uncontroversial among semantic externalists. The stronger claim is rather that the propositional content of a given memory state *continues to change* as S is slowly switched around. If such *content-switching externalism* is sustainable, the inference from (10) to (11) fails. She may fail to know introspectively at t_2 what she was thinking at t_1, while knowing introspectively at t_1 what she was thinking then, without having forgotten anything. Moreover, if all the contents of S's memories have changed, then she obviously cannot explicate the difference between the two sets of thoughts. Nobody can discriminate between two sets of thoughts if only one set is graspable.[20]

The problem with this conception of memory is that S's beliefs at t_2 about her beliefs at t_1 are all rendered false. Suppose that at t_1 S forms the true belief that twin-water is wet. At t_2 S tries to retrieve her belief – a belief she would express with the sentence 'water is wet', but if what S now believes is that she believed that water is wet, then that belief about her past belief is false. In the light of the general character of the content of that belief, that may be no bitter pill to swallow. But the problem can be sharpened. Consider instead S's belief at t_1 that some twin-water in the neighbourhood is polluted. As this belief makes a reference to S's specific environment, it would seem imperative that it be tokened on Twin Earth rather than Earth. When S at t_2 attempts to recover that belief using 'some water in the neighbourhood is polluted', S's second-order belief comes out false. Moreover, memories presumably resemble other content-bearing mental states in being individuated by their contents such that no single state can survive a change in its content. Recall Burge's initial extension of the Twin Earth argument from Section 3.3. If that is right, then the same memory state cannot change its content through time. Note finally that memory is factive: S cannot remember a falsehood. So, given that S did not believe that some water in the neighbourhood is polluted, she cannot now remember that she believed just that. She has at most an apparent memory of her past thoughts. The upshot is that S's memory at t_2 should preserve the contents of her thoughts at t_1, i.e. she must retain the beliefs involving **twin-water** that she acquired at t_1 if we are to credit her with true memory beliefs at t_2.[21]

Another objection is to deny the relevant alternative conceptions of knowledge when it comes to self-knowledge. Thus Bar-on (2005: Ch. 5) and S. Goldberg (2005: 141–42, 2006a: 304–7), following Burge (1988, 1996), argue that since S judging that she is thinking that p involves thinking that p, S is perfectly reliable with respect to p yet is unable to discriminate between p and some relevant alternative q. Failure to discriminate, however, is not indicative of a lack of self-knowledge. What matters is that S has the highest degree of objective justification for her judgement, where objective justification is understood in terms of probability of truth. Moreover, when S reflectively appreciates that she thinks the thought that p in the very act of self-ascribing that thought, she has reflective grounds for thinking that her thought is self-verifying. So, the fact that her self-verifying judgement enjoys this ultimate kind of truth-conducive justification is reflectively accessible to S, and so this judgement amounts to knowledge. Goldberg's (2005) dialectical point is that the slow switching argument does nothing to discredit Burge's original case for why S can know introspectively at t_1 what she was thinking at t_1. Goldberg does not directly challenge any of the premises in the slow switching argument. Burge (1988, 1996), however, makes the related but stronger point that the relevant alternatives conception of knowledge is irrelevant when it comes to S's introspective knowledge at t_2 of what S thought at t_1. The key point is to realize that memory can work through *preservation of content* rather than discrimination between relevant alternatives. Burge (1988: 660, 1998: 361, cf. 1993c) concedes that S may be unable to discriminate between **water**-thoughts and **twin-water**-thoughts, and thus unable to know whether she was thinking the former thoughts rather than the latter thoughts, but such discriminatory knowledge is neither here nor there. She can know her thoughts in some privileged manner without knowing very much about them. As Burge (1998: 355) puts it, there is no "need to *identify* the content of our thoughts in such a way as to be able to rule out relevant alternatives to what the content might be". Perception requires identification of the perceived object, which involves exclusion of relevant alternatives, but there is no neat analogy between perception and introspection in this respect. As Bar-on (2005: 172–73) stresses, telling what content our thoughts have is not a matter of telling it apart from other candidate contents in a way analogous to recognitional identification of external objects. Burge, Bar-on, Davidson, Falvey and Owens and many other semantic externalists are united in opposing such perceptual, or observational, or inner-sense models of self-knowledge, which in their view lie behind much incompatibilist thinking. In particular, Burge's ideas (1988, 1993c, 1998) about the role of content preservation in memory conflict with such models. Through causal memory chains, the content of S's belief about what she was thinking at t_1 is fixed by the content of what she was in fact thinking at t_1. Activating memory automatically brings up the past content, thus allowing S to redeploy that same content in practical or theoretical reasoning, regardless of whether S has identifying knowledge. Compare with anaphoric pronouns, as in:

(12)   Anna suffered from chronic fatigue. She was granted an essay extension.

When S utters (12), she uses 'she' to refer back to the individual that 'Anna' refers to regardless of any ability to identify the referent of the pronoun. The speaker S is relying on certain mechanisms in the discourse securing back-reference in much the same way she is relying on memory mechanisms securing content preservation when recalling an earlier thought. And as long as S's memory is in fact working properly, S is epistemically entitled to rely on the deliverances of her memory. In particular, S need not be able to empirically defend the reliable workings of her memory. And for S to be epistemically entitled to believe what she was previously thinking puts her in a position to know what she was previously thinking. This means that (7) is false: S can know introspectively at t_2 that she was thinking **twin-water**-thoughts at t_1 even though S is unable to introspectively discriminate her thinking those thoughts from the relevant alternative **water**-thoughts. In claiming that S knows what she is thinking only if she has an introspective ability to discriminate between relevant alternative thoughts, the incompatibilist assumes a flawed model of self-knowledge.

A final objection is to concede the relevant alternatives conception of knowledge but argue that slow switching is irrelevant. Thus Warfield (1992) correctly objects that as presented the slow switching argument is invalid. What follows from (7)–(9) is merely the much weaker:

(10*)   If the Twin Earth switching case is actual, then S does not know introspectively that she is thinking **water**-thoughts.

But since there is no reason to think that this fanciful switching case actually takes place, there is no reason to think S cannot know by introspection that she is thinking thoughts containing **water**. Transportation back and forth between Earth and Twin Earth is simply too far-fetched to constitute a relevant alternative. What slow switching shows is merely that (Epistemic Transparency) is compromised: the difference between thoughts containing **water** and **twin-water** is epistemically opaque to S in that she could have both sets of thoughts and yet lack introspective knowledge of their difference. But nothing of intuitive value need be lost. The compatibilist can safely concede that self-knowledge encompasses only the contents of S's contemporary mental states and not the identity conditions of their contents over time. She can know the contents of her thoughts without knowing about sameness or differences between those contents.[22] The incompatibilist aims to draw the stronger conclusion that not only would S not know whether her **water**-thoughts are identical to her **twin-water**-thoughts, S would not even know that she thinks **water**-thoughts. The reason being that S can know the latter only if she can rule out the relevant alternative that she thinks thoughts containing **twin-water**. So, much hangs on what it takes for an alternative to count as relevant.

In response, Ludlow (1995: 46) has objected that (9) misstates the conditions under which there might be relevant alternatives to **water**-thoughts. Consider instead:

(9*)   If switching cases in general are prevalent, then cases of S thinking **twin-water**-thoughts are relevant alternatives to her thinking **water**-thoughts.

And Ludlow (1995) argues that the antecedent in (9*) is plausible. We frequently slide from one language community to another, or from one social group or institution to another. If we defer to those communities, groups or institutions, and if Burge-style social externalism is true, then moving from one to another implies that the contents of our thoughts shift undetectably as well. Ludlow offers the example (1995: 47) of Biff who travels back and forth between the UK and the US. Biff eschews leafy vegetables, but as his knowledge is partial he defers to the linguistic community when speaking of them. He knows that radicchio and arugula are such vegetables, although he cannot distinguish them. Unbeknownst to Biff, when he says 'chicory is healthy' in the UK he expresses a proposition different from the one expressed when he utters the same sentence in the US. Biff has become a victim of a slow switching case.[23]

In such real-life cases, speakers lack introspective knowledge of what they believe, because they cannot rule out a relevant alternative to what they believe. Their belief about what they believe is based on evidence that is compatible with it being the case that they hold this alternative belief.[24] As Warfield (1997: 283–84) remarks, Ludlow shows that actual speakers are occasionally in no epistemically advantageous position with respect to these wide-content aspects of their thought activity. Ludlow has not shown that semantic externalism implies lack of self-knowledge across the board. To show that is to show that no speakers in any possible world can have self-knowledge of any wide states. In other words, Ludlow has at most established weak incompatibilism. But of course, as Ludlow (1997: 286) counters, this result is bad enough for the semantic externalist, because slow switching potentially covers a range of realistic cases in the actual world.[25]

5.5 Reasoning

Recall our speaker S who unwittingly is the victim of a series of slow switches between Earth and Twin Earth. On Earth S's tokens of sentences containing 'water' express **water**-thoughts, but then when she is transported to Twin Earth her tokens of the same type of sentences will eventually express **twin-water**-thoughts. As mentioned, in response to the slow switching argument from Section 5.4, most semantic externalists concede that (Epistemic Transparency) (p. 130, above) has to be jettisoned. On Earth S believes at t_1 that some water in the neighbourhood is polluted, but then having been shifted up to Twin Earth and spent enough time there she comes to believe at t_2 that some twin-water in the neighbourhood is polluted. Assuming that memory retains S's Earthly beliefs when on Twin Earth, she will thus hold two beliefs whose contents she cannot tell apart from the inside. As far as S is concerned the sentence 'some water in the neighbourhood is polluted' will express the same proposition. This means that when S uses that sentence to express her belief, she is not in a position to know purely by reflection that she expresses distinct propositions: **some water in the neighbourhood is polluted** on Earth and **some twin-water in the neighbourhood is polluted** on Twin Earth. To wit, the propositions that S expresses, which are the contents of her respective beliefs, are epistemically opaque to her. But, as we saw in Section 5.4, semantic externalists take that concession to constitute no embarrassment to their view. The reason is that (Epistemic Transparency) is an unduly strong principle that goes beyond anything commonsensical about self-knowledge.

Boghossian thinks otherwise. He argues (1992: 21–22) that if (Epistemic Transparency) is false then our slow traveller S will be unable to judge a priori the logical properties of her inference. And since semantic externalism is committed to the rejection of (Epistemic Transparency), this view is inconsistent with 'the *a priority of logical abilities*'. Intuitively, the logical properties of the inferences S engages in are judgeable a priori, but if semantic externalism is true, then S cannot detect the validity of her inferences without recourse to empirical investigation. Here are some examples. First, let's consider a case involving *theoretical reasoning*. When on Earth S went on a trip to the undeveloped countries where she learned about the shortages of water supplies. Now back on Twin Earth S recalls the unpleasant experience of widespread drought while thinking to herself:

(13)   Water is a rare commodity in those areas I visited during my trip.

Given that her Earthly experience is about water, then so is the thought in (13). While still on Twin Earth S then recalls yesterday's pleasant experience of quenching her thirst after finishing a marathon by indulging in a cold glass of what she calls 'water', thus thinking to herself:

(14)   Water is the liquid I drank after yesterday's marathon.

Given that this twin-Earthly experience is about twin-water, then so is the thought in (14). But now S can put these two pieces of information together by inferring that:

(15)   The liquid I drank after yesterday's marathon is a rare commodity in those areas I visited during my trip.

To S the deductive inference from the premises (13) and (14) to the conclusion (15) will seem valid, but in actual fact the reasoning succumbs to the *fallacy of equivocation*.[26] The first premise is true if interpreted as about water, and so is the second premise if interpreted as about twin-water, but the conclusion is patently false. Hence, the argument is invalid. The problem for the semantic externalist is that S is in no position to notice this fallacy by reflection alone, and is therefore not to blame for her fallacious reasoning. Only empirical scrutiny of her external physical environment will enable her to detect the conflation in question.

Let's now consider a case of *practical rationality* instead. While S was on Earth she drank some water from a dispenser at the office. Now back on Twin Earth she remembers that experience while thinking to herself:

(16)   Water is the liquid I drank from the dispenser at the office.

Still on Twin Earth, S desires after an exhausting run some of the liquid that she calls 'water' but is in fact twin-water. She therefore thinks to herself:

(17)   I want to drink some water.

Finally, by reflecting on the content of her desire and the content of the thought she had when she remembered drinking from the dispenser, she puts the two pieces of information together:

(18)   I shall set off to drink some of the liquid I drank from the dispenser at the office.

As the first premise (16) expresses an Earthly memory, it is about water, but the second premise (17) expresses a present desire, and so is about twin-water. The conclusion in (18) is intuitively false: now that S has spent long enough time on Twin Earth she has no intention to drink the liquid that she drank from the dispenser when she was on Earth. Indeed even if there is a true reading of (18), (18) does not follow from (16) and (17), because of the equivocation on 'water'.

The upshot is that as far as S can tell just by reflection, the reasoning in both the theoretical and the practical case looks valid when in fact it is leading S astray. But intuitively S's logical abilities should furnish her with reflective knowledge of whether these arguments are truth-preserving. The question of an argument's validity is ordinarily one that S can settle a priori. After all, validity is merely a question about whether the conclusion must be true if all the premises are true. But the concern is here that although S can know a priori that if the first argument has the form 'a is b, a is c; therefore b is c', then it is logically valid, she cannot know a priori whether it satisfies that form. For in order to determine whether her reasoning equivocates, she would need to empirically investigate her external environment.

One may well ask why S's logical acumen should issue in such a priori knowledge. Boghossian's answer (1992: 26–28) is that unless logic is a priori in this way, our propositional attitudes cannot *rationalize* our practical and theoretical reasoning. When I am interested in finding out why you behave the way you do, or why you hold certain beliefs rather than others, I am seeking an explanation that cites the reasons for which you behave or believe as you do. Such explanations are rationalizing if they show why believing or acting as you do makes sense from your point of view in light of what you desire and what else you believe.[27] Now take the case of practical rationality. Why does S intend to drink some of the liquid she drank from the dispenser at her office? Because she wants to drink some water and she takes it that water is the liquid she drank from the dispenser at the office. We make sense of S's intention to behave by explaining it in terms of her beliefs and desires. These propositional attitudes constitute reasons which rationalize her behavioural intentions – they explain why behaving in a certain way makes sense for her. Likewise in the case of theoretical rationality. Why does S believe that the liquid she drank after yesterday's marathon is a rare commodity in those areas she visited during her trip? Because S believes both that water is a rare commodity in those areas she visited during her trip, and that water is the liquid she drank after yesterday's marathon. These last two beliefs make up the reasons for which S holds the first belief, and so explain why having that belief makes sense from her point of view. It would in both cases be wrong to say that S lacks reasons for her beliefs and behavioural intentions. But if semantic externalism is right, we have only S's wide states and they seem not to provide any reason-giving explanations. We do not rationalize S's belief that the liquid she drank after yesterday's marathon is a rare commodity in those areas she visited during her trip by citing her widely individuated beliefs that water is a rare commodity in those areas she visited during her trip, and that twin-water is the liquid she drank after yesterday's marathon. Nor do we rationalize S's behavioural intention to drink some of the liquid she drank from the dispenser at the office, by citing her widely individuated belief that water is the liquid she drank from the dispenser at the office, in conjunction with her widely individuated desire to drink some twin-water. For such explanations to do the job of making sense of S's belief and behavioural intention we would need to ascribe to S the additional belief that water is twin-water – something S clearly does not believe.[28]

Let's delve deeper into S's reasoning. Take the first argument again. In response to Boghossian's argument, Schiffer (1992: 34) recommends that the second premise (14) in the first argument involving theoretical reasoning be restated as follows:

(19)   Water, the liquid that is a rare commodity in those areas I visited during my trip, is what I drank after yesterday's marathon.

If prompted, S would surely be willing to rephrase the second premise in this way. Nothing in the way the example is presented indicates that S would resist (19), indeed S's intention is to tie the term 'water' as used in (13) together with the term 'water' as used in (14). But in that case, the deductive argument from (13) and (19) to (15) is clearly valid. It is just that (19) is false. That is to say, although S applies 'water' unambiguously to pick out water, and so engages in flawless reasoning, she falsely believes that water is what she drank after yesterday's marathon.

Likewise, Burge (1998: 363–68, cf. 1993c) emphasizes the importance of preservative memory in deductive reasoning. Assuming S's memory is working properly, she is entitled to rely on her memory preserving her thoughts in the course of engaging in deductive reasoning. But this means that S's argument from premises (13) and (14) to the conclusion in (15) is protected from undetectable equivocation. True, the term 'water' as it occurs in the first premise (13) expresses the concept **water**. But given that S's intention is to connect the two premises in a way that supports the conclusion, she should be interpreted as using 'water' in the second premise (14) to also express **water**. And S's memory allows her precisely to hold constant the concept **water** when she thinks the second premise. Put differently, S reasons in such a way that there are links between the occurrences of 'water' in the two premises that secure sameness of reference. Boghossian's mistake is to assume that because twin-water caused S to think the proposition expressed in (14), that proposition must contain the concept **twin-water**. But, as was emphasized in Section 3.1, causation is distinct from individuation: some external features of the environment can cause S to be in a certain mental state without that state being individuated in terms of those features. This means that (14) is false: water was not the liquid S drank after yesterday's marathon. She commits no mistake in reasoning, but her memory merely misidentifies the liquid in question. So, while S's memory preserves the same content throughout the reasoning from (13) and (14) to (15), her memory fails to preserve the content of her original thought in (14).

One concern about the Schiffer–Burge reply to Boghossian's argument that semantic externalism is incompatible with the 'a priority of logical abilities' is whether S's intention to use 'water' univocally, or to think the same thoughts by 'water', thereby guarantees that S indeed does so. This concern arises for semantic externalism, because on this view S expresses distinct concepts when she travels back and forth between Earth and Twin Earth. Let's continue to focus on the first argument involving deductive reasoning. At the time of reasoning, S is on Twin Earth. So, in the second premise, why does her intention to use 'water' to refer to and express whatever 'water' refers to and express in the first premise override the fact that that term ought to pick out twin-water as S is now on Twin Earth, and hence express the concept **twin-water**? Well, as S. Goldberg (2007a: 182–83) remarks, that intention would not secure univocality in reference or thought if the semantic externalist held that once S thinks a given thought, it retains its original content as long as S would use the same sentence to express that thought. But the semantic externalist rejects that claim. She first thinks the thought that she would express with 'water is the liquid I drank after today's marathon' while on Twin Earth. Thus she referred to twin-water and expressed **twin-water**. But now the day after she engages in deductive reasoning which draws on thoughts she had while back on Earth. It would thus be reasonable to interpret her as expressing by 'water' the same concept that she expressed while on Earth, namely the concept **water**.

Still, a worry lingers on. Forget about deductive reasoning. The semantic externalist is happy to concede that the contents of S's thoughts change as she is being whisked off to Twin Earth. As S is entirely unaware that she is a victim of these transportations, it would seem that S's intentions univocal with respect to the reference and meaning of 'water' remain the same on Twin Earth. Whatever S intends to refer to and express by 'water' on Earth is what S intends 'water' to refer to and express on Twin Earth. It certainly seems plausible that S has such standing intentions to use language univocally through time even when she is not engaged in deductive reasoning. The problem is now the following. On the one hand, if these standing intentions suffice to ensure that S on Twin Earth refers to and expresses by 'water' what she refers to and expresses by 'water' on Earth, then the semantic externalist cannot account for content changes in cases of slow switching. On the other hand, if these standing intentions do not trump the external factors that individuate content, then why do the specific univocality intentions do so in the context of deductive reasoning? Either the semantic externalist would have to reject the existence of such standing univocality intentions, or else provide some explanation as to why they differ from the specific univocality intentions at play in deductive reasoning.[29]

Chapter summary

In this chapter we initially summarized self-knowledge: individuals typically have privileged access to their own occurrent mental states which gives rise to a priori knowledge of these states and their contents. An asymmetry in psychological discourse between first- and third-person utterances reflects this phenomenon. There are three characteristics: authority, non-inferentiality and salience. Assuming competence, sincerity and attention, one need not provide reasons in support of one's claim to be in some basic mental state, one does not infer from one's behaviour that one is in that state, and if one is in some such state one will be disposed to notice that one is. Self-knowledge contrasts with the stronger claim that individuals can know a priori whether any two propositions they understand are identical or distinct. To say that one can have a priori knowledge of the logical properties of contents in this manner is to say that these contents are epistemically transparent. We then proceeded to show that the strong claim that semantic externalism and self-knowledge can never be reconciled is false. Burge's self-verifying judgements are counterexamples: if one knowledgeably judges that one is currently thinking that water is wet, then one is thereby thinking that water is wet. Just as with Descartes' *cogito*-thoughts, a gap between the first-order thought and the second-order thought is ruled out, because the first-order thought is contained as the object of the second-order thought. But self-verification is not what accounts for knowledge of *cogito*-like thoughts. Instead we expanded on Burge's entitlements as the special kind of warrant that attaches to second-order judgements in virtue of their role in critical thinking. It was emphasized how Burge's account diverts from inner-sense or perceptual models of self-knowledge. We then scrutinized arguments for the weaker claim that self-knowledge and semantic externalism are occasionally irreconcilable. Boghossian asks us to imagine cases in which an individual unwittingly undergoes a series of switches between Earth and Twin Earth, sufficiently slow to acquire the distinct wide-content thoughts. If knowledge requires an ability to discriminate between relevant alternatives, and thoughts containing the concept **twin-water** are relevant alternatives to thoughts containing **water**, it looks like an individual in this predicament cannot know a priori that she thinks thoughts containing **water**. From her internal perspective there are no detectable differences between thinking these distinct sets of thoughts. In response, some reject the relevant alternatives conception of knowledge when it comes to self-knowledge. Following Burge and others, this conception relies on an illicit, perceptual model of self-knowledge. Others accept that conception but maintain that these transportations are too outlandish to count as actually relevant. There is some consensus though that slow switching cases prove epistemic transparency false but many are happy to eschew this unduly strong principle. The last section was devoted to another putative problem for semantic externalism about how to avoid the consequence that certain intuitively valid arguments do not succumb to the fallacy of equivocation. Boghossian imagines our traveller going through an argument. The occurrence of 'water' in one premise expresses the concept **water**, since it refers to experiences had while on Earth, but the occurrence of 'water' in another premise expresses the concept **twin-water**, since it refers to experiences had while on Twin Earth. When the traveller draws the conclusion on the basis of these two premises, she equivocates on 'water'. The problem is that she has no a priori way of detecting the fallacy. In response, some appeal to preservative memory in deductive reasoning. If the traveller's memory is working properly, she is entitled to rely on her memory preserving the same unequivocal thoughts in the course of engaging in deductive reasoning.

Annotated further reading

There are by now several competing accounts of self-knowledge in the philosophical literature, e.g. Dorit Bar-on's (2005) *Speaking My Mind: Expression and Self-knowledge*. Many of the most classical articles can be found in (1994) *Self-knowledge*, edited by Cassam Quassim. We aimed at finding fairly common ground between these various accounts. For a survey and critical discussion of the recent literature see Aaron Zimmerman (2008) and Brie Gertler's (2010) *Self-knowledge*. Burge's papers on self-verifying judgements and entitlement to self-knowledge are collected in (1998) *Externalism and Self-knowledge*, edited by Peter Ludlow and Norah Martin, chapters 4 and 15. Part V and part VI in the same anthology include many important articles on the slow switching argument. Other influential articles are brought together in (1998) *Knowing Our Own Minds*, edited by Crispin Wright, Barry Smith and Cynthia Macdonald, in (2003b) *New Essays on Semantic Externalism and Self-knowledge*, edited by Susana Nuccetelli, and in (2004) *The Externalist Challenge*, edited by Richard Schantz. Jessica Brown's excellent (2004) *Anti-individualism and Knowledge* discusses in chapters 2–4 the slow switching argument and attendant epistemological issues pertaining to discrimination, relevant alternatives and reliability. In chapter 5 she specifically addresses the question of whether semantic externalism is incompatible with competent speakers' ability to a priori detect the validity of their deductive reasoning. In this context, it is also worth mentioning the recent interest in whether semantic externalism is compatible with epistemological internalism, and whether semantic internalism is compatible with epistemological externalism. Thus Sanford Goldberg (2007b) has edited a fine collection of articles devoted to these questions, entitled *Internalism and Externalism in Semantics and Epistemology*.

6

SCEPTICISM

6.1 Scepticism about self-knowledge

In Chapter 5 we examined various arguments purporting to show the incompatibility between semantic externalism and self-knowledge. In this chapter we will explore the implications that semantic externalism has for knowledge of the external world. But let's first probe deeper into the reasoning underlying scepticism about self-knowledge. Brueckner (1990, 1994a) has argued that semantic externalism provides the basis for such scepticism. The *content sceptic* argues that S's introspective belief that she is thinking that water is wet cannot constitute a priori knowledge. For if S knows a priori that she is thinking that water is wet, then S also knows a priori that she is not thinking that twin-water is wet. Since S does not know a priori that she is not thinking that twin-water is wet, S does not know a priori that she is thinking that water is wet. Despite being located on Earth S lacks a priori knowledge that she is thinking **water**-thoughts, i.e. thoughts containing the concept **water**. We can put this line of reasoning as follows – call it the content sceptical argument:

(1) S does not know a priori that S is not thinking that twin-water is wet.
(2) If S knows a priori that S is thinking that water is wet, then S knows a priori that S is not thinking that twin-water is wet.
(3) S does not know a priori that S is thinking that water is wet.

Note that what the content sceptical argument shows is not that S could not possibly know which thoughts she is thinking, but rather that S could not possess such knowledge introspectively. (Remember, we call knowledge by introspection 'a priori'). And that is bad enough. If the only way S can know what she is thinking is by empirical investigation, then content scepticism is vindicated. Note also that the content sceptical argument is clearly valid as it is just an instance of *modus tollens* (p → q, ¬q; therefore ¬p). The question is then what justifies the premises. The second premise (2) is underwritten by an instance of the epistemological principle that *knowledge is closed under known entailment*:

(Closure)   If S knows that p and S knows that if p then q, then S knows that q.

The thought is that S knows everything that she knows to be entailed by what she knows. So, in this case: if S knows a priori that she is thinking that water is wet, and S knows a priori that she is not thinking that twin-water is wet if she is thinking that water is wet, then S knows a priori that she is not thinking that twin-water is wet. There is no question that S knows a priori the conditional that if she is thinking that water is wet, then she is not (now) thinking that twin-water is wet. Given the Twin Earth thought experiment, thinking that water is wet is inconsistent with (simultaneously) thinking that twin-water is wet. So, (2) is justified if (Closure) holds. However, (Closure) has obvious counterexamples. Think of cases where S fails to form the belief that q. Since belief is arguably necessary for knowledge, S thus fails to know that q. But it may well be that S still knows that p and knows that if p then q.[1] Consider instead the principle that *knowledge is closed under competent deduction*:[2]

(Closure*)   If S knows that p and competently deduces q from p, thereby coming to believe that q, while retaining S's knowledge that p, then S comes to know that q.

This more plausible principle captures the intuitive idea that S can extend her knowledge by competently performing deductive inferences from what she already knows. She can acquire new knowledge by reasoning from old knowledge. Whether there are counterexamples to (Closure*) is a vexed issue. Suppose S knows by visual perception that there is wine in the bottle. She then comes to believe that there is not coloured water in the bottle by competent deduction. Assuming S retains her knowledge that there is wine in the bottle, does S thereby come to know that there is not coloured water in the bottle? That seems odd. She can only know that there is not coloured water in the bottle by, say, gustatory perception or testimony. Be that as it may, (2) is not obviously susceptible to similar kinds of counterexample. If S knows a priori that she is thinking that water is wet, and comes to believe that she is not thinking that twin-water is wet by competent deduction while preserving her a priori knowledge that she is thinking that water is wet, then she arguably does come to know a priori that she is not thinking that twin-water is wet. Obviously, this assumes that while on Earth S can think **twin-water**-thoughts. So, there must be a way for S to possess the concept **twin-water** while on Earth. We can again envisage S being subject to a series of slow switches between Earth and Twin Earth, or just that the content sceptic presents S with the possibility of her undergoing such transportations, thereby enabling S to pick up that concept.

What supports the first premise (1) then? One reason S does not know a priori that she is not thinking that twin-water is wet might be that if S were thinking that twin-water is wet, then everything internal would seem exactly the same to her. As far as self-knowledge is concerned there are no characteristic experiential marks that would enable S to reflectively distinguish between thoughts containing **water** and thoughts containing **twin-water**. Indeed, in the absence of empirical investigation, everything external would also seem exactly the same to S. If S were located on Twin Earth thinking **twin-water**-thoughts without empirically investigating the underlying nature of her physical environment, the perceptual experiences S would have would be qualitatively indistinguishable from the ones S has on Earth. To borrow Bar-on (2005: 158) words, "thought contents do not wear marks of their hidden nature on their perceptible sleeves". Suppose against this backdrop that S's evidence for her belief that she is not thinking that twin-water is wet consists in the totality of her first-person experiences – both her perceptual experiences of the external world and the experiences, if any, she undergoes when thinking thoughts about water. This suggests, Brueckner (1990: 448) contends, that S lacks knowledge that she is not thinking that twin-water is wet. More precisely, Brueckner (1994a: 333) argues that S lacks knowledge that she is not thinking that twin-water is wet as that hypothesis is underdetermined by her evidence (see underdetermination). The idea is that knowledge requires evidence in the sense that S lacks knowledge unless S has evidence that favours what she believes over any hypothesis that she knows is incompatible with what she believes.[3] Consider the special case involving a sceptical hypothesis:

(Underdetermination)   If S knowingly considers a hypothesis H and a competing incompatible sceptical hypothesis H_S and S's evidence does not favour H over H_S, then S does not know that not-H_S.

In our example the content sceptic first asks S to contemplate both the hypothesis (H) that she does not think that twin-water is wet and the competing alternative (H_S) that she does think that thought. Then the content sceptic challenges S to produce evidence on the basis of which S can accept one over the other of these hypotheses. But unless S empirically investigates her environment, the totality of her evidence does not favourably speak to one rather than the other. Neither S's perceptual experiences nor her introspective evidence discriminate between the two hypotheses. That is, without empirical investigation, S's total evidence underdetermines her choice of hypothesis. The principle of (Underdetermination) then dictates that S lacks knowledge that she is not thinking that twin-water is wet.

Falvey and Owens (1994: 118–23) and Gibbons (1996) think otherwise. Suppose again that without empirical investigation S's evidence comprises the totality of her perceptual and introspective experiences, and suppose also that S bases her belief that she is not thinking that twin-water is wet on that experiential evidence. Then consider the following principle, due to Falvey and Owens (1994: 116) embodying a *relevant alternatives conception of knowledge*:

(Relevant Alternatives)   If q is a relevant alternative to p, and S's evidence for her belief that p is such that if q were true S would still believe that p, then S does not know that p.

Let q be that S is thinking that twin-water is wet, and let p be that S is not thinking that twin-water is wet. On the assumption that S has undergone a series of switches between Earth and Twin Earth, the possibility that S is thinking that twin-water is wet is a relevant alternative to S not thinking that twin-water is wet. The problem is now that S's evidence is not such that if S were thinking that twin-water is wet, then S would still believe that she is not thinking that twin-water is wet. For if S were on Twin Earth thinking about twin-water, then S would believe that she is thinking that twin-water is wet. The reason is that the contents of S's beliefs about her thoughts are locked onto the contents of those thoughts in such a way that the former contents will be determined by the external environment in just the way the latter contents are externally determined; or so Falvey and Owens (1994: 122) maintain. Because S would truly believe that she was thinking that twin-water is wet rather than falsely believe that she was thinking that water is wet if she had been on Twin Earth, this relevant alternative is, as Gibbons (1996: 298) puts it, a *knowledge-consistent* rather than a *knowledge-precluding* one. This means that semantic externalism fails to undermine self-knowledge: appeal to Twin Earth yields cases where S forms a true belief with a content different from what she believes on Earth rather than a false belief with a content identical to what she believes on Earth. The antecedent of the relevant instance of (Relevant Alternatives) is therefore not satisfied, and so there is no reason why S cannot know that she is not thinking that twin-water is wet.[4]

This is not the place to adjudicate between (Relevant Alternatives) and (Underdetermination).[5] What is worth bearing in mind is that those content sceptical arguments that deploy (Closure*) succeed only if they describe a sceptical hypothesis (H$_S$) which is incompatible with the truth of what S believes. If the content sceptic relies on (Relevant Alternatives), she must show in addition that (H$_S$) is compatible with S believing what S actually believes, whereas if the content sceptic relies on (Underdetermination) she need only establish that (H$_S$) is compatible with the totality of S's actual evidence. But one might wonder whether content scepticism so much as makes sense. Thus Ebbs (2001, 2005) has argued that the content sceptical argument (1)–(3) is *self-undermining*. Ebbs (2005: 239) uses the notion of a 'subjectively equivalent world', which is a possible world in which S receives the same sensory stimulation that she receives in the actual world despite her environment being different from what S takes her environment to be in the actual world. In particular, some subjectively equivalent worlds are *weird worlds*: worlds in which utterances of the sentences in (1) and (2) express false propositions due to the nature of the environment in those worlds. So, in subjectively equivalent weird worlds, the content sceptical argument is unsound. The problem for the content sceptic is now that if the conclusion (3) of the content sceptical argument is true, then S does not know whether she is in one of these weird worlds, and so S does not know whether the premises (1) and (2) are true. The reason for this is that if S is in a weird world, then she expresses thoughts that are very different from the ones she thinks that she expresses. This means that S does not know whether (1)–(3) expresses a sound argument, and so S has no reason to accept the conclusion that she does not know a priori what she is thinking.

In response Brueckner (2003, 2007a) argues that the possibility of S being in a subjectively equivalent weird world poses no difficulty for the content sceptic. The conclusion (3) follows even though S does not know whether uttering the sentences in the content sceptical argument expresses a sound argument. For either (i) S's utterance of 'water is wet' expresses the proposition **water is wet**, or (ii) that utterance expresses some other proposition in virtue of S being in a weird world. If (i) holds, then S can take the sentences in the content sceptical argument at face value. This means that that argument is sound, whence that S does not know what she is thinking. If (ii) holds, then the same conclusion (3) follows regardless of whether the content sceptical argument is sound. For if S's utterance of 'water is wet' fails to express the proposition **water is wet**, then S cannot know that she expresses that proposition by uttering that sentence. The reason for this is that knowledge is factive: S knows that p only if p is true. Brueckner (2007a: 313–14) provides an illustrative analogy. Suppose S finds the following sentences written on a whiteboard that look like English:

(4)   If you know that I am speaking English, then you know which language I am speaking.
(5)   You do not know which language I am speaking.
(6)   You do not know that I am speaking English.

Let S be told that the writer may well be speaking a superficially similar language called 'twin-English'. This possibility, however, has no bearing on the argument. For either (i) the writer speaks English, or (ii) she speaks some other language such as twin-English. If (i) holds, then the argument is sound, because both premises (4) and (5) are true and the conclusion (6) follows via *modus tollens*. If (ii) holds, then the writer is not speaking English. Because knowledge is factive, S cannot know that the writer is speaking English. So, (6) follows either way.

6.2 External world scepticism

Semantic externalists have argued that if our thoughts have their contents in virtue of our standing in certain relations to our external environment, then introspective knowledge of those contents can afford us similar knowledge of relevant environmental features. This could mean either that semantic externalism furnishes us with the resources to fend off certain kinds of epistemological scepticism about the external world. Whether that is ultimately good news depends on how hard the sceptical problem is supposed to be. Some maintain that rebutting external world scepticism cannot be that easy. Or it could mean that semantic externalism provides a priori knowledge of specific, empirical propositions about the external world. Most semantic externalists admit that it would be too good to be true if their view implied that one could know via introspection and reflection that, say, water exists. Of course, all these arguments assume the existence of self-knowledge in one form or another. In Section 6.1 we examined arguments for the startling claim that semantic externalism provides the basis for scepticism about knowledge of the contents of our thoughts. Indeed the incompatibility arguments from Sections 5.3 and 5.4 can also be viewed as constituting forms of such content scepticism. If these arguments are cogent, that is rather bad news for the semantic externalist. In any case, it thus looks as if semantic externalism can safeguard our knowledge of the external world only at the expense of depriving us of knowledge of the internal world.

In this section we present a simple argument for *external world scepticism* and then review a familiar epistemic response to that argument. In this and the next section we will then examine whether there ultimately is any good news in the offing for the semantic externalist with respect to external world scepticism. Finally, in Section 6.4 we assess the problem of whether semantic externalism provides an a priori route to specific, empirical features of the external world.

Putnam (1981: 5–6, 1999) famously asked us to imagine the following sceptical scenario. Without your knowledge, your brain has long since been skilfully removed from the rest of your body, immersed in a vat full of nutrient fluid, and hooked up to a supercomputer. This computer, as controlled by an evil neuroscientist, feeds your envatted brain sensory experiences just as if you were a perfectly normal embodied human being. As normal embodied experiences and brain-in-a-vat BIV experiences are qualitatively indistinguishable, everything seems the same to you. The only difference between these experiences is causal: while your embodied experiences are caused by objects in your immediate external environment your (BIV) experiences are caused by features of the computer program. But such a difference in aetiology is undetectable from within those experiences.

The BIV is a sceptical hypothesis: a predicament to the effect that you are radically deceived in some undetectable way. If you were a BIV you would have experiences qualitatively indistinguishable from those you actually have when you perceive the external world. It would all be the same to you whether you were a BIV or not. Then it seems you cannot know that you are not a BIV. And if you lack such knowledge, you have granted the first premise in a sceptical argument with devastating consequences for your putative knowledge of the external world. For if you do not know that you are not a BIV, the external world sceptic will be quick to point out that you do not know any proposition that you know is incompatible with your being a BIV. For this purpose the external world sceptic avails herself of the principle from Section 6.1 that knowledge is closed under known entailment:[6]

(Closure)   If S knows that p and S knows that if p then q, then S knows that q.

Take again the proposition that you have hands. You know that being a BIV is incompatible with having hands. It follows via (Closure) that if you do not know that you are not a BIV, you do not know that you have hands. To clearly see why, we need to *contrapose* (if p then q; therefore if not-q then not-p) on (Closure):

(Contrapositive   If S does not know that q, then it is not the case that S
Closure)   knows that p and that if p then q.

Given that you most certainly know the entailment from having hands to not being a BIV, lack of knowledge that you are not a BIV entails lack of knowledge that you have hands. The external world sceptical argument can now be phrased as follows:

(7)   S does not know that S is not a BIV.
(8)   If S does not know that S is not a BIV, then S does not know that S has hands.
(9)   S does not know that S has hands.

The conclusion in (9) is problematic by any reckoning. Still, the argument has limited scope, because the second premise (8) relies on (Closure), and so will only rob S of knowledge of propositions that are inconsistent with S being a BIV, e.g. that S has hands, feet, knees. It shows at most that S does not know the negation of any proposition that S knows is entailed by being a BIV. The argument says nothing about alleged knowledge of propositions not pertaining to S's body. To broaden its scope we need to follow Putnam (1981: 6) in envisaging increasingly more radical sceptical hypotheses to the effect that all human beings are BIVs, or that all sentient beings are

BIVs, or that "the universe just happens to consist of automatic machinery tending a vat full of brains and nervous systems".

An epistemic response to the external world sceptical argument is one that draws on epistemic states, processes or principles. The one that shall occupy us rejects (Closure). On Nozick's view (1981: Ch. 3), *knowledge requires sensitive belief*:

(Sensitivity)   S knows that p only if: were p false S would not believe that p.

So, S knows that she is not a BIV only if: S would not believe that she is not a BIV if she were a BIV. But, according to Nozick, that *counterfactual* is false. If S were a BIV, she would still believe that she is not a BIV. The reason is that if S were a BIV the evil scientist would feed her sensory experiences in every way as if she were an embodied normal human. So, S does not know that she is not a BIV, because S's belief is insensitive. But on Nozick's view, S does know that she has hands. For if it were false that S has hands, she would not believe that she has hands. In the closest possible worlds in which S does not have hands, she has stumps (or something similar), and so in those worlds S does not believe that she has hands. The possible worlds in which S has stumps are closer to the actual world than the world in which she is a BIV. This means that on Nozick's view although S cannot know that she is not a BIV, she can know that she has hands. But S also knows that if she has hands, then she is not a BIV. The principle of (Closure) therefore fails in this case.

Note also that our two epistemic principles from Section 6.1 would seem to entail that (Closure) is going to fail. Consider again the requirement that Falvey and Owens (1994: 116) place on knowledge:

(Relevant   If q is a relevant alternative to p, and S's evidence for her
Alternatives)   belief that p is such that if q were true S would still believe
                that p, then S does not know that p.

This principle resembles (Sensitivity) by imposing a *modal constraint* on knowledge: in order for S to know that p, S's belief that p, or evidence for that belief, must be sensitive to possible variations in the truth-value of p. Knowledge requires *tracking* the truth across possible worlds. Just as with (Sensitivity), (Relevant Alternatives) implies that S cannot know that she is not a BIV. Assume that S's evidence for her belief that she is not a BIV consists in her sensory experience as of having hands, and assume that a relevant alternative to not being a BIV is being a BIV. Then S's evidence is such that if she were a BIV, she would still believe that she is not a BIV.[7] But S can know that she has hands. Take again S's evidence to be S's sensory experience as of having hands, and let having stumps be a relevant alternative. Then S's evidence is not such that if she had stumps, S would still believe that she has hands. If S had stumps, she would have a sensory experience as of having stumps, and so would believe that she has stumps. Again (Closure) fails: S knows that she has hands, and S knows that if she has hands then she is not a BIV, but S does not know that she is not a BIV.

Remember the content sceptical argument from Section 6.1. Brueckner and Falvey and Owens disagreed over how best to reconstruct the content sceptic's reasoning. In particular, Brueckner (1994a: 330–33) objects that since (Relevant Alternatives) implies the failure of (Closure), it is uncharitable to interpret the sceptic as relying on this principle, since it would prevent her from getting either the content sceptical argument or the external world sceptical argument off the ground. Instead Brueckner argues (1994a: 333–34) that (Underdetermination) (see p. 160) does not imply that (Closure) fails in the content sceptical argument. Be that as it may, Vahid (2003: 375–76) points out that (Underdetermination) has that implication when it comes to the external world sceptical argument. Suppose S knowingly considers the hypotheses that S has hands and that she is a BIV. These hypotheses are incompatible, because BIVs are handless by stipulation. Again if S's evidence is confined to the totality of her sensory experiences, then that evidence does not speak favourably to the hypothesis that S has hands as opposed to being a handless BIV. The principle of (Underdetermination) thus dictates that she does not know that she is not a BIV. But (Underdetermination) allows S knowledge that she has hands. Suppose S knowingly considers the hypotheses that she has hands and that she has stumps. The principle of (Underdetermination) is silent over the range of sceptical hypotheses that can be considered alongside the hypothesis that S has hands, and so we may include only the relevant hypothesis that S has stumps. But if what S has to go on is the totality of sensory experiences, then S's evidence does favour the hands hypothesis over the stumps hypothesis. The upshot is that (Closure) fails: S knows that she has hands, and S knows that if she has hands then she is not a BIV, but S does not know that she is not a BIV.

6.3 Putnam's proof

In Section 6.2 we surveyed some epistemic responses to the external world sceptical argument to the effect that (Closure) fails. The common feature of

(Sensitivity) and (Relevant Alternatives) is that knowing that p requires sensitivity to possible variations in the truth-value of p. In this section we will review a *semantic* response – one that draws on truth, reference or meaning – to that argument. Interestingly, it transpires that once semantic externalism is on-board these modal conceptions of knowledge can be understood to issue in a rather different response to that argument.

Putnam (1981: 7–8) aimed to show that the BIV hypothesis cannot possibly be true, because it is *self-refuting*. To say that a statement is self-refuting is to say that its truth implies its own falsehood. Take the general statement that all general statements are false. That statement is false, because its truth implies its falsehood. The following is a truth of logic: if p then not-p; therefore not-p. But Putnam's claim was that the BIV hypothesis is self-refuting in a stronger sense: the supposition that the hypothesis is as much as comprehensible entails its falsehood. How so? Putnam offers an illustration (1981: 1–2): as an ant is crawling on a patch of sand it traces a line that accidentally curves and recrosses itself in such a way that it ends up looking like a caricature of Winston Churchill. But the ant has not thereby depicted Churchill, because it has no intention to do so. Nor is there any causal or counterfactual dependency between Churchill and the indentation in the sand, e.g. the imprint would remain the same even if Churchill had looked very different. The intrinsic similarities between that imprint and a picture of Churchill fall short of making that imprint represent Churchill. As shown in Section 4.4, the moral is that representational properties are not intrinsic, or with Putnam's words (1981: 18), " … signs do not themselves intrinsically refer". For a start, something instantiates a representational property only if it sustains requisite causal connections with what it represents. As highlighted by the Twin Earth argument, in order for my use of 'water' to refer to water, there must be some adequate causal-historical connections between that use and water. As my fellow Earthly speakers and I are causally insulated from Twin Earth, my tokens of 'water' fail to refer to twin-water, and so these tokens represent water rather than twin-water.

Given this causal constraint on reference, the question is what the BIV refers to when it utters a word like 'tree'.[8] After all, the BIV sustains no causal connections with tress, at least if BIVs are envatted from birth. One proposal is that BIVs simply fail to refer to anything. Compare with Davidson's Swampman (1987: 451–54) from Section 3.5. This example was designed to show that unless one has a causal history comprising the right causal connections between the external physical environment, the speech community and oneself, one is incapable of having thoughts or communicate meaningful sentences. Both the BIV envatted from birth and the Swampman are precisely in that kind of predicament.

The problem for the BIV, however, is not being devoid of a causal history, but rather that its causal history is radically different from ours. What causes its tokens of 'tree' are not tress, but rather features of the computer program or electronic impulses or whatever. So, Putnam suggests (1981: 14–15) that the BIV's tokens of 'tree' might be referring to trees-in-the-image, or to the electronic impulses that cause the experience as of there being a tree, or to those features of the computer program that are causally responsible for those impulses. The key point is that it cannot refer to an actual tree. So, the BIV might think the proposition **there is a tree-in-the-image** when it utters 'there is a tree', and that proposition may well be true. If the BIV is really having an experience as of there being a tree rather than it merely seeming to the BIV that it is having such an experience, then that utterance is true. The BIV need not be radically mistaken about the nature of its strange environment. But the BIV cannot refer to trees, and so its utterance of 'there is a tree' cannot express the proposition that our tokens of the same sentence type express, namely **there is a tree**. Consequently, the BIV cannot think that proposition truly.

The foregoing sits well with semantic externalism. This view, remember, has it that when S uses a referring term, she refers to whatever typically causes her uses of that term.[9] As the BIV refers systematically to entities distinct from those ordinary English speakers refer to, the BIV is best interpreted as speaking a different but syntactically and phonologically indistinguishable language – call it vat-English (or BIVese). Similarly, in vat-English tokens of 'BIV' do not refer to BIVs, but rather to BIVs-in-the-image (or something related). The BIV has no causal connection to real brains or vats. One might object that since BIVs are brains immersed in vats containing nutritious liquid, there are trivial causal connections between them and brains and vats. There are three things to say in response. Firstly, the example could be changed so that no vats were involved. Secondly, the causal connections that matter are those between the BIV's tokens of 'brain' and 'vats' and their causal origin. What causes the BIV to utter 'BIV' is not the brain or the vat, but rather features of the computer program or whatever. Thirdly, there is a causal connection between the use of every word in vat-English and the particular vat that the BIV is in, but there is no special causal connection between the BIV's use of the particular word 'vat' and vats.

Now, having set the stage, let's turn to Putnam's proof that we are not BIVs (1981: 15). We know that if we were BIVs, then by 'we are BIVs' we would mean **we are a BIV-in-the-image** (or something similar). But we also know that the BIV hypothesis is not about BIVs-in-the-image. What we are supposed to hallucinate is that we have hands when in fact we are BIVs, not that we are BIVs when in fact we are BIVs-in-the-image. It follows that if we are BIVs, the sentence 'we are BIVs' is false. If, however, we are not BIVs, then by 'we are BIVs' we mean **we are BIVs**. So, if we are not BIVs, then 'we are BIVs' is false. As that sentence is therefore false whether or not we are BIVs, it is necessarily false. That we are BIVs is physically possible, but it is a precondition for referring to and hence thinking about BIVs that we are not BIVs. A physical possibility has thus been shown to be a conceptual impossibility. How best to understand Putnam's reasoning is a vexed issue, but recent discussion of Putnam's proof is centred on the idea of *disquotation*.[10] To say that my language disquotes means that I can use any meaningful, referring term 'N' to characterize its own reference: 'N' refers to N. Knowing such semantic features as the meaning of 'refers' and of quotation marks furnish me with a priori knowledge that my own language is subject to disquotation. Take Wright's succinct rendition (1992: 74):

(10)   My language disquotes.
(11)   In vat-English 'BIV' does not refer to BIVs.
(12)   In my language, 'BIV' is a meaningful expression.
(13)   In my language, 'BIV' refers to BIVs.
(14)   So, my language is not vat-English.
(15)   But if I am a BIV, my language is vat-English.
(16)   So, I am not a BIV.

Before we turn to objections, let's revisit our two modal constraints on knowledge from Section 6.2, namely:

(Sensitivity)   S knows that p only if: were p false S would not believe that p

and:

(Relevant   If q is a relevant alternative to p, and S's evidence for her
Alternatives)   belief that p is such that if q were true S would still believe
                that p, then S does not know that p.

As we saw in Section 6.2, (Sensitivity) and (Relevant Alternatives) can be used to show that S cannot know that she is not a BIV. But if the foregoing holds, it looks as if that is mistaken. Take (Sensitivity) first. If Putnam's take on the BIV scenario is correct, then S would not believe that she is not a BIV if she were a BIV. The reason is that in those counterfactual circumstances S *could not* believe that she is not a BIV. She would simply fail to grasp the concept **BIV** required for that belief. As S would then, by 'BIV', express the concept **BIV-in-the-image**, S would rather (truly) believe that she is not a BIV-in-the-image. Consequently, S's belief is sensitive, and so nothing stops her from knowing that she is not a BIV. Similarly in the case of (Relevant Alternatives). Let S's evidence for the belief that she is not a BIV embrace the totality of S's sensory experiences. Assume also that considering the intuitively remote BIV hypothesis suffices to render that possibility a relevant alternative to its negation. If Putnam is right about how to understand the BIV scenario, then it is not the case that S's evidence for her belief that she is not a BIV is such that S would still believe that she is not a BIV if she were a BIV. Not because of anything to do with the character of S's evidence, but because she *could not* believe that she was not a BIV if she were a BIV. The reason BIVs cannot believe that they are not BIVs is that they lack the requisite concepts. Accordingly, nothing pertaining to (Relevant Alternatives) prevents S from knowing that she is not a BIV. The lesson is that properly assessing the anti-sceptical implications of such epistemic principles as (Sensitivity) and (Relevant Alternatives) requires delving into issues about semantic externalism.[11]

In the remainder of this section we will discuss the cogency and scope of Putnam's proof. Consider first Brueckner's rejoinder (1986, 1999) that (13), and therefore (10), is *question-begging* in this context. My use of 'BIV' refers to BIVs only if my language is not vat-English, and my language is not vat-English only if I am not a BIV. But it is illegitimate to assume that I am not a BIV in support of a premise in an argument with the conclusion that I am not a BIV. You cannot use the device of disquotation in an argument against a sceptic who says you do not know you are not a BIV. For if you do not know you are not a BIV, you do not know that you do not speak vat-English, and vat-English is a language in which you cannot legitimately use the disquotation device.

In response, Wright (1992: 74–75) draws a distinction between being permitted to disquote one's own language and possessing identifying knowledge of reference and meaning. To allow a speaker knowledge that 'Aristotle' refers to Aristotle is not to attribute to her any knowledge that identifies Aristotle – she need not thereby know who Aristotle was. Likewise, given that 'BIV' is a meaningful expression in my language, I am entitled to say that 'BIV' refers to BIVs. There is no implication that I thereby possess knowledge that identifies BIVs. Likewise I can know that I have the thought **'BIV' refers to BIV** without being able to identify that thought, e.g. discriminate it from other pertinent thoughts. As we saw in Chapter 5 I can know the contents of my thoughts without knowing very much about them.

Similarly, Falvey and Owens (1994: 126–36) argue that any proficient English speaker has knowledge of the propositions expressed by a homophonic theory of truth for that language. For instance, I can know in virtue of being a competent user of English that my utterances have disquotational truth-conditions: 'I am a BIV' is true if and only if I am a BIV. Such disquotational knowledge is different from knowing the empirical propositions expressed by a non-homophonic truth-theory for English, i.e. that 'I am a BIV' is true if and only if I inhabit a world containing brains and vats, and I am one of those brains and live in one of those vats. Put differently, I am always entitled to homophonically state the referents of my words – 'BIV' refers to BIVs. But for me to also explicate the meaning of that word in my language – 'BIV' refers to certain definite physical objects in my environment – is to make an additional empirical claim about the nature of my environment. Importantly, since that empirical claim would be false if I were a BIV, it is not one I can legitimately make in the course of an argument that I am not a BIV. More generally, Falvey and Owens (1994: 126–36) argue that I can have introspective knowledge of the contents of my thoughts without knowing how to correctly explicate those contents. Thus I can know by introspection the content that my utterance of 'I am not a BIV' expresses without knowing introspectively whether that content would be different from or identical to the content a BIV would express when uttering that sentence. The latter knowledge of comparative content is at best empirical. Consequently, on the assumption that Putnam's proof appeals to knowledge of comparative content, it fails to constitute a cogent anti-sceptical argument. It would be question-begging to assume any empirical knowledge in an argument against a sceptic who questions all empirical knowledge.

Moreover, even if we disallow the use of disquotation in Putnam's proof, the sceptic is in trouble. Suppose I am running the external world sceptical argument from Section 6.2 in the first person. In order for the sceptic to justify the first premise that I do not know I am not a BIV, the sceptic must assume that I can actually think the proposition **I am not a BIV**. For if I could not think that proposition, the external world sceptic could not provide me with reasons why I should believe that I do not know that proposition. But the only way I can think that proposition is if I am not a BIV. That in essence was Putnam's original point that if I am able to so much as entertain the sceptical hypothesis that I am a BIV then that hypothesis must be false.

Compare with this simplified version of Putnam's proof due to Warfield (1999: 78):

(17)   I think that water is wet.
(18)   No BIV can think that water is wet.
(19)   So, I am not a BIV.

Here premise (17) is knowable a priori in virtue of having privileged access to the occurrent deliverances of my introspective faculty. By relying on self-knowledge of occurrent thoughts rather than the disquotation schema for reference, we avoid ontological commitment to terms having specific referents. In fact, Warfield (1999: 81) claims that if this schema is understood as saying that for all referring terms 'N' in my language, 'N' refers to Ns, then it has counterexamples as in: my tokens of 'unicorn' refer to unicorns. Further, Warfield (1999: 86–87) denies that this anti-sceptical argument begs the question against the sceptic: there is nothing problematic about appealing to a priori knowledge of mental content in the context of arguing against external world scepticism. But obviously against the backdrop of the BIV hypothesis, there is an intimate connection between external world scepticism and content scepticism. Thus Brueckner (1999: 48–49) claims that the semantic externalism underlying Putnam's proof engenders scepticism about knowledge of content. In short, if only we had a satisfactory response to scepticism about knowledge of the inner world, we could solve the problem of scepticism about knowledge of the outer world!

Let's finally consider two ways in which the sceptic can strike back even if Putnam's proof is sound. Firstly, as Wright remarks (1992: 76–77), it is imperative that the proof be formulated in the first person using the indexical expressions 'I' and 'my'. Suppose I want to figure out whether Mary knows that she is not a BIV:

(20)   Mary's language disquotes.
(21)   In vat-English 'BIV' does not refer to BIVs.
(22)   In Mary's language, 'BIV' is a meaningful expression.

(23)   In Mary's language, 'BIV' refers to BIVs.

(24)   So, Mary's language is not vat-English.

(25)   But if Mary is a BIV, her language is vat-English.

(26)   So, Mary is not a BIV.

The problem is that unless we know more about Mary, we do not know which language she speaks, and so we cannot know whether in her language 'BIV' refers to BIVs. Suppose Mary is in fact a BIV. Then (20), (21) and (22) are all true yet (23) is false. For in vat-English 'BIV' is a meaningful expression, yet it does not refer to BIVs. Although Mary herself cannot think the thought that she is a BIV, *we* can think that thought, and so we cannot successfully run the argument. Following Wright (1992: 93), the worry is now that just as we can wonder whether Mary is a BIV, there could well be a similar kind of disconcerting thought for someone to think about us. Putnam's proof provides no assurance that no such true thought exists, and so it fails to entirely refute the nightmare!

Secondly, the reason I could not think thoughts about tress or vats if I were a BIV is that I would sustain no appropriate causal connections with tress or vats, nor even have encountered others who have had such commerce with tress or vats. But what if, following Wright (1992: 90) and Christensen (1993: 314–15), I were only *very recently disconnected* from my body to be placed in the vat? If until now I have been interacting with tress and vats, then I would have been speaking English up until my recent envatment, and so my words will retain their referents to trees and vats at least for a while. Remember that in order for the slow switching argument from Section 5.4 to work the transportations had to occur slowly enough for the terms to change their referents. This means that Putnam's response from semantic externalism to the external world sceptical argument has limited scope. The best way for the external world sceptic to avoid this semantic response is instead to home in on Descartes' dreaming argument, which is in effect a recent envatment scenario. After all, the reference of your words does not change overnight while you are asleep.[12]

6.4 McKinsey's recipe

In Section 5.2 we were occupied with what Brown (2004: 234) calls the *achievement problem*: how can privileged access to mental states be achieved given that being in those states depend on features of the external environment to which nobody has privileged access? Now we will turn to what she (2004: 234) calls the *consequence problem*: what consequences follow from the joint assumptions of semantic externalism and privileged access? The consequence problem highlights another way of bringing out the apparent tension between these two doctrines: both are first assumed to be true, then an absurdity is derived using intuitively plausible inference rules, and finally at least one of these doctrines is concluded to be false. Such a line of reasoning is called a *reductio ad absurdum*: if an argument is valid and all its premises are true, then its conclusion must be true. So, if its conclusion is false on pain of absurdity, at least one of its premises must be false too.

The basic idea is simple. Assume that the thesis of self-knowledge holds. In that case S knows a priori that she thinks **water**-thoughts. But having convinced herself from the philosophical armchair that semantic externalism is sound, S can also know a priori that if she thinks **water**-thoughts, then water exists. Putting those two premises together, S is in a position to know a priori that water exists. All S needs is an instance of (Closure) specifically about a priori knowledge. That, however, is incredible: knowledge of the existence of water is a posteriori. And the argument seems impeccable given that (Closure) is independently motivated as sketched in Section 6.1. Unless the semantic externalist is bold enough to embrace privileged access to the external world, she is therefore compelled to jettison privileged access to the internal world. Due to McKinsey (1991) and Davies (1998), this incompatibilist argument is an exemplification of the M–C-form – also called *McKinsey's recipe*:

(27)   S has mental property M.
(28)   If S has mental property M, then S meets condition C.
(29)   So, S meets condition C.

To cook up an incompatibilist argument using McKinsey's recipe, C must be an external condition the obtaining of which makes M a wide-content mental state. For instance, if M is the state I am in when I think that water is wet, C might consist in having causally interacted with instances of the natural kind water. Thus McGinn (1989: 30–36, 47–48) thinks semantic externalists must embrace this constraint on concept possession:

(Strong Constraint)   If the concept of X is an atomic natural kind concept, then S cannot possess that concept unless S has causally interacted with instances of X.

As mentioned in Section 4.1, an atomic concept is one that lacks conceptual constituents. McGinn suggests that S can possess the composite natural kind concept **H₂O** without having had any causal encounters with instances of H_2O. Imagine that hydrogen and oxygen are too scarce and widely separated to have ever formed H_2O. If S has the concepts **hydrogen**, **oxygen** and **bonding**, she can compose the concept **H₂O** by theorizing that oxygen bonds with hydrogen to form H_2O. Still, if **hydrogen** and **oxygen** are atomic concepts, S must in addition have been acquainted with instances of these chemical kinds. Atomic natural kind concepts must have an extension with which possessors of those concepts have causally interacted.

Perhaps it is preferable not to require actual encounters by each and every possessor of the atomic natural kind concept in question. Maybe it would suffice that S be a member of a linguistic community in which other members have causally interacted with such-and-such instances. The following is less demanding:

(Intermediate   If the concept of X is an atomic natural kind concept, then
Constraint)   S cannot possess that concept unless S has causally interacted
                  with instances of X, or else S is a member of a linguistic
                  community in which other members have causally inter-
                  acted with instances of X.

In any case, both of these constraints have it that instances of X must exist in S's environment if S is to have an atomic natural kind concept of X. Now suppose mental property M is possession of the atomic natural kind concept **water**, and that external condition C is that water exists. In that case, **water** is an atomic natural kind concept of a composite natural kind (H_2O). Then consider the following exemplification of the M–C-form:

(30)   S has the concept **water**.
(31)   If S has the concept **water**, then water exists.
(32)   Water exists.

As the M–C-form is an instance of *modus ponens* ($p \rightarrow q$, p; therefore q), there is no question about its validity. And both premises would seem to be underwritten by purely non-empirical considerations. The first premise is a priori knowable by self-knowledge, and the second premise seems like a conceptual truth according to semantic externalism, and so is a priori knowable. Hence, assuming the applicability of (Closure) as pertaining to a priori knowledge, the conclusion can be deduced on purely a priori grounds. Yet this is intolerable since C embraces features of the external world to which S intuitively has no a priori access. The worry here is not that S could not know anything a priori about the external world and her location in it. Remember the simplified version (17)–(19) of Putnam's proof from Section 6.3, which is structurally identical to McKinsey's recipe. There is nothing intuitively problematic about S coming to know a priori that she is not a BIV in this way. The problem is rather that S can deduce a priori knowledge of specific, empirical facts about the external world. As McKinsey's recipe applies to all atomic natural kind concepts, the range of conditions C is potentially huge. So, if the reasoning is cogent, one or both of the premises cannot be a priori knowable. McKinsey's recipe is a *paradox* in that both premises are plausibly a priori knowable yet the conclusion that follows just by reasoning from those premises is at best a posteriori knowable. While commentators have interpreted McKinsey as attempting a *reductio ad absurdum* of semantic externalism, he (2002) is explicit that the original ambition was to present an inconsistent triad consisting of (30), (31) and the denial of (32). McKinsey's recipe has sparked a huge debate in recent years to which we cannot here do full justice. But here are three chiefly semantic objections.[13]

(I) The second premise (31) is false as it is insufficiently supported by the Twin Earth argument even if (Intermediate Constraint) is the right way of understanding the semantic externalist constraint on possessing the mental property in question. Consider the contrapositive of (31):

(33)   If water fails to exist, then S lacks the concept **water**.

As (33) makes clear, it is not enough to show that certain concepts depend for their individuation on the nature of the physical environment in which they are tokened. What must be shown is moreover that such concepts depend for their existence on the existence of appropriate objects in that environment. However, all the Twin Earth argument demonstrates is that in cases where a natural kind concept has an extension, that concept is individuated externally in terms of that extension. In order to sustain (31), it must be shown that the very existence of such concepts is dependent upon the existence of an extension. As Brown (2004: Ch. 8), Ball (2007) and others have argued, the Twin Earth argument fails to support that stronger claim. So, the semantic externalist can safely reject (31), because she is committed to external individuation but not kind-dependence of natural kind concepts.

One problem with objection (I) is, as we saw in Section 4.1, that weak semantic externalism – content depends for its individuation on external factors – seems to entail strong semantic externalism – content depends for its existence on external factors. That the weaker claim collapses into the stronger claim was precisely the upshot of Boghossian's (1998b) Dry Earth argument. So, although McKinsey's recipe does not directly attack weak semantic externalism, it does so indirectly via considerations about Dry Earth. But suppose the semantic externalist could find a way to block the Dry Earth argument. After all, as we saw in Section 4.1, Burge (1982) envisaged a Dry Earth scenario in which S has **water**-thoughts despite not knowing the chemical composition of water, and despite the absence of water in her global environment. What enables S to think such thoughts is the existence of sufficient knowledge of chemistry among the more informed members of her community to distinguish the concept **water** from concepts like **twin-water**.

Another problem with objection (I) is that even if Burge is right about Dry Earth, McKinsey's recipe remains a threat to strong semantic externalism, and that would still be an independently surprising result. At first blush, there is nothing incoherent about strong semantic externalism. Sawyer (1998), Putnam (1999) and Nuccetelli (2003a) all maintain that propositions expressed by sentences containing natural kind terms are kind-dependent. The Evans/McDowell view of object-dependent thoughts from Section 4.1 could reasonably be extended to embrace kind-dependent thoughts. Indeed, Davidson's Swampman from Section 6.3 seems to support this view: the Swampman's token sentences fail to express any thoughts at all since there are no external individuation conditions. If privileged access to this view's attendant notion of a kind-dependent thought entailed a priori access to the existence of that natural kind, then it looks as if something has gone awry.

(II) A popular objection, due to Gibbons (1996), McLaughlin and Tye (1998a, 1998b), S. Goldberg (2003b), Nuccetelli (2003a), Brown (2004: Ch. 8) and Brueckner (2001, 2007b), is to deny that the second premise (31) is a priori knowable. For instance, McLaughlin and Tye (1998a: 370–71, 1998b: 298–99, 311) argue that even if (Strong Constraint) is licensed by the Twin Earth thought experiment, and so is a priori knowable, it does not follow that S can know a priori that water exists. The reason is that although S can know a priori that she has the concept **water** and that her semantic intentions determine that her tokens of 'water' aim to express a natural kind concept, S cannot know a priori that **water** is a natural kind concept. For **water** is a natural kind concept only if 'water' has an extension, indeed only if that extension comprises water as a natural kind, and S cannot know a priori that 'water' is non-empty or that water is a natural kind. For all S can tell a priori, water could turn out to be like jade which comes as jadeite and nephrite, or even like phlogiston which failed to exist. The speaker can know a priori that she intends 'water' to name a natural kind but not that 'water' actually names such a kind. If being a natural kind concept is an extrinsic property of **water**, and as Gibbons (1996: 291) says, introspection affords reflective access only to the intrinsic properties of thoughts, S can only know a posteriori that **water** is a natural kind concept.[14] Moreover, as mentioned in Section 4.1, it is doubtful whether S can know a priori that **water** is an atomic concept rather than a compositional concept.

McLaughlin and Tye (1998a: 371) draw a comparison with singular thoughts, which as we saw in Section 4.1 are object-dependent. Suppose the thought **Cicero is an orator** is a singular thought individuated by Cicero himself. The concept **Cicero** as expressed by the proper name 'Cicero' is singular, and so to understand that name requires having *de re* knowledge of its referent. If that individual did not exist (timelessly), S could not think that thought. Their claim is then that although S can know a priori that she thinks the thought **Cicero is an orator**, she cannot know a priori that her thought is object-dependent. For to know the latter is to know that there is an individual, namely Cicero, such that **Cicero is an orator** is individuated in part by that individual, and that is only a posteriori knowable. In short, just as being an object-dependent thought is an a posteriori fact about the thought **Cicero is an orator**, being a natural kind concept is an a posteriori fact about the concept **water**.

The problem with objection (II) is fourfold. First off, McKinsey (1991, 2002, 2007) takes this objection to be committed to (31) being metaphysically necessarily true.[15] The upside is that knowledge of the relevant metaphysical necessities is a posteriori, e.g. water is H_2O, but the downside is that semantic externalism is trivialized. For my contentful mental states have all sorts of irrelevant metaphysical dependencies. Assuming with Kripke (1980) that individuals have their biological origins essentially, my belief that water is wet metaphysically necessitates the (timeless) existence of my mother, but the reason why the content of that belief is wide has nothing to do with my biological origin. Instead, McKinsey (2002, 2007) holds that although (31) is a posteriori knowable, the existence of water is conceptually implied by her having the concept **water**. On his view, (31) provides a counterexample to the claim that conceptual relations are knowable a priori. Instead he proposes that a priori knowledge be closed under conceptual implication:

(A Priori Closure)   If S knows a priori that p, and p conceptually implies q, then S knows a priori (or at least is in a position to know a priori) that q.

Given (A Priori Closure) and the above-mentioned conceptual implication, it follows that S knows (32) a priori if she knows (30) a priori. But, as Brueckner (2007b) notes, how could (32) be a priori knowable on the basis of (30) and (31) if only (30) is a priori knowable? It would seem that the conclusion of any *modus ponens* argument is a priori knowable only if both premises are a priori knowable.

Secondly, Pryor (2007: 189–96) observes that objection (II) has limited scope. For instance, it cannot accommodate the Evans/McDowell view of object- or kind-dependent thoughts according to which if S were to inhabit Dry Earth she would simply fail to think a content-bearing thought when she utters sentences containing 'water'.[16] If S knows a priori that such misfortune would afflict her were she on Dry Earth, and S also knows (30) a priori, it looks as if S has a priori knowledge of (32). Friends of this neo-Fregean view might respond with Brown (2004: Ch. 8) that S has a priori knowledge of (31) only if S can rule out a priori the possibility that she is suffering an illusion of content. But S cannot know a priori that she is not undergoing such an illusion, because if she were then she would still believe that she were not, were the question to arise. Brown here invokes (Sensitivity) from Section 6.2 – the idea that knowledge requires sensitive belief. Consequently, S cannot know (31) a priori. The problem is however that if S cannot know a priori that she is not the victim of such an illusion, it follows by (Closure) that S cannot know a priori that she is thinking a contentful thought. At this juncture, Brown recommends that (Closure) be jettisoned since it is incompatible with (Sensitivity).

Thirdly, as Gertler (2004: 46–47), Pryor (2007: 188) and Häggqvist and Wikforss (2007) remark, objection (II) concedes that S lacks comprehensive introspective knowledge of the nature of her concepts, and hence of propositions containing those concepts. The speaker can know a priori that she thinks the thought **water is wet**, but S cannot know a priori which concept is deployed in that thought. True, semantic externalists are typically happy to surrender (Epistemic Transparency) from Sections 2.4 and 5.1 – the idea that S can know a priori whether any two apprehended thoughts are distinct or identical. But what is jeopardized here is not just introspective access to such logical properties of thoughts, but introspective access to key semantic properties. For instance, prior to detailed scientific investigation of the environment, S does not know whether the concept expressed by 'water' has any descriptive content or is directly referential, which implies that prior to such investigation S knows next to nothing about its conceptual or logical connections.

Fourthly, Brown (1995) devised an even weaker constraint on concept possession, which appears to finesse objection (II) by circumventing the empirical assumption that **water** is a natural kind concept. Brown's thought is roughly that if S were in an environment containing neither water nor other speakers, then she could not possess **water** because nothing would then determine an extension for that concept:

(Weak Constraint)   If S has the concept of X, and S is agnostic about the application conditions of that concept, then either S is in an environment which contains instances of X and that concept is a natural kind concept, or S is part of a community which has the concept of X, whether or not that is a natural kind concept.

Brown's charge is that (Weak Constraint) suffices to spell trouble for the semantic externalist. Arguably, S can know a priori that she has the concept **water**, and S can also know a priori that she is unsure about its application conditions when such determinate conditions are in place. The latter follows from S's a priori knowledge that she lacks beliefs about the chemical composition of water. The speaker is thus in a position to know a priori that either she is in an environment containing water, or else there are other expert speakers in her speech community who possess **water**. But just as S intuitively cannot know a priori that water exists, she cannot intuitively know a priori that other speakers exist.

The principle of (Weak Constraint) has sparked considerable controversy. Falvey (2000: 140–42) and McLaughlin and Tye (1998b: 314–17) deny that Burge-style semantic externalists are committed to even that much. In particular, if **water** turns out to be a non-natural kind concept, S could possess that concept while being agnostic about its application conditions and yet not belong to a speech community. On their view, there simply is no external condition the obtaining of which follows a priori from the conjunction of privileged access and semantic externalism. Brown (2001) defends (Weak Constraint) by claiming that these compatibilists illicitly equate agnosticism with merely being unsure about how to apply **water** when it should rather be understood in terms of being unsure about whether **water** applies when there is a determinate fact of the matter whether that concept applies. Agnosticism thus understood is one type of incomplete understanding. Misunderstanding is another type of incomplete understanding. For instance, take Alf from Section 3.3 who misunderstands **arthritis** in that he has a mistaken view about which kinds of ailments that concept applies to. Importantly neither type of incomplete understanding seems a priori knowable. As regards agnosticism, S can know a priori that she is unsure whether a concept applies but she cannot know a priori that there is a determinate fact of the matter whether it applies. As regards misunderstanding, S cannot know a priori that her view about how a concept applies is mistaken. For instance, Alf learns that 'arthritis' is inapplicable to ailments other than the joints only after having spoken to his doctor.[17]

(III) A third objection is to pinpoint an acceptable way of embracing the a priori knowability of the conclusion (32). That there can be a class of a priori knowable, contingent statements is shown not only by such uninformative examples as 'I exist' or 'I am here now', but also by the very contents that we standardly credit ourselves with in self-knowledge. I can know a priori that I entertain the proposition **water is wet** even though I might not have done just that. So, maybe we should encompass certain informative aspects of the external world as well. Sawyer (1998) maintains there is nothing illegitimate about a priori access to such contingent features of the external world as the existence of water or other speakers. To see why, Sawyer (1998: 530) claims that according to semantic externalism S can acquire the concept **water** only if the right causal connections between S and her physical or social environment are in place. Here the relevant external facts are general – that water or other speakers exist – rather than specific – that this jug contains water or that Mary said so-and-so. But if such causal contact is necessary for the acquisition of **water**, there is no room for S possessing that concept in the absence of water or other speakers. Her concept is thus programmed in by its extension or the practices of her linguistic community, and so encodes such information about the external world. It should therefore come as no surprise that S can deduce a priori knowledge of the existence of water or other speakers from her a priori knowledge that she possesses **water**. That would only be a mystery if S could acquire that concept prior to any exposure to those features of the external world.

In response, it should first be noted that semantic externalists can allow for the possibility of possessing a natural kind concept in the absence of both instances of that natural kind and other speakers. As we saw in Section 4.1, semantic externalism is consistent with an entirely isolated scientist theorizing the existence of a compound of hydrogen and oxygen, both of which she has causally interacted with but only on separate occasions. While her chemical theory is false, she clearly does possess the concept H_2O. Secondly, it remains unclear how the mere existence of the right causal links alleviates the concern that S has no a priori access to contingent features of the external world. The fact that introspection will yield a priori knowledge only of those external features of which S could already have acquired perceptual knowledge is little comfort. If S did not in fact acquire such perceptual knowledge, then she could deploy McKinsey's recipe to come to know those features a priori for the first time.

An initially more promising way to bite the bullet is to accept Brewer's stronger claim (2000: §3) that in order for S to possess the (non-empty) concept **water**, she must already have demonstratively based knowledge of its extension. That could be perceptual-demonstrative knowledge that that water in the jug is refreshing, or else such knowledge as retained in memory but now expressed by 'the water in the jug was refreshing'. For if (30) requires that S has demonstratively based knowledge about the extension of **water**, then S is in a position to arrive at knowledge of (32) prior to inferring that conclusion from the two premises. McKinsey's recipe cannot therefore constitute an untoward source of new knowledge about contingent features of the external world – or so Brewer submits.

The first rejoinder that springs to mind is to question whether the semantic externalist is committed to Brewer's claim that if the concept **water** has an extension and S is in possession of that concept, then S must have some knowledge of its extension. What matters for individuation of **water** in cases where that concept has an extension is the obtaining of causal links between S or her fellow speakers and that extension, and not in addition that S has knowledge of those links. But even if Brewer's claim that (30) requires a posteriori knowledge of (32) is correct, that is consistent with S knowing (30) a priori, hence with S coming to know (32) a priori on the basis of knowing both (30) and (31) a priori. In that case, as Brueckner (2007b) remarks, (32) would be known both a priori and a posteriori. But the fact that (32) is also known a posteriori does not make a priori knowledge of (32) less problematic.[18]

Chapter summary

This chapter continued to explore the epistemological ramifications of semantic externalism. Focus was on how epistemological scepticism about the external world meshes with epistemological scepticism about the inner world of our mental states and their contents. Both forms of scepticism rely on the principle that knowledge is closed under known entailment: if S knows that p and that p entails q, then S knows that q. The content sceptic argues that S knows a priori that if she is thinking **water**-thoughts then she is not thinking **twin-water**-thoughts, but since S does not know a priori that she is not thinking **twin-water**-thoughts, S does not know a priori that she is thinking **water**-thoughts. Brueckner upholds the argument: S's belief that she thinks **water**-thoughts falls short of knowledge as it is under-determined by her experiential evidence. However, following Falvey and Owens and Gibbons, the alternative that S is thinking **twin-water**-thoughts is relevant but also consistent with her knowing that she thinks **water**-thoughts. Finally, Ebbs takes this content sceptical argument to be self-refuting. We then moved on to consider external world scepticism. While semantic externalism seemed to provide the basis for content scepticism, Putnam took semantic externalism to offer a swift semantic response to the external world sceptical argument: S knows that if she has hands then she is not a brain in a vat (BIV), but since S does not know that she is not a BIV, S does not know that she has hands. Those who endorse sensitivity or relevant alternatives accounts of knowledge reject the closure principle. Instead Putnam argued that if I am able to think that I am not a BIV then I am not a BIV. Since BIVs sustain no causal interactions with brains or vats, they cannot think **BIV**-thoughts. But I know a priori that I am thinking **BIV**-thoughts, and so I can deduce a priori knowledge that I am not a BIV. Various responses were adumbrated to do with the scope of the argument and whether Wright's use of the disquotation principle (I know a priori that term 'N' in my language refers to N) in setting up the argument is question-begging. While a priori knowledge of the negation of sceptical hypotheses seems pretty benign, we turned to other more troublesome cases. McKinsey argued that I know a priori via introspection that I think that water is wet, and that I know a priori via reflection on the Twin Earth argument that if I think that water is wet, then water exists. So, I can infer via (Closure) a priori knowledge that water exists. That is astonishing. Nobody can acquire armchair knowledge of contingent empirical propositions about the external world. Three responses were examined. Some deny the truth of the second premise. That premise assumes the kind-dependence of **water**-thoughts: if water did not exist I could not think **water**-thoughts. But semantic externalism is merely a claim about the external individuation of **water**-thoughts. Others, e.g. McLaughlin and Tye, maintain that the second premise is merely a posteriori knowable. I can know a priori that I think **water**-thoughts, but since I cannot know a priori that water exists, I cannot know a priori that my concept **water** is a kind-dependent, natural kind concept. Lastly, some embrace the a priori knowability of the existence of water. This bullet-biting response maintains that such knowledge is no embarrassment as the acquisition of **water** involves having perceptual-demonstrative knowledge of water.

Annotated further reading

Epistemological scepticism has traditionally been concerned to show that we lack knowledge of features of the external world. With the advent of semantic externalism, epistemologists were hopeful that a semantic response to such scepticism was forthcoming. For a recent collection of relevant articles see Keith DeRose and Ted Warfield's (eds) (1999) *Scepticism: A Contemporary Reader*. Part one of this anthology is precisely about semantic responses to epistemological scepticism, e.g. Putnam's proof that we are not brains-in-vats, and part three is about those epistemological views that entail the rejection of the closure principle. Jonathan Kvanvig's (2006) "Closure Principles" is a very useful survey of the recent debate on how best to formulate the closure principle. The following four collections all include important articles on McKinsey's argument that semantic externalism is incompatible with self-knowledge – what we called 'McKinsey's recipe': (1998) *Externalism and Self-knowledge*, chapters 6–11, edited by Peter Ludlow and Norah Martin, (1998) *Knowing Our Own Minds*, chapters 9–11, edited by Crispin Wright, Barry Smith and Cynthia Macdonald, (2003b) *New Essays on Semantic Externalism and Self-knowledge*, chapters 1–7, edited by Susana Nuccetelli, and (2004) *The Externalist Challenge*, part VI, edited by Richard Schantz. Jessica Brown's (2004) *Anti-Individualism and Knowledge* critically discusses various responses to Mckinsey's recipe in chapters 7 and 8. For a very recent, engaging exchange see Anthony Brueckner's and Michael McKinsey's contributions to *Contemporary Debates in Philosophy of Mind*, edited by Brian McLaughlin and Jonathan Cohen (2007). Kallestrup (2011) is a survey article on McKinsey's recipe.

7

MENTAL CAUSATION

7.1 The varieties of mental causation

In the preceding two chapters we have probed into the epistemological implications of semantic externalism. Here in the last chapter we will examine some metaphysical implications of this view, namely those pertaining to mental causation. Let's first ponder over the importance of the many facets of mental causation.

Suppose I accidentally touch a candle, subsequently experience a pain in my hand, and then quickly remove my hand. Intuitively, the candle causes the pain in my hand, which in turn causes the movement of my hand. After having experienced such a pain in my hand, I form on that basis the belief that touching burning candles gives rise to pain. That belief together with my desire to avoid pain then causes my future behaviour to be such that I refrain from touching burning candles. These cases illustrate *physical-to-mental* causation, *mental-to-physical* causation and *mental-to-mental* causation. At least five reasons can be adduced as to why these three kinds of causal relationships should be taken on-board.

(i) Suppose I am looking at the rain pouring down outside my office window. The light rays reflecting the rain stimulate my retinas. The rain thereby causes in me a visual experience as if it is raining. On the basis of undergoing such an experience I form the belief that it is raining. Given that my belief is both true and reliably formed I thus come to know just that. Without physical-to-mental and mental-to-mental causation, perceptual knowledge of the external world would be impossible.

(ii) I believe that Anna ate three apples for lunch and that apples are fruit. On the basis of these two beliefs, I infer, and thereby come to believe, that Anna ate three pieces of fruit for lunch. By inference one belief is causally generated by two other beliefs. Suppose also that my beliefs that Anna ate three apples for lunch and that apples are fruit amount to knowledge as they are true and reliably formed. By reasoning in the way I do I thus come to know that Anna ate three pieces of fruit for lunch.[1] Without mental-to-mental causation, knowledge by inference would be impossible.

(iii) Epiphenomenalism is the view that although the mental is caused by the physical, the mental itself is causally inefficacious with respect to both the physical and the mental. Nobody could be rationally persuaded to hold this view. Suppose the epiphenomenalist were to mount an argument in support of her view. The argument would be such that if the conclusion (the mental is causally inert) is true, then believing the conjunction of the premises cannot cause me to believe the conclusion. Something physical might prompt belief in the conclusion, but that belief would fail to be rationally based on belief in the premises. Our deductive inferences are both rational and causal in nature.

(vi) Suppose I undergo a severe pain in my knee as a result of a nasty football tackle. Leaving the field on a stretcher I utter 'the pain is in my kneecap'. Intuitively we would want to say that my pain causes my verbal phenomenal judgement. The problem is now that if my phenomenal property of being in pain were epiphenomenal, that property could not cause my judgement, and so we could hardly causally explain my judgement in terms of my pain: I said the pain is in my kneecap, because that is where I feel that pain. Without mental-to-physical causation, we are faced with the paradox of phenomenal judgement.[2]

(v) It is a truism in ordinary folk psychology that we tend to behave in such a way as to fulfil our desires if our means–end beliefs are true. Some refrain from actually behaving in ways that satisfy their desires even when their beliefs are true. Maybe they suffer from weakness of will, or maybe they are prone to known immoral desires. Not always though. I go into the pub because I desire a beer and I believe that by entering the pub I can drink one. I am subject to moral blame if I had promised to attend a meeting at the same time. Crucially, if this explanation were not causal such blame would make little sense. Without mental-to-physical causation, we cannot make sense of free human agency.

So much by way of motivating the importance of mental causation. Before pressing on to consider problems about mental causation, three general observations are worth making. Firstly, philosophers take different stances on what the *causal relata* are, i.e. what the two-place relation *cause c causes effect e* relates. Some believe in object causation, e.g. the football caused the window to shatter. Others prefer talk about event causation, e.g. the football match caused the street riot. What exactly events are is a tricky question. Davidson (1970) held that events are bare particulars, and Kim (1993a) equated events with property-exemplification, i.e. exemplifications of properties by objects at times. And others say that causation is a relation between facts, e.g. the fact that Jill drank red wine caused the fact that she has a migraine. Philosophers have variously portrayed facts as true propositions, as what makes propositions true, and as states of affairs that obtain. Some think there is a distinctive kind of agent causation, e.g. Jim caused the class to laugh. Finally, some take causes and effects to be properties, e.g. the jumper being yellow caused me to wear it. Here we must tread carefully though. If properties are universals, then properties as types can be causally relevant for effects, but only tokens of properties are candidates for causes and effects. Tokens of properties are property instances, but what are those? They could be the objects that have the properties, e.g. since I am six feet tall I am an instance of the property of being six feet tall. Or they could be tropes, i.e. abstract particulars such as my tallness. Or they could be events as property exemplifications.[3] Regardless of that dispute, there is consensus that not all properties of causes are causally relevant to their effects. A property of a cause causing some effect is causally relevant if the cause caused the effect in virtue of having that property.[4] Suppose my office window shatters as a result of Plácido Domingo singing "Flower of Scotland". The event that caused my window to brake has certain semantic properties pertaining to the lyrics, but they are causally irrelevant to the effect. Only some of the purely physical properties matter, say the pressure vibrations or other acoustic properties.[5]

Secondly, talk about mental causation is about one or both of the *causal relata* being mental, e.g. a mental event or mental-property token. There is no implication of a special kind of causation. What distinguishes purely physical causation from mental causation is merely that in the former case both *causal relata* are physical, e.g. physical events or physical-property instantiations. In this respect, mental and purely physical causation are, as Crane (1995) says, homogeneous.

Thirdly, the distinction between causation and causal explanation is crucial. As we have seen, causation is a relation between concrete external world entities such as events, facts or property instances. Causal explanation, however, is a representation in language or in thought of which such entities caused which such other entities. Causal explanation is thus a relation between sentences, statements or propositions. Nevertheless, in a wide range of cases, causation and causal explanation stand or fall together. Suppose the bottle shattered because Suzy threw a rock at it. Here the statement that the bottle shattered is the explanandum, i.e. that which is explained, and the statement that Suzy threw a rock is the explanans, i.e. that which explains.[6] If this causal explanation is true, then presumably Suzy's rock is what caused the shattering. Bill also threw a rock of the same size at the bottle, but Suzy's rock hit the bottle first. The reason it sounds odd to say that the bottle shattered because Bill threw a rock at it is that Bill's rock is not the cause of the effect. On the face of it, one causal statement 'c' explains another causal statement 'e' if and only if c causes e.

There are at least two problems about mental causation. One is about how mental states *qua mental* can cause something physical. This is a problem for dualism in the metaphysics of mind, which says that the mental is (numerically) distinct from the physical. Take property dualism. Suppose mental property M causes physical property P. The physical world is causally closed such that all physical effects have sufficient physical causes. This means that P has sufficient physical cause P*. Following property dualism, M and P* are distinct properties. But no effect has two distinct sufficient causes since that would imply a mysterious kind of causal overdetermination. So, P* excludes M as a cause of P. In short, how can a mental property cause a distinct physical property if every physical effect has a sufficient physical cause and no effect is caused twice over by distinct properties? This is called the *causal exclusion problem*, and is not our primary concern here.[7]

Another problem is about how mental states *qua contentful* can cause something physical. This problem thus assumes not only that mental states do bring about physical states, but also that they do so in virtue of their contents. Here as elsewhere attention is restricted to the truth-conditional content of propositional attitudes such as beliefs. Before delving into the details of this problem, it is worth briefly assessing that assumption. As the example of Plácido Domingo singing "Flower of Scotland" in my office highlights, not all properties of causes are causally relevant. Why then think the properties of having certain contents are causally relevant properties of beliefs and desires as opposed to various physical properties? Presumably, such mental states are physically realized by neurophysiological states, and the latter seem better candidates for causal relevance. In reply, note first that, as we saw in Section 3.3, mental states are individuated in terms of their contents. The content of my belief that today is Thursday is part of what makes it the belief that it is. Alteration in the content of a belief results in changes in the identity of the belief. The belief that today is Friday is clearly a different belief. In short, the contents of beliefs are essential to them. Note secondly that when the content of a mental state is shifted the explanatory value of that state is different. Differences in mental content provide for different causal explanations of behaviour. I switch on the TV today, because I want to watch Taggart and nothing else, and I believe that Taggart is on TV today. My belief–desire pair causally explains my behaviour. Had I believed that Taggart is on TV tomorrow, I would not have switched on the TV today. My switching on the TV today is not explained by my wanting to watch Taggart, and my belief that Taggart is on TV tomorrow. In the latter case, my belief–desire pair fails to provide a causal explanation of my behaviour. This suggests that desires and beliefs have the causal effects they have, because they have the specific contents they have.

Now we can explain the problem of how mental states can cause behaviour in virtue of their contents. This is primarily a challenge for semantic externalism. On this view, the propositional content of beliefs and desires is individuated by *distal* factors. What makes Mary's belief that water is thirst-quenching wide is an extrinsic property, such as sustaining causal encounters with water. But causation is *local*: the causes of behaviour must reside inside agents' bodies. What make Mary's arm move towards a glass of water are intrinsic neurophysiological properties. In a nutshell, how can a mental state cause some behavioural effect in virtue of having the content it has if that state's causal properties are intrinsic while its content is an extrinsic property of that state? If semantic externalism holds, how can a mental state's representational power be reconciled with its causal power? The problem can be phrased in terms of causal explanation in place of causation. The locality of causation allows us to appeal only to intrinsic properties of agents' bodies when causally explaining their behaviour, but semantic externalism dictates that mental content is determined by causal-historical factors that go beyond the boundaries of skin and skull. On this background it is hard to see how such widely individuated content could possibly play a role in causal explanations of agents' behaviour. We shall call the problem of reconciling the locality requirement on causation with the externality of mental content *the problem of causal relevance of content*.[8]

Here is an illustration. On Earth, Mary's **water**-thoughts are dependent on her, or her fellow speakers, sustaining causal-historical connections with instances of the natural kind water. As Mary's doppelgänger, i.e. internal duplicate, on Twin Earth stands in causal-historical relations to twin-water, twin-Mary thinks **twin-water**-thoughts. The different propositional contents of their respective thoughts are fixed by distal relations which they bear to their respective external environments, i.e. factors that extend spatially and temporally beyond the here and now. The way in which Mary and twin-Mary behave – drinking a glass of what they call 'water', jumping in the swimming pool, etc. – is however entirely determined by proximal factors, i.e. their internal physical make-up. The causes of the movements of their arms or legs must reside inside their bodies. Some neural processes take place in their identical brains, and then signals are sent to the relevant muscles to contract. A full account of the behavioural causes specifies only local properties about what is happening here and now. It makes no appeal to what goes on in other more or less remote parts of space-time.

7.2 The modal argument for narrow content

In presenting the problem of causal relevance of content, we talked about belief–desire pairs causing behaviour in virtue of their contents. 'Behaviour' should here be understood as *action*. Behavioural activity falls short of action if not *intentional*. My arm suddenly moving upwards as a result of a nervous twitch does not constitute a greeting, because I did not intend to greet anyone. Because the movement of my arm is not caused by intentional states, it does not count as intentional behaviour. It is merely a bodily movement. As Davidson (1971) said, an action is something an agent does that is "intentional under some description". As with tics or automatism, bodily movements caused in the wrong way fall short of being actions. They are not purposeful or goal-directed. How best to understand the role of intentions in action is a thorny question which shall not be settled here. Davidson (1963) also famously argued that the reasons for which an agent acted in the way she did are the causes of that action. Reasons explain, hence rationalize, action in virtue of causing action. So, explanations in terms of reasons for action are causal explanations. The relevant reasons are those that motivate the agent to act, and these are complexes of beliefs and desires. *Motivating reasons* facilitate causal as well as rationalizing explanation of the agent's action. As mentioned in Section 5.5, reason explanations cite belief–desire pairs as the reasons for which the agent acted as she did, and thus render her action intelligible. They contrast with *normative reasons* which are those an agent has when her action is justified. Obviously, there can be a (normative) reason for an agent to act without that being the (motivating) reason for which she acts, and in that case the former reason is non-explanatory. Suppose there is a good reason (to do with helping those in need) why you ought to donate money to Oxfam, but the reason why you donate stems from certain tax benefits. If instead you are practically rational and have the right beliefs about those normative reasons, you will act for the reason you have. So, although normative reasons primarily provide justification for the agent's action, they can also play a role in causally and rationally explaining her action.[9]

Let's now revisit the problem of causal relevance of content. A natural thought is that only narrow states can be causally efficacious. If causation is local and content-bearing mental states are causally efficacious, the causal powers of such states must supervene on intrinsic properties of individuals who are in them. As Fodor (1987: 44) says, "causal powers supervene on local structure. In the psychological case, they supervene on local neural structure". But mental states with narrow content are precisely those states that supervene on such intrinsic properties. It seems to follow that the content of mental states must be narrow if they are causally efficacious.

Suppose by way of comparison that John inserts a quarter in a vending machine. The coin has a certain size, shape and density common to quarters, but having those intrinsic properties is insufficient for being a quarter since they could be shared by a good counterfeit. A coin is a quarter only if it has the right causal history.[10] But the machine reacts only to the coin's intrinsic properties. It is insensitive to whether the coin was produced in a bona fide mint or by ingenious counterfeiters. As we shall see in Section 7.4, extrinsic properties clearly enter into causal explanations. To say that the machine broke down due to overuse is an adequate causal explanation, but that is not yet to hold the extrinsic property of being overused causally responsible for the breakdown. Be that as it may. The analogy is that humans are in some respect similar to vending machines. We produce behavioural responses to incoming sensory stimuli wholly in virtue of our internal make-up. If the content of our mental states is individuated in terms of causal-historical relations to our environment, then these distal relations play no role in generating our behaviour. Only narrow states could have a chance of playing such a role, because proximal features of our physical bodies fix only such states.

The foregoing is somewhat sketchy, but Fodor (1987, 1991) attempted to mount a more compelling case for narrow content based on considerations about how mental states are taxonomized for the purpose of causal explanation of behaviour in cognitive psychology. The remainder of this section elaborates on this argument and the ensuing notion of narrow content, but first it is worth pausing to briefly sketch the background against which Fodor presents his argument. The received view was that cognitive psychology must make essential explanatory appeal to beliefs and other mental states which are individuated by their content. Stich (1978) and others then argued that such theory is committed to incompatible claims. On the one hand, it is a methodological principle that individuals differ in psychological explanatory states – states that explain behaviour in virtue of their content – only if they differ in some internal physical way, but on the other hand the Twin Earth argument, or an extension thereof, shows that internal physical duplicates may be in different content-bearing mental states. Stich's (1983) own solution was to recommend that cognitive psychology abandon the appeal to content-individuated, explanatory states. Owens (1987), Burge (1989) and others denied instead that cognitive psychology is constrained by the methodological principle. If behaviour is intentionally characterized then individuals may differ in psychological explanatory states even though they are indistinguishable in terms of their internal physical features, i.e. internal physical duplicates may be in different psychological states that explain different behaviours, thus understood. Cognitive psychology can thus allow for such states to be individuated by their wide contents. In contrast, Fodor's argument can be seen as an attempt to resolve this tension within cognitive psychology by invoking narrow content. More precisely, Fodor's original idea (1982) was that while the truth-conditions of ordinary propositional attitude ascriptions fail to supervene on internal physical features, psychological explanatory states do supervene on such features. Such states are individuated by a kind of narrow, non-propositional content. The belief content that explains behaviour is firmly in the head, but such content does not determine truth-conditions. Truth-conditions are not fixed by what is in the head.[11]

Fodor (1987: 42) starts out by defining *methodological individualism* as "the doctrine that psychological states are individuated *with respect to their causal powers*". This means that any two such distinct states M_1 and M_2 have different causal powers: M_1 is capable of causing behaviour B_1 and M_2 is capable of causing B_2 if and only if M_1 and M_2 are distinct. The rationale for this doctrine is that psychology aims at causal explanation, and should therefore be methodologically constrained to adopt taxonomies which are sensitive only to the causal powers of the states classified. We need a scientific taxonomy that makes distinctions between mental states only insofar as they have different causal powers. Methodological individualism contrast with *methodological solipsism* which is the stronger doctrine that "psychological states are individuated *without respect to their semantic evaluations*" (1987: 42).[12] This means that belief states M_1 and M_2 are not individuated by their truth-conditions: despite M_1 and M_2 differing in truth-value in some contexts, they could well count as identical belief states. Semantic evaluation is an external matter: whether Mary's belief that water is an abundant liquid is true depends on how things are water-wise in her environment. Methodological solipsism thus rules out such extrinsic properties from individuating mental states. Methodological individualism, however, is consistent with mental states being individuated extrinsically. It requires merely that individuating properties are those that affect the causal powers of the mental states in question. So, extrinsic properties can individuate mental states when they make a difference to those states' causal powers. Fodor (1987: 33–34, 1991: 5) offers the following modal argument in support of methodological individualism:

(1)   Mary on Earth and twin-Mary on twin-Earth are molecular duplicates.
(2)   Therefore their (actual and counterfactual) behaviours are identical inrelevant respects.
(3)   Therefore the causal powers of their mental states are identical in relevant respects.
(4)   Therefore Mary and twin-Mary belong to the same natural kind for purposes of psychological explanation, and methodological individualism is true.

On the face of it, the second premise (2) seems the most contentious. Granted, Mary's behaviour and twin-Mary's behaviour are identical under some intentional descriptions: they both reach for a watery stuff. Call behaviour common to doppelgängers 'narrow behaviour'. But their behaviour will differ under other such descriptions: Mary reaches for water, but twin-Mary reaches for twin-water. Call behaviour not shared by doppelgängers 'wide behaviour'. It looks as if only appeal to wide states can explain differences in wide behaviour.

In response, Fodor (1991: 6, 14) acknowledges the causal power of wide states to cause wide behaviour. These mental states are by no means causally idle. But consider first *non-intentionally described, wide behaviour*: Mary gets (or grabs or drinks) water but twin-Mary gets (or grabs or drinks) twin-water. Their wide behaviours differ when non-intentionally characterized, but this is compatible with their wide states playing no distinctive causal role. For judging whether the causal powers of these states differ, certain counterfactuals across contexts must be assessed. Causal powers are dispositional properties that govern interaction with actual as well as possible environments. It is true that: had Mary with her **water**-states been whisked off to Twin Earth, she would have got twin-water, and also that: had twin-Mary with her **twin-water**-states been whisked off to Earth, she would have got water. For any context (Earth, Twin Earth, etc.), if they were in that context, their non-intentional wide behaviour would be similar. With regards to such behaviour these states have identical causal powers. The only difference is that Mary and twin-Mary actually inhabit distinct environments.

Now consider instead *intentionally described wide behaviour*: Mary reaches (or searches or drills) for water, but twin-Mary reaches (or searches or drills) for twin-water. Here Mary is trying to get water, and her behaviour counts as trying for water only if it is caused by her **water**-states. Likewise, twin-Mary is trying to get twin-water, and her behaviour counts as trying for twin-water only if it is caused by her **twin-water**-states. In this case, the counterfactuals across contexts are to no avail. For since Mary will be in **water**-states on both Earth and Twin Earth (at least for a while), her behaviour will count as a trying for water on both Earth and Twin Earth. Similarly, since twin-Mary will be in **twin-water**-states on both Twin Earth and Earth (at least for a while), her behaviour will count as a trying for twin-water on both Earth and Twin Earth. Their behaviours thus remain relevantly different under these wide intentional descriptions even when we consider them located in different contexts. As we can put it, **water**-states invariably cause water-behaviour, and **twin-water**-states invariably cause twin-water-behaviour.

To solve this problem Fodor (1987: 43, 1991: 19–21) asks us to contrast wide content mental properties with the property of being a planet. This latter property is also an extrinsic property yet is one that science can use to classify objects.[13] A chunk of rock constitutes a planet only if it produces Keplerian orbits. An intrinsically identical duplicate of a planet is not a planet if it does not revolve around a star in the way Kepler discovered. Being a planet is a property with causal powers in virtue of its ability to produce Keplerian orbits. But given that planets might not have had Keplerian orbits, it is contingent that being a planet has these, or indeed any, causal powers. Not so in the case of wide states. As with Mary and twin-Mary, **water**-states cause water-behaviour and **twin-water**-states cause twin-water-behaviour. But having **water**-states rather than **twin-water**-states are not causally responsible for water-behaviour rather than twin-water-behaviour, i.e. the difference in states is not a causal power in virtue of its being causally responsible for water-behaviour rather than twin-water-behaviour. The reason is that it is conceptually necessary that **water**-states cause water-behaviour and that **twin-water**-states cause twin-water-behaviour. Water-behaviour is just behaviour caused by **water**-states, and twin-water-behaviour is just behaviour caused by **twin-water**-states. But as Hume taught us, what causal powers something has is determined by what contingent, not conceptual, connections it enters into. The upshot is that the difference between the causes counts as a difference in causal powers only if the difference between the causes is contingently connected to the difference between the effects. This happens in the case of being a planet and being merely a chunk of rocks, but not in the case of **water**-states and **twin-water**-states. Consequently, the difference between those latter states is not a causal power in virtue of its responsibility for those behavioural properties which are taxonomically relevant for purposes of causal explanation in psychology, i.e. that difference does not entail a difference in natural kinds for explanatory purposes.[14]

By showing that distinct wide states share causal powers so that differences between such states are irrelevant for purposes in psychology, the modal argument makes an indirect case for the existence of narrow states. In particular, the argument does not speak directly to methodological solipsism. Nevertheless, Fodor (1987: 43–44) explicitly endorses this view according to which content-bearing mental states are not individuated by their truth-conditions.[15] Suppose both Mary and twin-Mary utter the sentence 'there is water in the jug'. What Mary said is true if and only if there is H_2O in the jug, but what twin-Mary said is true if and only if there is XYZ in the jug. So, the thoughts they express by those utterances differ in truth-conditions. And if those thoughts have different truth-conditions, they will also differ in truth-value. If there is actually H_2O in the jug, Mary's thought is true but twin-Mary's thought is false. Yet those thoughts are identical on the assumption that they supervene on the intrinsic properties common to Mary and twin-Mary. And if those thoughts are identical, so are their contents. Changes in the content of a mental state imply changes in the identity of that state. This means that although the content of Mary's thought is identical to the content of twin-Mary's thought, the two contents differ in truth-value. So, it looks as if content does not determine truth-value – or extension generally. But content supposedly supervenes on extension such that differences in extension entail differences in content. That was Putnam's problem about Twin Earth.

Fodor's remedy (1987: 46–48) is to make the connection between content and extension context-relative such that content determines extension relative to a context. A context comprises those external features that determine what the thought is about, e.g. sustaining causal encounters with water is what determines that her **water**-thought is about H_2O. Fodor then proposes to think of the content of a thought as a function from a context and a thought onto the thought's truth-condition in that context. That is what narrow content is. The wide content of a thought, however, is truth-conditional, and can only be determined once the narrow content is specified and a context is fixed. So, the wide, truth-conditional content of Mary's thought and twin-Mary's thought are different due to the difference in contexts. But the narrow contents of their thoughts are identical, because they assign the same mapping of thought and context onto truth-conditions. Mary's thought on Earth is true if and only if there is H_2O in the jug, but her thought is true on Twin Earth if and only if there is XYZ in the jug. Similar for twin-Mary's thought.[16]

Narrow content, on this view, is not subject to semantic evaluation. The pressing worry is then that such content is not genuine. Content represents the world as being a certain way, and so is true if the world is that way. Content that cannot be assessed for truth is at most potential content: it is what delivers genuinely semantic content once a context is fixed. How might Fodor bolster his notion of narrow content? He explicitly rejects the identification of narrow content with Putnam's *stereotypes*. The latter are not by Putnam intended to determine extension, but narrow content is meant to do so albeit relative to contexts. Moreover, Fodor eschews any attempt to come up with sentences that actually specify what narrow content amounts to – what content Mary and twin-Mary have in common in virtue of which their thoughts have different truth-conditions when embedded in different contexts. The content of such sentences as actually uttered by us Earthlings is all wide since they are uttered in a specific context, namely Earth. What can be said using sentences is semantically evaluable in a context-independent way, but what Mary and twin-Mary have in common is not. Consequently, narrow content is somewhat inexpressible. All we can do by way of approximating narrow content is specifying what truth-conditions a thought actually has, and what truth-conditions it would have were the context different.

7.3 The doppelgänger challenge

In Section 7.2 we examined Fodor's modal argument which aimed to show that wide states have no distinctive causal power. In this section we will dwell on arguments levelled at the causal explanatory power of object-dependent mental states.

As mentioned in Section 7.1, in ordinary folk psychology, we causally explain an agent's intentional behaviour using the following desire–belief principle: if S desires F and believes that doing A will help secure F, then *ceteris paribus* S will do A. Suppose my doppelgänger and I are confronted with distinct yet subjectively indistinguishable apples – call them 'apple$_1$' and 'apple$_2$' respectively. For all we can tell by looking at them, they are identical apples. I reach for that apple$_1$, because I desire something wholesome, and I believe that that apple$_1$ is wholesome. My doppelgänger reaches for that apple$_2$, because she desires something wholesome, and she believes that that apple$_2$ is wholesome. As we saw in Section 4.1, perceptual-demonstrative thoughts are not only widely individuated, they are also object-dependent: the thought **that apple$_1$ is wholesome** is individuated in terms of the demonstratively identified apple about which I am thinking, but is also available for me to think only if apple$_1$ is actually there for me to demonstrate. Moreover, since my doppelgänger and I are presented with distinct apples, our behaviours differ if widely described in terms of those apples. As said in Section 7.2, our wide behaviours differ when relevant features of our environments do. So, the example seems to show that object-dependent states can causally explain wide behaviour.

The semantic internalist need not claim that object-dependent states are explanatorily idle. All she needs to show is that such states are explanatorily redundant: whatever they do explain is equally well explained by narrow states in conjunction with relevant features of the environment. This in essence is the so-called *doppelgänger challenge*.[17] Obviously, narrow states causally explain narrow behaviour, i.e. behaviour shared by doppelgängers. I reach for an apple, because I desire something wholesome, and I believe that apples are wholesome. Similarly, my doppelgänger reaches for an apple, because she desires something wholesome, and she believes that apples are wholesome. Neither of our behaviours makes reference to specific features of our respective environments. And the shared content of our mental states would be available regardless of which apple is being reached for. Indeed that common content is object-independent: we would both be in those states with that content were we to perceptually hallucinate the existence of an apple.

Narrow states do not all by themselves causally explain wide behaviour. My desire for something wholesome together with my belief that apples are wholesome cannot explain why I reach for that apple$_1$ as opposed to that apple$_2$. But those mental states, in conjunction with the relevant external facts, do explain wide behaviour. I reach for that apple$_1$ rather than that apple$_2$, because apple$_1$ is the one with which I am actually confronted. Had I instead been presented with apple$_2$, I would have reached for that one, assuming my mental states stay fixed. So, while my object-dependent states explain the way I actually behave, my narrow states explain the way I would behave if I had been in a different environment. But once the actual environment is known, we have an explanation of the way I actually behave in terms of my narrow states. On this *dual-component conception of causal explanation*, object-dependent states have no distinctive explanatory role: a combination of narrow states together with pertinent environmental features will equally well explain wide behaviour.

The foregoing is somewhat sketchy, but there are ways to sharpen the charge that object-dependent states are superfluous in the causal explanation of behaviour. Noonan envisages two cases: an actual case (A) in which S, based on a veridical perception, lashes out at a tiger above her, and a counterfactual case (C) in which S, based on a perceptual hallucination, lashes out into thin air. Noonan (1993: 285–88) then mounts the following redundancy argument:[18]

(5)   What explain S's behaviour in (A) are her object-dependent states containing the perceptual-demonstrative concept **that tiger**.

(6)   What explain S's behaviour in (C) are her object-independent states containing the concept **there is a tiger**.

(7)   S's object-dependent states in (A) are unavailable in (C), but S's object-independent states in (C) are also available in (A).

(8)   S's behaviour in (C) is rationally explicable by reference to S's object-independent states.

(9)   Reference to S's object-independent states in (C) suffices to explain S's behaviour in (C).

(10)   So, reference to S's object-independent states in (C) suffices to explain S's behaviour in (A).

(11)   So, reference to the additional object-dependent states in (A) is redundant.

Note that the redundancy argument rules out neither the existence nor the causal efficacy of object-dependent states. What it shows is merely that such states are explanatorily redundant if they exist. Here are two objections:

(I) The inference from (9) to (10) assumes that the behaviours in (A) and (C) are identical. But while S makes exactly the same bodily movements in (A) and (C), their behaviours differ under some intentional descriptions: to hit a tiger is distinct from lashing out wildly into thin air.

In response, Noonan takes that behavioural difference to be merely extrinsic: S lashes out in both situations but only in (A) does she make contact with a tiger. As S's narrow behaviour in (C) can be explained by S's object-independent states in (C), S's wide behaviour in (A) can also be explained by those same states, together with the presence of the tiger. This response thus assumes that wide behaviour is causally explained by the conjunction of object-independent states and pertinent environmental features. But as Crawford (1998) has argued, there are problems with this dual-component conception of causal explanation. Let (C*) be a counterfactual case in which S suffers a *veridical hallucination*: S hallucinates a tiger above him yet luckily manages to make contact with a tiger when she lashes out. Intuitively, S's intentional wide behaviour in (A) is distinct from S's intentional wide behaviour in (C*) in that only in (A) did S deliberately lash out at that tiger. But the dual-component conception cannot distinguish the two cases: the causal explanation will in both cases consist in citation of S's object-independent states together with the presence of the tiger. That allows for an explanation of why, as in both (A) and (C*), S lashed out at that tiger, but not of why, as in (A) only, S intentionally lashed out at that tiger. To explain the latter appeal must be made to S's object-dependent states. So, to account for the difference in intentional wide behaviour between (A) and (C*) such states must be invoked.[19]

(II) Premise (10) talks about S's object-independent states in (C) being sufficient to explain the behaviour in (A). But that is compatible with S's object-dependent states in (A) being what sufficiently explains the behaviour in (A). Just as being causally sufficient is distinct from being a sufficient cause, being sufficient for a causal explanation is distinct from being a sufficient causal explanation. Suppose I form the desire to use the next available computer, whichever that is, in the computing lap. When number 7 suddenly becomes vacant I form the desire to use that computer. Then I take a seat and log on. In conjunction with certain beliefs, my behaviour is sufficiently causally explained by the latter desire, which causally pre-empts the former desire, but the former desire would have sufficiently causally explained my behaviour had the latter desire not done so.

In reply, Noonan points to a disanalogy between the two cases. In the computer case, either one of the two desires might have been present without the other. But in the tiger case, it could not be that the concept **there is a tiger** is unavailable when S entertains the perceptual-demonstrative concept **that tiger**. So, the object-dependent state does not causally pre-empt the object-independent state. Now, Noonan adduces nothing in support of the claim in (7) that S's object-independent states in (C) are also available in (A). Be that as it may. There are other cases of causal pre-emption in which there is a dependency between the putative causes. Suzy and Bill both throw a rock towards a bottle. Bill throws his rock first, but Suzy's rock hits the bottle first since she throws much faster than Bill. And Suzy only throws her rock if Bill throws his first. So, Suzy's rock is the cause of the shattering, but Bill's rock is causally sufficient. Had Suzy not thrown her rock, Bill's rock would have caused the bottle to shatter. Yet Suzy would not have thrown her rock had Bill not thrown his rock.

Suppose the redundancy argument is right, and that object-dependent states are explanatorily superfluous. Premise (6) says that the concept **there is a tiger** is object-independent, but presumably **tiger** is a natural kind concept and therefore subject to a Twin Earth argument. At this juncture the proponent of the redundancy argument might concede that **tiger** is not shared by doppelgängers yet maintain its object-independence. Recall the distinction from Section 4.1 between weak and strong semantic externalism. As the redundancy argument would then be compatible with concepts having wide but object-independent contents, it would pose no immediate threat to the indispensability of wide states in causal explanations. The redundancy argument would simply provide no support for narrow content. Alternatively, the friend of that argument might try to spell out **tiger** in terms of purely descriptive properties: **the yellow-brown, black-striped, carnivorous, maneless feline**. Let's scrutinize this proposal. The thought is that not only is the content of this descriptive concept narrow, it is also fine-grained enough for purposes of psychological explanation. It specifies how the possessor of that concept conceives of tigers, and is therefore suitable to appear in belief–desire explanations of why she behaves the way she does when tigers are involved. Semantic internalists typically take narrow content to be what essentially plays a certain *cognitive role* in our psychological lives. It is content that facilitates causal explanation of our sayings and doings.

Nevertheless, as we saw in Sections 2.2 and 2.3, there are ample difficulties. Firstly, on the basis of what are some but not other descriptive properties selected for inclusion in the narrow content of the concept **tiger**? For instance, why leave out being furry, animate, indigenous to India, and fierce? Intuitively, being animate is definitive of 'tiger', but being indigenous to India is not. Tigers are necessarily animals, but might not have been indigenous to India. Where and how is the line drawn between what defines 'tiger' and what is empirically known for certain about tigers? Secondly, pretty much all of these descriptive properties that supposedly constitute the narrow content of **tiger** would most certainly get the extension of 'tiger' wrong. Think of actual or possible albino tigers, stripeless tigers and maned tigers.

In response, the semantic internalist could leave out all the superficial properties, and embrace only the essential ones. But if only such properties as being an animal, carnivorous or feline are included, the *cognitive content* of **tiger** cannot be accounted for, where that is content suitable to appear in causal explanation of behaviour. Speakers conceptualize tigers differently from leopards and panthers, but leopards and panthers are also carnivorous felines. Moreover, 'animal', 'carnivorous' and 'feline' are themselves natural kind terms susceptible to Twin Earth arguments. The relevant properties can of course be restricted even further to include only those that specify the essential genetic code for tigerhood. This will get the extension right by including albino tigers and excluding leopards. But these properties fail to capture the cognitive content. Surely speakers could possess **tiger** without knowing anything about the genetic make-up of tigers. Scientific essences are not widely known by ordinary speakers who competently master **tiger**.

Let's try a different tack at construing the content of S's mental states in (C) so as to vindicate their narrow content. Contrast with the perceptual-demonstrative concept **that tiger**. One proposal is that the narrow content of these states includes the character associated with the demonstrative expression 'that tiger'. Characters are linguistic meanings which speakers know when they grasp indexical or demonstrative expressions. As mentioned in Sections 2.3 and 4.1, while characters are functions from contexts of utterance to propositional contents in those contexts, propositional contents are in turn functions from circumstances of evaluation to referents, extensions or truth-values. When it comes to indexical expressions, propositional content is context-dependent, and thus not shared by doppelgängers.

Which singular proposition is expressed by an utterance of 'that tiger is fearsome' depends on which tiger is demonstratively identified. If tiger$_1$ is what S points to, then S expresses the singular proposition **tiger$_1$ is fearsome**. If tiger$_2$ is what S's doppelgänger twin-S demonstratively identifies, then twin-S expresses the singular proposition **tiger$_2$ is fearsome**. But characters are context-independent and thus shared by doppelgängers. The character of 'that' maps any context onto the demonstratively identified object in that context. Regardless of whether tiger$_1$ or tiger$_2$ is the contextually salient tiger, 'that tiger is fearsome' as used by S and twin-S is associated with the character **the demonstratively identified tiger is fearsome**.

Perry (1993) and Kaplan (1989) argued that the *cognitive significance* of a content-bearing mental state consists in its character (what Perry called 'sense') rather than its singular propositional content (what Perry called 'thought'). If Paul utters 'I am about to be attacked by a bear', and Peter utters 'you are about to be attacked by a bear', they express the same singular proposition **Paul is about to be attacked by a bear** containing Paul and the property of being about to be attacked by a bear as constituents. But they do so under different characters, namely **the speaker is about to be attacked by a bear** and **the hearer is about to be attacked by a bear**. Put differently, Paul and Peter believe the same thing in different ways. Consequently, they behave differently. Paul rolls up in a ball and lies still. Peter fetches the park warden. But if Peter and Paul both utter 'I am about to be attacked by a bear', then they express different singular propositions: **Paul is about to be attacked by a bear** and **Peter is about to be attacked by a bear**. However, they do so under the same character: **the speaker is about to be attacked by a bear**. In other words, Paul and Peter believe different things in the same way. Accordingly, they behave alike in that both roll up in a ball. In short, same singular propositional content with different character will imply different behaviour, but different singular propositional contents with the same character will imply same behaviour. So, it looks like only character plays an explanatory role, at least under some intentional descriptions.

In reply, Segal (2000: 108) objects that characters are too coarse-grained to play the role of cognitive content. Compare: 'yesterday', 'the day before a present utterance of this sentence' and 'yesterday, or if today is Sunday, the most recent Saturday'. These three expressions map any context onto the same referent, but they obviously have different cognitive significance. To think it was raining yesterday need not involve any thoughts about Sunday or about uttering a sentence. This means that these thoughts will give rise to different kinds of verbal or physical behaviour.

Another problem is whether *general concepts* such as **water** or **arthritis** have any obvious character. Any competent speaker knows that 'I' picks out the speaker of the context, but what about 'water'? Kaplan (1989) allows for indexical expressions to have a *context-sensitive* character in that their propositional content varies with context of utterance, but insists that non-indexical expressions have a *fixed character* since the same content is invoked in all such contexts. If 'water' is non-indexical, it will have the same character as 'H_2O': both will map any context onto the same referent. That would prevent their characters from being cognitively significant, because **water**-thoughts and **H_2O**-thoughts give rise to different kinds of behaviour.

Suppose instead 'water' is construed as short for 'the actual watery stuff', where 'actual' is an indexical that picks out the world of the context of utterance. Suppose also that the parameters of contexts of utterance include a *centred world*, i.e. a world with a designated speaker and environment. Then 'water' has something like a context-sensitive character consisting in a function from such an extended context to referents. Assuming 'H_2O' incorporates no such indexical element, its character will be fixed. Given that 'water' and 'H_2O' will then be associated with distinct characters, these may then constitute cognitive contents. This proposal bears resemblance to Chalmers' notion (2002, 2003, 2011) of an epistemic intension of a term as a mapping of worlds considered as actual onto referents in those worlds. As explained in Section 4.3, the epistemic intensions of 'water' and 'H_2O' are clearly different, and so can serve the purpose of being cognitively significant and hence explanatorily relevant.

However, Segal's problem (2000: 111) remains that even context-sensitive characters are not suitably fine-grained to play the role of cognitive content. Suppose 'water' is short for 'the actual watery stuff'. This gets the reference right on Earth and on a counterfactual Twin Earth. But so does 'the actual watery stuff that is or is not H_2O'. Importantly, these two rigidified descriptions have the same context-sensitive character, because they yield the same mapping of extended contexts or worlds considered as actual onto referents. They pick out H_2O if Earth is considered actual, but XYZ if Twin Earth is considered actual, and nothing if Dry Earth is considered actual. Yet they have different cognitive contents. Someone might competently think that water is wet without having any thoughts containing the concept **H_2O**. Consequently, thoughts involving **the actual watery**

stuff and thoughts involving **the actual watery stuff that is or is not H$_2$O** will give rise to different kinds of behaviour.

7.4 The explanatory value of wide content

So far we have been concerned with the causal relevance and explanatory power of wide-content or object-dependent states. The semantic externalist might try to show that these problems afflict narrow-content states too. In Section 4.5 the contention was that not even narrow content is intrinsic. Narrow content supervenes on intrinsic properties, and is thus shared by doppelgängers. Wide and narrow content are both extrinsic but in importantly different ways. While wide content has a particular world-dependency, narrow content merely has a general world-dependency in much the same way dispositional properties do. For a sugar cube to be water-soluble is for the environment in general to be such that it would dissolve if immersed in water. A solute retains its solubility even if never dissolved in any particular solvent. But only local or intrinsic properties are causally efficacious. What makes my arm move is a bunch of neurological and physiological properties. The problem about causal relevance of content thus seems to generalize to narrow content thus understood.

If the semantic internalist could somehow establish the causal efficacy of dispositional properties, she might therefore be able to avoid this problem. How so? Dispositional properties such as solubility or fragility are defined in terms of eliciting certain outputs given certain inputs. But they are also (always or typically) grounded by categorical base properties. Distinguish between *first- and second-order properties*. Second-order properties are those of having some first-order properties that stand in certain causal relations to inputs, outputs and possibly one another. To be clear, a second-order property is not a property of a property, but a property of the object that instantiates the first-order property. An object has a second-order property just in case it has a first-order property that plays a certain causal role. The second-order property is the *role-property*, and the first-order property is the *filler-property*. Take solubility. The role-property is that of having a property that causes solutes to dissolve if immersed in a solvent. The filler property is the microstructural property which plays that role, e.g. when a sugar cube is placed in water intermolecular bonding results in the dissolution of that cube.

Dispositional properties are often seen as identical to the role properties. Sugar and salt share the dispositional property of being water-soluble. What these solutes have in common is the property of having a property that causes solution when put in water. But they share that same role property in virtue of distinct microstructural filler properties. This raises a problem about how dispositional properties can be causally efficacious or explanatory. In particular, they seem not to cause the effects in terms of which they are defined. Suppose the property of being fragile is that of having a property that causes breaking if dropped. To say the glass broke when dropped because the glass is fragile is then to say that the glass broke when dropped because the glass has a property that causes it to break when dropped. That sounds odd. The filler properties do all the causal work. Better to say that the glass broke when dropped because the glass has a certain molecular bonding property. What is causally responsible for the shattering is this microstructural property together with the dropping. Or take Block's example (1990: 155–56). What provokes the bull is the redness of the bullfighter's cape, i.e. it is the first-order property of being red which causes the bull's anger.[20] The cape also has the property of being provocative. This is the second-order property of having a first-order property, e.g. redness, which causes anger in the bull. But the provocativeness of the cape causes no anger in the bull. The bull is simply too stupid for that. At most it might cause an animal rights group to take action against bullfighting. So, the lesson is that second-order role properties are not causally efficacious of the effects in terms of which they are defined.[21]

Even if dispositional properties are deemed causally inefficacious, there is no doubt that such properties frequently enter into causal explanations in science. Following Richard Feynman, what caused the space shuttle *Challenger* to blow up was the failure of an O-ring seal in one of the solid rocket boosters at lift-off. These O-rings are used to prevent hot gas from escaping and damaging other parts, but this particular O-ring failed to expand with the rest of the booster parts when the temperatures fell. So, Feynman explained the disaster in terms of the loss of elasticity at low temperatures of that O-ring. Being elastic is a dispositional property of an object to return to its original shape after the stress that made it deform is removed. Think of a rubber band. Non-elastic objects are rigid by way of resisting deformation. So, being rigid is a dispositional property of an object not to bend, fold or flex under an applied force. These dispositional properties are causally relevant in some sense. Feynman was right just in case the basis of the O-ring's rigidity at low temperature caused the disaster. Jackson (1996: 397) suggests that causal explanations by dispositional properties provide two kinds of information: (i) the effect was caused by the categorical basis of the disposition, and (ii) the effect is one of the outputs in terms of which the disposition is defined. The kind of information described by (ii) is required because some base properties can ground more than one disposition, e.g. electrical and thermal conductivity in metals share the same categorical basis. What Feynman discovered was that the categorical basis of the rigidity caused the disaster, and the disaster resulted from the kind of output distinctive of rigidity: the O-ring failed to expand after compression and its failure led to the disaster.

Now let's return to narrow contents. How can the causal efficacy of narrow states be vindicated if such content is best viewed as dispositional in nature? Suppose belief-ascribing sentences are defined extrinsically in terms of sensory inputs and behavioural outputs: 'S believes that p' is true if and only if S is in a physical state which causes characteristic behavioural output given a certain sensory stimuli. That is a thesis about the truth-conditions of such sentences, and as such does not speak to the metaphysical question of which state is identical to the mental state in question. One option is to identify a narrow (belief) state with a second-order role state: the state of being in a physical state that plays that causal role. The semantic internalist might then assimilate what Jackson says about dispositional properties to narrow states. That will preserve the explanatory power of narrow states, but rob them of any causal power to produce the effects in terms of which they are defined. All the causal work will be carried out by the first-order filler states. To settle the metaphysical question in a way that underpins the causal efficacy of narrow states, they should instead be identified with these filler states. This is not to say that mental states are second-order states which are identical to first-order physical states, but rather that 'S believes that p' refers to these physical states. In effect, this amounts to a version of the mind–body identity theory: mental states are identical to physical states of the brain (and body). Since such neuro-physiological states are local features, there is no mystery about how they can be causally efficacious in bringing about behaviour.[22]

In the remainder of this section, we will briefly discuss three ways for the semantic externalist to strike back. The first is due to Williamson. Assume with him that propositional knowledge – knowledge that p – is a *sui generis* mental state, not decomposable into true belief plus something else. Knowledge is factive: S knows that p only if p is true. This means that when p characterizes the external world knowledge will be a wide state solely in virtue of the attitude in question. Indeed just as there are object- and kind-dependent mental states, knowledge is a fact-dependent mental state. Contrast with beliefs which are non-factive: it is possible for S to believe a falsehood. If belief states are wide, they are so in virtue of their content. Williamson (2000: 60–64) propounds that knowledge plays an irreducible role in causal explanation of behaviour. Consider this explanation: John dug up the treasure because he knew that it was buried under the tree (and he wanted to get rich). Wide behaviour is explained by the wide state of knowing. Substituting 'believe' for 'know' weakens the explanation for it does not entail that the treasure was where he believed it to be. The explanans – John believes that it was buried under the tree – does less to raise the probability of the explanandum – John dug up the treasure. Williamson (2000: 62, 86–87) suggests a different response, namely to substitute 'believe truly' for 'know' in the original explanation. To be sure, if John believes truly that the treasure is under the tree, the explanation does entail that the treasure is where he believes it to be. But there are supposedly also counterexamples to this type of explanation: a burglar spends all night ransacking a house, because he knows that there is a diamond in the house. Substituting 'believes truly' for 'knows' entails loss of explanatory power. The reason is that his true belief may have been derived from the false premise that the diamond was under the bed when in fact it was in a drawer. Upon discovering that the diamond was not under the bed, the burglar would give up his true belief, and thus abandon his search. Not so if he knows that the diamond is in the house.

One might object to this last case as follows. When substituting 'believes truly' for 'knows', the agent's other mental attitudes should be fixed. But in this case, the burglar's true belief is supposed to derive from a false belief, which his knowledge could not derive from. So, the difference in explanatory power is due to a difference in these other mental states. Not just any isolated true belief will do the explanatory job equally well. If knowledge can explain a piece of behaviour, then so can a corresponding true belief provided all other pertinent mental states remain the same. For instance, if the burglar's knowledge that there is a diamond in the house is based on testimony that somewhere there is a diamond in the house, his true belief based on the very same testimony will also make him search the house all night.[23]

The second rejoinder on behalf of semantic externalism is due to Jackson and Pettit (1988, 1990). They proposed that causal explanations cite features that *program* without actually *producing* anything. Here is one of their examples (1988, 397–98). Suppose object X is pressed into damp clay. The clay is allowed to harden with the impression of X's shape recorded in it.

Object Y is then placed in the impression and fits perfectly. Why is that? Here is a process explanation in terms of a narrow state of the clay: X left a round impression of 5 cm in diameter in the clay and Y fitted the impression because it too is 5 cm in diameter. Having a round impression of 5 cm in diameter is a property the clay shares with all its doppelgängers. Here is a program explanation in terms of a broad state of the clay: Y fitted the impression, because the impression was caused by an object that has the same shape as Y. Having an impression caused by an object which is the same shape as Y is not a property the clay shares with all its doppelgängers. The first explanation tells us which particular shapes were actually involved, and thus yields a sense in which the particular shapes do matter, whereas the second tells us what matters is that X and Y have the same shape, and thus yields a sense in which the particular shapes do not matter. Of course Y fits all the duplicates of the clay – even those in which the impressions are not caused by an object with the same shape as Y. What the program explanation says is that if we vary the shape of Y and of the object causing the impression but keep constant their relationship, we still get a snug fit.

By analogy, explanations that cite wide states are program explanations. The speaker S reaches for a particular glass because she has the wide content belief that that glass is desirable. The glass has a bunch of descriptive properties: being a certain colour, shape, distance and direction from S. Call these 'the F'. What actually causes S to reach for the F is S's narrow content belief that the F is desirable – assuming the glass being the F causes S to believe that the F is desirable. The F is that glass, so what actually causes S to reach for that glass is S's narrow content belief that the F is desirable. But had the glass had slightly different descriptive properties – call them 'the G' – then S would have believed that the G is desirable – assuming the glass being the G causes S to believe that the G is desirable. And then that belief would have caused S to reach for the G. Because the G would then have been that glass, S would then have reached for that glass. So, there is an aspect of S's behaviour – reaching for that glass – which remains constant under a range of possibilities about which narrow states do the causing.

One problem with the foregoing is that although wide states may play an irreducible role in some causal explanation, they are devoid of causal efficacy. According to this proposal, all the causal work is done by narrow states – the broad states only come along for the ride. One could reply with Burge (1993b) that our concept of causality is fundamentally explanatory in that causally relevant properties are those that figure in the best causal explanations. Our understanding of mental causation gains purchase only from our understanding of mentalistic explanation. Since wide states figure in causal program explanations, they must be deemed genuinely causal.[24]

The last proposal is due to Dretske (1988, 1993b). It relies on a distinction between *structuring and triggering causes*. Here is one of his examples. By pressing a key on the keyboard, S moves the curser on a computer screen. Pressure on the key is the triggering cause of cursor movement. Knowing this, suppose S asks why the cursor moves when pressing the key. Now S is looking for a structuring cause. She wants to know what caused the machine to occupy a state in which pressing the key has this effect. The causal explanation will be given in terms of what produced the hardware conditions, e.g. certain electrical connections in the computer, and maybe also relevant software conditions. There is a *causal regularity* between triggering causes (c_T) and effects (e): whenever c_T occurs (in certain circumstances), e occurs. But structuring causes (c_S) are not regularly followed by e: it is not the case that whenever c_S occurs (in certain circumstances), e occurs. Additionally, the structuring causal relationship between c_S and e is one–many, while the triggering causal relationship between c_T and e is one–one. A distinct press of the key produces each movement of the cursor, but the same hardware will cause all the cursor movements. Instead of c_S being a cause of e, maybe c_S is better characterized as a cause of the background conditions in which c_T causes e. A software programmer and a hardware engineer together create a computer which enables the operator to move the cursor by pressing a key. The triggering cause c_T is the single cause of e, but c_S is the cause of c_T's causing e.

Now, let's turn to the mental case. Dretske proposes a *dual-explanandum strategy* according to which the triggering causes are responsible for mere *bodily movement*, while the structuring causes are responsible for *intentional behaviour*. Behaviour is a process of mental states causing bodily movement. When S reaches for a glass of water, because S wants to quench her thirst and she believes that reaching for a glass of water fulfils that desire, her behaviour is not her hand moving, but the process of this belief–desire pair causing her hand to reach out. Dretske takes triggering causes to be mental states, and structuring causes to be the contents of these states. He admits that when a mental state triggers a process ending in motor output, it does so only in virtue of its intrinsic physical properties. Nevertheless, the wide content of that state has a causal role to play as structuring the causal processes that are behaviour. It is because S's belief has the content it has – that reaching for a glass of water is a way of quenching thirst – that it gets recruited (together with the desire) as a cause of hand movement. So, while S's purely internal physical states cause the movement of her hand, that content causes those states to cause that movement.

In response, Block (1990: 153–54) and Kim (1993b: 302–3) objected that it is doubtful whether the wide contents of wide states do in fact play a causal role in structuring causal processes in the brain. Such content is meant to shape those processes by causing neurophysiological states to cause bodily movement. But bringing about the conditions in which such processes can take place is distinct from actually causing anything here and now. Surely, the physical states of S's brain would seem to be causally amendable only to their local or intrinsic properties. No highly extrinsic features enter the causal story resulting in bodily movement.

Chapter summary

We began this chapter by surveying various aspects of mental causation. Mental states are caused by physical states and in turn cause behavioural and other mental states. In particular, we tend to behave in such a way that we fulfil our desires if our beliefs are true. Folk psychology abounds with causal explanation of behaviour in terms of beliefs and desires, and such explanation seems to assume the causal efficacy of these mental states with respect to behaviour. The question is: how can these mental states cause behaviour in virtue of having the contents that they do? This problem about the causal relevance of content is especially worrisome for the semantic externalist. For on her view, the propositional contents of beliefs and desires are individuated by distal environmental factors. But causation is local: the causes of behaviour must reside inside agents' bodies. So, how can a mental state cause some behavioural effect in virtue of having the content it has if that state's causal properties are intrinsic while its content is an extrinsic property of that state? We scrutinized Fodor's modal argument. As psychology aims at causal explanation, it should be methodologically constrained to adopt taxonomies of mental states which are sensitive only to their causal powers. While wide states have the causal power to cause wide behaviour, i.e. externally individuated behaviour, the difference between two different wide states in causing different wide behaviours is not a difference in causal powers. What causal power a state has is determined by what contingent connections it enters into, but the connection between **water**-thoughts and water-behaviour is conceptually necessary. Fodor aimed to make a case for narrow content, but his attempt at spelling out this notion was found problematic. We then looked at Noonan's redundancy argument against the causal explanatory power of object-dependent mental states. Such states are causally explanatory of wide behaviour, but their explanatory power is redundant: whatever they do explain is equally well explained by narrow states in conjunction with relevant features of the environment. However, this dual-component conception of causal explanation seems incapable of handling veridical hallucination cases where someone hallucinates a particular object yet luckily manages to make behavioural contact with a distinct but similar object. Further attempts at substantiating narrow content as what plays a certain cognitive role were critically discussed. While there seems to be a need for narrow content in accounting for similarities and differences in behaviour among internal duplicates, semantic internalists have found it difficult to say what exactly it amounts to. We discussed whether there is a corresponding problem about the causal efficacy of narrow states if these are also extrinsic features. Finally, we offered three proposals concerning the explanatory value of wide content. Williamson argued that knowledge as a wide mental state plays an irreducible role in causal explanation of behaviour. Jackson and Pettit took causal explanations that cite wide states to be program explanations: they program for the effect without actually producing anything. Lastly, Dretske proposed a dual-explanandum strategy according to which mental states are triggering causes of mere bodily movement, while the wide contents of these states are structuring causes of behaviour, understood as a process of mental states causing bodily movement.

Annotated further reading

There is a vast philosophical literature on mental causation, and one should be mindful to disentangle the many different but often related problems. For an accessible introduction to the many facets of mental causation and the underlying metaphysical issues see John Heil's (2004a) *Philosophy of Mind. A Contemporary Introduction*. Tim Crane's (1995) "The Mental Causation Debate" and Frank Jackson's (1996) "Mental Causation" are slightly more challenging but still very helpful in this respect. In *Mental Causation* (1993) John Heil and Alfred Mele have collected a number of outstanding articles specifically on the causal relevance of mental contents. Other hugely influential articles on this topic can be found in *The Twin Earth Chronicles*, part III, edited by Andrew Pessin and Sanford Goldberg. Chapter 2 in Robert Wilson's (1995) *Cartesian Psychology and Physical Minds: Individualism and the Sciences of Mind* is a critical discussion of Fodor's modal argument. See also Frederick Adams (1993)

"Fodor's Modal Argument" and other fine articles in a fine symposium on that argument in *Philosophical Psychology* 6 (1). Gabriel Segal's (2000) *A Slim Book about Narrow Content*, chapter 5, defends the role of narrow content in psychological explanation. Frances Egan's (2009) "Wide Content" argues that considerations about the explanatory role of content attributions fail to support the existence of narrow content. Chapters 14–16 in Tyler Burge's (2007b) *Foundations of Mind* defend the claim that wide states play an irreducible role in such explanation. When it comes to the role of knowledge in causal explanation of behaviour chapter 2 of Timothy Williamson's (2000) *Knowledge and Its Limits*, is essential reading, but chapters 1 and 3 are worth scrutinizing as well. The distinction between program explanation and process explanation is developed in a series of co-authored papers by Frank Jackson and Philip Pettit, e.g. their (1988) "Functionalism and Broad Content," and (1990) "Program Explanation: A General Perspective". Dretske's dual-explanandum strategy and the distinction between triggering causes and structuring causes is expounded in his (1993b) "Mental Events as Structuring Causes of Behaviour" and in his (1988) *Explaining Behaviour: Reasons in a World of Causes.*

GLOSSARY

analytic/synthetic A sentence (or statement or proposition) is analytic if and only if it is true in virtue of the meaning of its constituent expressions or concepts. A synthetic sentence is one that is not analytic. For instance, the sentence 'vixens are female foxes' is analytic. Being a female fox is simply what 'vixen' means. Traditionally, analytic truths are knowable a priori. Understanding what 'vixen' means suffices for knowing that 'vixens are female foxes' is true. In contrast, the sentence 'vixens weigh around 5.2 kilograms' is synthetic. Weighing around 5.2 kilograms is not even part of what 'vixen' means. Merely understanding what 'vixen' means does not put one in a position to know that 'vixens weigh around 5.2 kilograms' is true. One needs empirical information, e.g. by looking up an encyclopedia. That sentence is thus only a posteriori knowable.

a priori/a posteriori A proposition (or fact) is a priori knowable if and only if it is knowable independently of empirical investigation or sense experience. An a posteriori knowable proposition is one that is knowable but not a priori knowable. For instance, the proposition **red is a colour** is a priori knowable. Note that some philosophers think one cannot possess the (phenomenal) concept **red** unless one has had an experience as of something red. This does not render that proposition a posteriori knowable. The question about whether one can know a proposition a priori only arises once one is able to grasp that proposition. The fact that certain experiences are required in order to grasp a proposition is irrelevant to settling that question. In contrast, the proposition **Jill's car is red** is a posteriori knowable. One cannot know the truth of that proposition until one has had a visual experience of her car, or received reliable testimony from others who have had such an experience.

aetiology The aetiology of some event or fact pertains to its causal history: the antecedent factors that causally contributed to the occurrence of that event or obtaining of that fact.

causal explanation An explanation consists of an *explanans* – that which explains – and an *explanandum* – that which is explained. To causally explain an event is to cite some other events which in some sense are causally responsible for the former event. Causal explanations answer 'why'-questions, e.g. why did Jones put salt in the water? Because he wanted to boil some pasta. Here the question signifies the explanandum, and the answer signifies the explanans. Some philosophers maintain that events can feature in causal explanations of other events without being causally efficacious of those other events. Causal explanations are rife in the cognitive and special sciences as when behaviour is causally explained by citing belief–desire pairs. They should be distinguished from reductive explanations which answer 'how'-questions, e.g. how does salt dissolve in water? The sodium chloride lattice dissociates into individual ions surrounded by water molecules. The special sciences frequently call upon lower-level properties in reductively explaining higher-level properties.

causal relevance Some properties of an object (or event) are causally relevant to some effect of that object (or event) while others are causally irrelevant. Suppose the baseball bat smashed the window. The weight, speed and direction of the bat are causally relevant to the shattering, but the colour, price and ownership are causally irrelevant. The bat caused the shattering in virtue of having the first three properties, but the last three properties made no difference to the effect. Some philosophers use 'causal relevance' in a loose sense to mean that some object (or event) can play a role in the causation of some effect without actually producing that effect.

closure of knowledge To say that knowledge is closed under known entailment is to say that if one knows that p and that p entails q then one knows that q. However, that simplified version of the closure principle has obvious counterexamples when one knows that p and that p entails q but simply fails to form the belief that q. A better proposal is to say that if one knows that p and competently deduces q from p, thereby coming to believe that q, while retaining one's knowledge that p, one comes to know that q. Several sceptical arguments in epistemology hang on the closure principle. Rejecting that principle as many sensitivity and relevant alternatives accounts of knowledge have advocated thus paves the way for a swift response to scepticism.

context of utterance/circumstance of evaluation Contexts of utterance consist of the speaker, hearer, time and place at which the expressions in question are uttered. If a sentence containing indexical expressions is uttered, contexts of utterance are needed to determine which proposition is expressed. Take 'I am bald'. If John is the speaker of the context, he expresses the proposition **John is bald**, but if Brian is the speaker, he expresses the proposition **Brian is bald**. Circumstances of evaluation are indices consisting of contextual features that need not go together in any possible context. They are needed to evaluate the truth-value of the propositions expressed. If evaluated with respect to circumstances in which John is bald but Brian is not, the proposition John expressed is true, but the proposition Brian expressed is false. If evaluated with respect to circumstances in which neither is bald, both propositions are false. And so on.

contingent/necessary To say that a proposition (or sentence) is contingent is to say that it is true but possibly false. For instance, the proposition **Edinburgh is the capital city of Scotland** is contingent. As things are Edinburgh is the capital city of Scotland, but had the historical facts been slightly different Glasgow or Stirling would have been the capital city of Scotland. A contingent proposition is true at the actual world but false at some other possible world. To say that a proposition (or sentence) is necessary is to say that it is true at all possible worlds including the actual world. Depending on which possible worlds are considered, different notions of necessity arise. The proposition **the boiling point of water is 100°C at standard pressure** is nomologically necessary: true at all possible worlds consistent with the actual laws of nature. To find a possible world where that proposition is false you have to change the laws of nature. The proposition **water is H_2O** is metaphysically necessary: true at all metaphysically possible worlds. It remains true at a possible world with deviant laws of nature or different particular matters of fact.

counterfactuals A counterfactual is a subjunctive conditional of the form 'if p had been the case, then q would have been the case'. This conditional is true if and only if either p is necessarily false, or q is true in the closest possible worlds in which p is true, where closeness is a question about conformity to natural laws and match of particular facts. Consider the following counterfactual 'if the course had been waterlogged, the horse race would have been called off'. Since the course might have been waterlogged, the antecedent is not necessarily false, and so the counterfactual is not vacuously true. But given that horse races are invariably cancelled when the courses are waterlogged, the closest possible worlds in which the course is waterlogged are worlds in which the race is called off. There are possible worlds in which the race goes ahead despite the course being waterlogged, but these are more remote than the worlds in which the course is waterlogged and the race is cancelled. The former worlds require more changes in matters of particular fact than the latter worlds, e.g. changes in the regulations governing such races. Counterfactual conditionals contrast with material conditionals of the form 'if p is the case, then q is the case'. These are true if and only if p is false or q is true.

de re/de dicto The de re/de dicto distinction is often applied in connection with beliefs and knowledge. De re belief/knowledge has the form 'S believes/knows of an object that it is F'. De dicto belief/knowledge has the form 'S believes/knows that an object is F'. While 'de re' indicates an object, 'de dicto' indicates a proposition.

descriptivism/descriptive theory of reference The descriptive theory of reference, or descriptivism, says that referring terms have associated descriptive meanings which are both what competent speakers know when they understand them and what determine the reference if any of these terms. This view in philosophy of language applies to singular referring terms, e.g. proper names such as 'Robert Burns', and general referring terms, e.g. natural kind terms such as 'rhinoceros'.

disquotation To say that one's language disquotes is to say that one can use any meaningful, referring term to characterize its own reference. If one knows the meaning of 'refers' and of quotation marks, then one has a priori knowledge that one's own language is subject to disquotation. For instance, since the proper name 'Sir Alex Ferguson' is meaningful in my language, I know a priori that 'Sir Alex Ferguson' refers to Sir Alex Ferguson. Being permitted to disquote one's own language does not imply the possession of identifying knowledge of reference. It is a further question whether I know exactly who Sir Alex Ferguson is, e.g. that he is the Scottish manager of Manchester United. Similarly, I know in virtue of being a competent language user the propositions that are expressed by a homophonic theory of truth for my language, i.e. I know that a sentence 's' in my language has disquotational truth-conditions: 's' is true if and only if s. That is different from knowing the empirical propositions expressed by a non-homophonic truth-theory for my language. I can only know a posteriori that 's' is true if and only if r, where r is an explication of 's'.

epistemological scepticism Epistemological scepticism is the claim that we lack knowledge of some aspect of reality, typically the external world as such or confined to the past, other minds or unobservable scientific entities. The sceptic is a fictional character and scepticism is best viewed methodologically – as a way of doing epistemology. The best sceptical arguments are paradoxes: they argue from intuitively plausible premises to an intuitively implausible conclusion via intuitively plausibly inference rules or epistemic principles. A satisfactory response should therefore not only reject either one of the premises or the reasoning, it should also explain why that premise or reasoning seemed so plausible in the first place.

fallacy of equivocation The fallacy of equivocation occurs in arguments when a term is used ambiguously, shifting into having different referents during the course of the argument. Consider the following: Sam went to the nearest bank to collect seaweed. The nearest bank is the Bank of Scotland on South Street. So, Sam went to the Bank of Scotland on South Street to collect seaweed. This argument in invalid: both premises can be true when the conclusion is false. It commits the fallacy of equivocation because 'bank' is used to designate riverbank in the first premise but money bank in the second premise, and that ambiguity is used to reach the conclusion. If an argument contains ambiguous terms but nothing turns on the ambiguity, it may be misleading without being guilty of the fallacy of equivocation.

first-order/second-order property A second-order property is the property of having a first-order property. For instance, having the same colour as the sky is a second-order property, and being blue is a first-order property. Second-order properties are not properties of properties, but rather properties of the objects that instantiate the first-order properties. My jeans have the property of being blue, and they also have the property of having the same colour as the sky. Second-order properties are distinct from first-order properties. If the sky suddenly turns gray, my jeans still have the property of being blue, but they no longer have the property of having the same colour as the sky. Some functionalists in philosophy of mind think that mental properties are second-order functional properties: they are properties of having first-order properties that play a characteristic causal role. This allows for different species sharing the same type of mental states in virtue of being in distinct physical states playing the same causal roles. That is to say, it is possible to share the same type of role states in virtue of different filler states.

incompatibilism Incompatibilism is any view in philosophy that two prima facie plausible theses are incompatible. In the present context, it is the view that semantic externalism is incompatible with self-knowledge. Slow switching arguments attempt to show that speakers who unwittingly undergo a series of slow transportations between Earth and Twin Earth do not know a priori that they are thinking **water**-thoughts, because they are incapable of ruling out the relevant alternative that they are thinking **twin-water**-thoughts. Another set of arguments aim to show that if speakers know a priori both that they are thinking **water**-thoughts and that water exists if they are thinking **water**-thoughts, then they can deduce a priori knowledge that water exists.

intentional context/extensional context A referring term '*a*' occurs in an intentional context if '*a*' is embedded inside the scope of an intentional operator such as a belief operator. A referring term '*a*' occurs in an extensional context if '*a*' is not embedded inside the scope of such an operator. For instance, the proper name 'Bono' occurs in an extensional context in the sentence 'Bono is the lead singer of U2', but in an intentional context in the sentence 'Liz believes that Bono is the lead singer of U2'. It is natural to think that co-referring terms can be substituted in extensional contexts but not in intentional contexts without change in truth-value. 'Bono is the lead singer of U2' is true, and so is 'Paul David Hewson is the lead singer of U2'. But it seems possible that 'Liz believes that Bono is the lead singer of U2' is true while 'Liz believes that Paul David Hewson is the lead singer of U2' is false. This can happen when Liz only knows that man under his stage name.

intrinsic/extrinsic property An intrinsic property is a property an object has solely in virtue of the way that object is, independently of which properties other objects have, indeed independently of whether there exist any other objects. An extrinsic property is one that is not intrinsic, and so an object having an extrinsic property depends on the existence of other objects and their properties. For instance, having a certain mass is an intrinsic property, but having a certain weight is an extrinsic property. The mass of an object is a question about the amount of matter in that particular object. The weight of an object is a question about the force of gravity pulling on its mass. When one moves an object on the surface of the Earth, its mass will remain constant but its weight will vary with changes in the gravitational field.

linguistic meaning/speakers' meaning. Linguistic (or lexical or conventional) meaning is the meaning of a type of expression, independent of any particular context of utterance. In contrast, speakers' meaning is what the speaker intended to mean in uttering an expression in a particular context. It is commonplace that speakers can say one thing but mean something else. Suppose I use the sentence 'there's a wine store around the corner' in order to tell you where you can buy wine. Here the speaker's meaning is what I mean or implicate – that you can buy wine around the corner – by way of saying something else, namely the linguistic meaning that there is a wine store around the corner. As we share knowledge of salient features of the context, and both rely on certain presumptions about what successful communication requires, you will be able to grasp what I intend to communicate – what I conversationally implicate.

methodological solipsism/methodological individualism Methodological individualism is the view that mental states are individuated with respect to
their causal powers such that two mental states are distinct if and only if
they have distinct causal powers. The causal powers of a mental state
consists in the effects an individual who is in that state would cause in
certain circumstances. Methodological solipsism is the view that mental
states are individuated without respect to their truth-conditions such
that it is possible for two otherwise identical mental states to differ in
truth-value.

mind–body identity theory The mind–body identity theory in philosophy of
mind says that mental states are numerically identical to physical states
of the brain or body. The identity in question can be either token–token
or type–type. The token-identity theory says that for every token mental
state M_{Token}, there is some token physical state P_{Token} such that M_{Token}
is identical to P_{Token}. The stronger type-identity theory says that for every
type (that is actually tokened) mental state M_{Type}, there is some physical
type P_{Type} such that M_{Type} is identical to P_{Type}.

possible worlds A possible world is roughly speaking a way things might have
been. Some take possible worlds to be maximal consistent sets of sentences. Some treat them as maximal possible states of affairs. Yet
others think possible worlds are irreducible and just as real as the actual
world. Regardless of that dispute, possible worlds can be used to better
understand the semantics of modal sentences. Take the sentences 'it is
possible that pigs fly' and 'it is necessary that heat is mean molecular
energy in gases'. The modal operators 'it is possible that' and 'it is
necessary that' can be treated as quantifiers over possible worlds. The
first sentence is true if and only if there is a possible world in which pigs
fly, and the second sentence is true if and only if for all possible worlds
heat is mean molecular energy in gases. Here 'there is' and 'for all'
indicate the existential and universal quantifier, respectively.

pragmatics/semantics Pragmatics deals with utterances or tokens of expressions in particular contexts. In contrast, semantics deals with types of
expressions independently of particular contexts of utterance. Another
way of drawing the distinction is to say that semantics is concerned with
linguistic meaning, and pragmatics is concerned with speakers' meaning or use. Another demarcation says that semantics deals with truth-
conditions or content that is truth-conditionally relevant, and pragmatics
deals with elements of meaning that go beyond truth-conditions. These
three distinctions, however, do not line up. For instance, the personal
pronouns 'I' and 'she' are context-dependent but their truth-conditional
contents are studied by semantics.

proposition A proposition is what is semantically expressed by a declarative
sentence such as 'Nicole Kidman was born in America'. Propositions

are also often taken to be the primary bearers of truth-values. Because the proposition **Nicole Kidman was born in America** is true, the sentence expressing that proposition is also true. Finally, propositions have been equated with the contents of beliefs and other propositional attitudes. A simple view of the semantics of belief-ascribing sentences says that the sentence 'Brian believes that Nicole Kidman was born in America' is true if and only if Brian is belief-related to the proposition expressed by the 'that'-clause. Some philosophers think that propositions are structured entities. For instance, referentialists say that the singular proposition **Nicole Kidman was born in America** consists of Nicole Kidman and the property of being born in America. Other philosophers think that propositions are functions from possible worlds to truth-values. Suppose Nicole Kidman was born in Germany in possible world *W*. Then that proposition maps the actual world onto the true, and *W* onto the false.

referentialism/direct reference theory The direct reference theory, or referentialism, says that referring terms refer to their referents directly, i.e. unmediated by the satisfaction of any associated definite descriptions. Such descriptions may play a role in fixing the reference of a term but they do not give that term its meaning. On this view, the meaning of a referring term is nothing over and above its referent. A causal-historical account explains why the term has the reference it has: at some point back in time the term was introduced into language by a ceremonial act of baptism, and was then passed on via some causal chain of communication.

relevant-alternatives account of knowledge The relevant alternatives account of knowledge says that knowledge consists in the elimination of all relevant alternatives to what is known. On this view, it is thus possible to know without being able to rule out all alternatives. Proponents disagree about what it takes for an alternative to be relevant. For instance, some say that relevance is fixed by features of the context of utterance such that an alternative may count as relevant in one context but not in another context.

rigid designation A rigid designator is a term that refers to the same object in all possible worlds in which that object exists (and not to any other objects in possible worlds in which that object does not exists). All directly referential terms are rigid, but not all rigid designators are directly referential. Directly referential terms are rigid *de jure* in that their rigidity is secured by semantic rules. But some definite descriptions, e.g. mathematical descriptions, are de facto rigid in that they happen to pick out the same object in all possible worlds. Most philosophers of language agree that ordinary proper names and natural kind terms are rigid designators. A non-rigid definite description can be rigidified using the indexical 'actual'. The description 'the winner of the 2006 FIFA World Cup' picks out Italy in the actual world, but other countries in different possible worlds depending on who won the 2006 FIFA World Cup in those worlds. When rigidified, 'the actual winner of the 2006 FIFA World Cup' picks out Italy in all possible worlds. There is no possible world in which Italy lost the 2006 FIFA World Cup in the actual world.

self-knowledge Self-knowledge is the kind of privileged access one has to one's own mental states and their contents, which yields a priori knowledge of those states and their contents. It applies in the first instance to occurrent phenomenal states such as pains and to occurrent beliefs and desires. Self-knowledge is characterized by authority, non-inferentiality and salience. Assuming competence, sincerity and attention, one need not provide reasons in support of one's claim to be in some occurrent mental state, one does not infer from one's behaviour that one is in that state, and if one is in some such state one will be disposed to notice that one is. Self-knowledge contrasts with the stronger claim that individuals can know a priori whether any two grasped propositions are identical or distinct. To say that one can have a priori knowledge of the logical properties of contents in this manner is to say that these contents are epistemically transparent. While most semantic externalists maintain a priori knowledge of the contents of occurrent mental states, they reject the claim that these contents are epistemically transparent.

semantic deference To say that a referring term is used with semantic deference is to say that one defers to the expert speakers in one's linguistic community when it comes to the application conditions of that term. This phenomenon is ubiquitous in natural language. It enables speakers whose mastery of a referring term is incomplete to use that term correctly in communication and to be ascribed beliefs involving its reference. Suppose I have many true beliefs about tomatoes: they are red, savory in flavour, used in pizzas, 5–9 centimetres in diameter. But, like many others, I also assent to 'tomatoes are vegetables'. I use 'tomato' deferentially, so when the experts point out to me that tomatoes are fruit, I correct my usage. Despite the mistake, my utterance is best understood as being about tomatoes, thus expressing my (false) belief that tomatoes are vegetables.

semantic externalism/semantic internalism Semantic internalism is the view that linguistic or mental content supervenes on internal features of individuals – it is content shared by doppelgängers or internal duplicates. Semantic externalism is the opposing view that linguistic or mental content fails to supervene on internal features of individuals – it is content that varies between those doppelgängers or internal duplicates who are situated in relevantly different external environments.

sensitivity account of knowledge A sensitivity account of knowledge states that one knows that p only if one's belief that p is sensitive, where one's belief that p is sensitive if and only if one would not believe that p if p were false. As sensitivity is understood in modal terms as a counterfactual, a sensitivity account of knowledge is a modal or tracking account of knowledge. To know that p requires that one tracks the truth across a range of possible worlds.

supervenience: a set of properties A supervenes on another set of properties B just in case no two objects can differ in respect of A-properties without also differing in respect of B-properties. If they differ in their A-properties, they must also differ in their B-properties. Put differently, if the two objects share the same B-properties, they must also share the same A-properties. Indiscernibility in regards to their B-properties entails indiscernibility in regards to their A-properties.

Swampman Swampman is an imaginary physical replica of Donald Davidson coincidentally made out of different molecules as a result of lightning striking a dead tree. Swampman is supposed to also be a functional duplicate of Davidson who behaves in every way just as Davidson does. Despite the functional and physical similarities between Swampman and Davidson, teleosemantics and other historical views of content predict that Swampman should be incapable of thinking any thoughts at all. The reason for this is that Swampman has no causal history. He is not of human descent, indeed he lacks any history of natural selection. Moreover, he has never been part of any physical or social environments.

teleosemantics Teleosemantics, or the teleological view of content, says that the propositional content of mental states is given by their biological function, where such function is understood in evolutionary terms, i.e. in terms of what these states were selected for by some historical process of natural selection. By identifying representational states with biological states, teleosemanics counts as a naturalist theory of content.

type/token A type is a general kind of thing, and a token is a particular concrete instance of that general kind of thing. Types are abstract, intangible entities, and tokens are concrete particulars in space-time. In the word 'letter' there are four types of letters, but six token letters.

Twin Earth Twin Earth is an imaginary distant planet just like Earth except that the clear, potable stuff that falls from the sky, runs out of taps, fills the oceans, etc., has a radically different microstructure, abbreviated XYZ. On Twin Earth each of us has a doppelgänger who is as ignorant about chemistry as we are supposed to be. The Twin Earth thought experiment is designed to establish semantic externalism. When I use 'water' on Earth I refer to H_2O, but when my doppelgänger on Twin Earth uses 'water' she refers to XYZ. Given that a difference in reference entails a difference in meaning, our respective tokens of 'water' have different meanings. But since my doppelgänger and I are internally alike, what we mean cannot be a function of our internal features. Meaning must rather depend for its individuation on the possibly unknown nature of our distinct physical environments.

two-dimensional semantics Two-dimensional semantics relies on two distinct ways of conceiving of possible worlds. One can consider a possible world as counterfactual. Then one asks: given the way the actual world is, what if it had been such-and-such a way? Or one can consider a possible world as actual. Then one asks: what if the actual world turns out such-and-such a way? Correspondingly, one can assign two distinct functions to a statement or a referring term depending on how the possible worlds are conceived. The epistemic intension of a statement/ term is a function from possible worlds considered as actual to truth-values/referents. The subjunctive intension of a statement/term is a function from possible worlds considered as counterfactual to truth-values/referents. Subjunctive intensions are a posteriori knowable, because they require knowledge of which possible world is actual. More contentiously, epistemic intensions are a priori knowable, because they are knowable independently of which possible world is actual.

underdetemination To say that a theory or hypothesis is underdetermined by evidence is to say that the evidence available at a given time is insufficient to determined whether that theory or hypothesis is true or acceptable. There could well be another theory or hypothesis incompatible with the first, which equally well accommodates all the available evidence at that time. Here's an example from the natural sciences (*New Scientist* 19 September 2009). Why do some female animals have horns? Horns on cloven-hoofed animals are believed to have evolved for fighting each other but most female cattle and deer engage in no such fighting. The evidence is that horns are most likely in species living in open habitat and large enough to be visible to predators. One theory says that horns evolved as defensive weapons, but another rival theory equally compatible with the evidence says that female competition for food is the reason why horns evolved.

NOTES

1 Descriptivism

1 Single quotes are used throughout to avoid use/mention confusion. To illustrate, 'Brown' indicates talk about the name that refers to the man Brown, e.g. 'Brown' contains five letters, but there are no letters in Brown.

2 To simplify matters, we shall occasionally talk about 'water' referring to H_2O, but what that means for now is that 'water' refers to the instances of the natural kind H_2O which constitute its extension. A competing view says that natural kind terms refer to the abstract kinds themselves rather than their concrete instances. We shall set this view aside until Section 4.4.

3 By 'sentence' we shall henceforth mean a declarative sentence, i.e. a sentence that can be used to make an assertion.

4 When we say that an expression 'expresses something' we shall henceforth mean semantic expression. Speakers can also use expressions to convey other kinds of meanings, e.g. non-literal meaning or pragmatic implicatures.

5 Frege (1994a/1892) called the view that operates only with objects and referring terms 'the objectual view', but nowadays it also goes under the name 'Millianism' after Mill. Chapter 2 is devoted to referentialism.

6 Frege actually used the names 'the morning star' and 'the evening star', but we will continue to use the proper names 'Hesperus' and 'Phosphorus' instead.

7 We shall henceforth use bold text to indicate talk about concepts and propositions.

8 Frege (1994a/1892: 143) talked about " ... the sense of the sign, wherein the mode of presentation is contained". We can also think of sense as the way the reference is determined or as a route to the referent. Evans (1982: 16–17) talks about " ... there being a particular way of thinking about its reference, shared by competent users of the language who understand the term".

9 Burge (1977) and Salmon (1986) take Frege's senses to be designed to play (i) a psychological role: they serve as the purely conceptual representation of an object which a fully competent speaker associates with the term, (ii) a semantic role: they serve as the mechanism by which the reference of the term is secured, and (iii) a cognitive role: they serve as the information value of the term – the contribution made by the term to the information content of sentences containing the term.

10 Following Kripke (1980), we shall conveniently talk about water being identical to H_2O although that is strictly speaking misleading. For instance, water is a liquid but some compounds comprised of H_2O come as water vapour or ice. Moreover, a single H_2O molecule is not a liquid. We can say instead that water is a macroscopic entity which is both (predominantly) composed of H_2O molecules and has certain dynamic structures to do with hydrogen bonds and oligomers. See also Needham 2000.

11 Types are general kinds whereas tokens are concrete particular instances of those kinds. To illustrate the distinction between types and tokens consider 'letter'. This word has six token letters but only four types of letters. Or suppose I say that you and I have the same BMW. I might mean that you and I share the very same token car, or that we each have a token car of the same type of car. For more on the distinction between semantics and pragmatics see Bach 2008.

12 See also Section 3.2.

13 Frege's solution is not unproblematic. For instance, it violates the principle of semantic innocence: embedded sentences in belief attributions express just the propositions they would if not embedded. In particular, referring terms appear to exhibit the same semantic behaviour whether they occur inside or outside the scope of a belief operator. In Chapter 2 we argue that names always refer to the same object, and so cannot be used to refer to the senses associated with them. For discussion see Forbes 1990.

14 In Section 2.4 we elaborate on a referentialist response, and Section 3.4 discusses an application of Kripke's paradox in the context of social externalism. For further discussion see Kallestrup 2003.

15 For details see Goldman 1967.

16 Jackson (2004) seems to defend a view similar to (D) on which, when a speaker intends to communicate a proposition *p*, she has successfully communicated *p* only if the hearer both knows that the speaker intends to communicate *p*, and also ends up having *p* in mind when the communication is over. In response, Kroon (2004) seems to opt for (B): all successful communication requires is that speaker and hearer know that they are referring to the same object, but such knowledge of co-reference can be secured without assuming that they share any descriptive contents.

2 Referentialism

1 For more details see Kaplan 1978, 1989, Recanati 1993, Marti 1995 and Soames 2002.

2 See Evans 1973 for critical discussion. We shall elaborate on the referentialist semantics for natural kind terms in Section 4.4.

3 Some descriptivists accept that names and natural kind terms are not synonymous with definite descriptions, yet their reference is always fixed by such descriptions. While Kripke (1980: 83–92) allows for some such terms to have their reference fixed in this way, his Gödel–Schmidt example is supposed to illustrate that as a matter of fact the reference of most ordinary proper names is not fixed by definite descriptions. Hence, even this weaker form of descriptivism is untenable.

4 Not any true propositional knowledge ascription will do. The content of that ascription must both (i) explicate the independent way in which *S* identifies Aristotle and (ii) connect that way with the property of being the bearer of 'Aristotle'. The speaker *S* cannot know of Aristotle that 'Aristotle' refers to him, unless for some property *G* distinct from being the bearer of 'Aristotle', *S* identifies Aristotle as the *G* and knows that the *G* is the bearer of 'Aristotle'. For instance, *G* could be the property of being the teacher of Alexander the Great. For more details and discussion see Dummett 1978: 125–27 and Stalnaker 1997: 547.

5 We should add that a rigid designator is one that refers to the same object in all possible worlds in which that object exists and not to other objects in possible worlds in which that object does not exist. That leaves it open whether a rigid designator refers to the same object even in possible worlds in which that object does not exist, or alternatively lacks a reference in such worlds.

6 Which object 'Aristotle' actually refers to depends of course on which contingent conventions govern that name. In the language we actually

speak 'Aristotle' is used to denote Aristotle, but in some possible language 'Aristotle' denotes someone else. However, these possibilities are irrelevant when determining whether 'Aristotle' is rigid or not. All that matters is the way we actually use 'Aristotle'. See also Kripke 1980: 77.

7 Or so Kripke argued in 1980: fn. 56.

8 For more discussion see Stanley 1997 and Salmon 2003.

9 Other objections levelled against descriptivism include the following. Suppose the proper name 'Peano' is simply shorthand for 'the discoverer of the Peano axioms'. This means that that name refers to whoever discovered those axioms. The semantic argument goes as follows. Intuitively, the sentence 'Peano is Italian' is true, but the sentence 'the discoverer of the Peano axioms is Italian' is false. Dedekind discovered those axioms and he was German. And the epistemic argument runs as follows. Intuitively, the sentence 'If Aristotle exists then Aristotle wrote *Nicomachean Ethics*' is a posteriori knowable. But if the propositional content of 'Aristotle' is given by 'the author of *Nicomachean Ethics*', then that sentence should be a priori knowable, because semantically equivalent to 'If the author of *Nicomachean Ethics* exists, then the author of *Nicomachean Ethics* wrote *Nicomachean Ethics*', which clearly is a priori knowable. For more details see Salmon 1986 and Soames 2002.

10 *Pace* Jackson (2004: 273–74) who proposes that the relation between water and H_2O be viewed like that between diamond and carbon: in order for H_2O to count as water it must have some watery properties. Microstructure matters but so does form.

11 Putnam (1990: 70) believes that the question of what the metaphysically sufficient and necessary conditions for something to be water are makes no sense. Once we change the laws of nature it becomes indeterminate what the extension of 'water' is.

12 See also Kripke 1980: 10–15.

13 In Section 1.2 we considered a compositionality principle (ComProp) to the effect that the proposition expressed by a sentence is determined by the propositional contents of its component expressions and the way in which these contents are combined. The modal substitution principle (ModSub) is in effect a consequence of such a compositionality principle as pertaining to modal sentences.

14 Bear in mind from fn. 9 in Chapter 1 the three roles that Fregean senses are supposed to play. One might take the modal argument to show that senses *qua* descriptive modes of presentation cannot constitute the semantic mechanism that secures reference. That is consistent with

senses still playing other psychological or cognitive roles. What the modal argument shows is at most that no single notion of sense can play all three roles. See also Salmon 1986 and Burge 1977.

15 See Stanley 1997: 574 and Jackson 2004: 260 for further discussion.

16 We return to cases involving semantic deference in Sections 3.3 and 3.4.

17 See Kripke 1980.

18 For more details on the distinction between contexts of utterance and circumstance of evaluation see Kaplan 1989: 494. As we shall see in Section 4.3 this distinction bears a resemblance to the distinction Chalmers (2002, 2003, 2006) draws between two ways of considering a possible world.

19 For more on indexical expressions see Sections 4.1 and 7.3. Perry (1993) interpreted Frege (1994b/1918) as saying that the sense of 'I' is private and incommunicable, which supposedly contradicts his thesis that senses are generally accessible and shareable. Anna cannot use (18) to express what Thomas expresses when he uses (18). Nor can Anna use 'the speaker feels elated' or 'Anna feels elated'. As we shall see in Section 4.2, the content of indexical beliefs is irreducibly egocentric. Imagine that Anna suffers from severe amnesia so that she has no idea who the speaker is or what her name is. Still, she can competently use 'I' to directly refer to herself. Evans (1981) remarked that even though some Fregean senses are not shareable, they might still be objective in that they exist and have their truth-value independently of the speaker entertaining them.

20 The following owes much to Soames 1998: 15–16, 2002: 43–46, and 2005: 304–5, although he uses proper names as examples. For critical discussion see Kallestrup (forthcoming).

21 We take the concept **water** to consist in the propositional content expressed by 'water'.

22 Indeed objects can have their intrinsic properties in the absence of any other objects. Examples of intrinsic properties include the properties of being square and being six feet tall. An extrinsic property is a property that is not intrinsic. Examples include the properties of being east of Glasgow and being taller than my sister. This definition of intrinsic works in most cases, though consider the property of being lonely. Alternatively, an intrinsic property of an object can be defined as one that is shared by all internal or perfect duplicates of that object. A problem for that account is the property of being identical to Mary, which is intuitively intrinsic but not shared by any internal duplicates such as Mary's identical twin. For more details see Langton and Lewis 1998. An object that looses or acquires an intrinsic property undergoes a real change, but an object that looses or

acquires an extrinsic property may just undergo what Geach (1969: 71) called a 'Cambridge change'. When I cease to be taller than my sister solely in virtue of my sister's growth, she undergoes real change while I undergo a mere Cambridge change. Often the distinction between intrinsic and extrinsic is taken to be identical to the distinction between non-relational and relational. But consider the property of having longer legs than arms. Being relational is better seen as a property of concepts rather than a property of properties. For instance, there are relational ways of picking out intrinsic properties.

23 For more on rigidification and Perfect Earth see Section 3.4 and Kallestrup (forthcoming).

24 For more details see Salmon 1986 and Soames 1987, 1989. Soames' (2002) more recent view is that sentences containing names semantically express singular propositions, but speakers can also use such sentences to assert partially descriptive propositions. Likewise, Thau (2002) holds that speakers communicate descriptive propositions by using sentences that conventionally implicate those propositions despite semantically expressing singular propositions. The intuition that (21) and (22) differ in truth-value is then explained by the fact that despite those sentences expressing identical singular propositions, speakers use them to communicate descriptive propositions that (they believe) differ in truth-value. Ordinary speakers are simply not always sensitive to the distinction between semantic expression and assertion/conventional implication. For critical discussion of so-called *Millian descriptivism* see Braun and Sider 2006 and Caplan 2007. Kroon (2004) holds the related but different view that while the propositional content of a referring term is its referent, that referent is determined by descriptive properties associated with that term by competent speakers.

3 From language to thought

1 The metaphysics of natural kinds is a complex issue which we shall not delve into here except to note that Salmon (1981) argued that only trivial forms of essentialism could be inferred from the semantic arguments of Putnam and Kripke.

2 Physicalists hold that mental properties are identical to, or at least strongly determined by, physical properties. If physicalism is false, we need to add that these doppelgängers on Twin Earth are also identical to Earthlings with respect to their non-physical mental properties such as fundamental qualitative properties of what it is like to undergo experiences.

3 Putnam (1975: 152) held that 'water' has an "unnoticed indexical component". To what extent, if at all, natural kind terms are indexical will be explored in Section 4.4.

4 To be clear, when Putnam talks about 'meaning' he means propositional content: the meaning of a referring term consists in the contribution it yields to determine the proposition expressed by sentences containing it.

5 Cf. also Burge 1986.

6 A set of properties A supervenes on a set of properties B just in case no two objects can differ in respect of their A-properties without also differing in respect of their B-properties. Put differently, supervenience says that if two objects are indiscernible with respect to their B-properties, they must also be indiscernible with respect to their A-properties. Supervenience is thus consistent with the possibility that two objects have the same A-properties while differing in their B-properties.

7 In the literature the view also goes under the names 'anti-individualism' and 'content externalism'. Thus Burge (2010: 61) defines 'anti-individualism' as the claim that "the natures of many mental states constitutively depend on relations between a subject matter beyond the individual and the individual that has the mental states", where these relations include causal, non-representational relations.

8 Note that in setting up the Twin Earth thought experiment water was assumed to be uniformly H_2O, but some H_2O may lack many of the watery properties while other chemical compounds may possess some of these properties – think of impure water, heavy water and so on. In response, the reference of 'water' can be determined by the underlying nature of local paradigm instances of water, e.g. the tap water that runs out of our faucets at home.

9 See Burge 1989: 305.

10 Farkas' (2003: 76–77) meningitis example shows that the internal/external distinction should not always be drawn around the skin or skull. You and I both have symptoms typical of meningitis, but where mine are caused by meningitis, yours are caused by a different bacterium. So, we are physically distinct yet inhabit identical environments. Without our knowledge, our token sentences containing 'meningitis' express distinct propositions. Instead Farkas suggests that internal duplicates should be not physical but phenomenal duplicates. Note also that semantic internalism may hold even if, as Clark and Chalmers (1998) maintain, cognitive processes extend beyond the boundaries of the skin and skull. If their extended mind thesis is true, the pertinent question

then becomes whether propositional content supervenes on the conjunction of internal features and whatever augmenting, technological devices extend the mind. See also Chalmers 2002: fn. 22, and Jackson 2003.

11 We shall henceforth continue to use the 'semantic externalism/semantic internalism' terminology to distinguish these views from epistemic externalism and epistemic internalism, respectively. See S. Goldberg 2007b for a collection of articles on the intriguing relationships between these views in philosophy of mind and epistemology.

12 See also Stalnaker 1990: 133.

13 Or take a different example. In criticizing this interpretation of Putnam's dictum, Yablo (1997: 269) remarks that "[Putnam] might as well have said that pennies ain't in the pocket, since events within the pocket do not suffice to make them *pennies*". Nothing is a penny unless produced in a bona fide mint, but that is not to say that all pennies are located where they were minted. For further examples and in-depth discussion see Burge 2010: Ch. 3. For more on this example see Section 7.3.

14 See Segal 2000: 25.

15 Remember fn. 2 from Chapter 1. When we say that 'water' refers to a natural kind we mean that instances of that kind fall within the extension of 'water'. A natural kind is an abstract entity, whereas its instances are concrete entities in space-time. Similarly, when we say in the following that we causally interact with water we mean concrete samples of water, not the abstract kind itself.

16 The last example is due to Segal 2004: 338. See also Mellor 1977: 303, Crane 1991: 10–13, Lewis 2002: fn. 2, and Jackson 2003.

17 For more on causal descriptivism see Searle 1983: 204–5, Kroon 1987, Lewis 1997, Jackson 1998a, 2003, 2004: 274. See also Section 4.2. As Jackson (2003: 106) remarks, causal descriptivism seems to have whatever results the causal theory of reference from Section 2.1 has: there is a causal-historical chain linking 'water' with H_2O if and only if H_2O satisfies the description 'the stuff that is linked by a causal-historical chain with "water"'.

18 See Segal 2000: 122–32, and 2004: 339–43, and Jackson 2004: 326. S. Goldberg (2002) defends semantic externalism against the charge that ascriptions of wide-content mental states are unfaithful to the individual's perspectival conception of the world.

19 Counterfactuals (formalized: $p \;\square\!\!\rightarrow q$) take the form: if p were (or had been) the case, then q would be the case. They are true if q is true in the

closest possible worlds – the worlds most similar to the actual world – in which p is true, where closeness is evaluated in terms of conformity to natural laws and match of particular facts. The more a possible world resembles the actual world with respect to particular matters of fact and laws of nature, the closer it is to the actual world. For more details see Lewis 1973.

20 See Jackson 2003 for more on this response.

21 See White 1982 and Block and Stalnaker 1999.

22 We shall henceforth use the terms 'intentional state' and 'representational state' interchangeably.

23 Perhaps some beliefs are linguistically inexpressible, e.g. to the extent that animals have beliefs then they presumably are. But for competent speakers most if not all beliefs do seem to be in principle expressible in language.

24 Note that beliefs and desires are non-factive mental states: one can believe or desire that p even if p is false. Contrast with regrets and admissions which are factive: one can regret or admit that p only if p is true. Knowing and seeing that p are also factive. Knowing, seeing, admitting or regretting that p are all wide states in that being in them depends on p being true. Importantly, unlike believing or desiring that p, these latter states are wide in virtue of the attitude rather than the proposition towards which one bears that attitude. See also Section 7.4.

25 In fairness it should be added that Putnam (1975) himself offered a Twin Earth argument purporting to show that linguistic content depends on sociolinguistic facts. Putnam is incapable of distinguishing elms from beeches, and so is his doppelgänger on a Twin Earth which is exactly like Earth except the words 'elm' and 'beech' are switched. Still, when Putnam says 'elm' he means **elm**, but when his doppelgänger says 'elm' he means **beech**.

26 That is not to say that intentional states are identical with those external conditions. The extended mind thesis, as in Clark and Chalmers (1998), is the claim that in certain circumstances features of the proximal environment can be regarded as constituting part of the cognitive system, and not the claim that distal facts about water or the use of 'arthritis' literally constitute mental states.

27 For more on conceptual errors in the context of social externalism see Wikforss 2001 and Sawyer 2003. See Tye 2009: 186–87, for a putative argument that Burge-style social externalism extends to our introspectively applied, general concepts for phenomenal character.

28 See also Burge 1993a: 313–19.

29 Note that following Burge (1979) incomplete understanding can consist in either misunderstanding or agnosticism. Alf exemplifies the former in that he correctly takes 'arthritis' to apply to joints, but also mistakenly thinks it applies to his thigh. An example of the latter would be someone who correctly used 'arthritis' to apply to joints, but was unsure about whether it could pick out ailments elsewhere. Agnosticism as a kind of incomplete understanding requires being unsure whether a concept applies when there is a determinate fact of the matter whether it applies. See also Brown (2000) who argues that there must be a limit on the extent to which we can incompletely understand the concepts we think with given our self-conception as critical reasoners.

30 In 1975, Putnam only took the division of linguistic labour to show that reference is determined socially, not that meaning is also determined socially. Note that social determination can mean either of two things. In the case of natural kind terms such as 'water' ordinary speakers defer to the experts for the correct extension which is determined by the underlying nature of the kind in question. In the case of social, artefactual or functional terms such as 'carburettor', the extension is determined by the experts' best opinions to which such speakers defer. As any device blending air and fuel for an internal combustion engine counts as a carburettor, there is no underlying nature that determines reference. This means that while semantic deference is essential to Burge's arthritis argument, nothing in Putnam's Twin Earth argument hangs on this phenomenon: the extension of 'water' can itself play a role in individuating the natural kind concept. More controversially, Burge (1979) also believed that colour concepts are deferential, and recently Tye (2009: 64) argues that if colour concepts are deferential, then so are the phenomenal concepts that pick out the phenomenal character of experiences of colour. For more on deferential concepts and believing incompletely understood propositions see Recanati 1997, 2000.

31 See for instance Fodor 1982: 106. At this juncture Jackson (2004: 271–72) invokes implicit knowledge of the relevant other-dependent description. Indeed the knowledge of any properties that are associated with terms like 'water' as determining their reference is mostly implicit. Donnellan (1993: 167) defends a version of the metalinguistic view on which Alf expresses **arthritis** by 'arthritis' yet the content of his belief involves the different concept **a condition called 'arthritis' by the experts**. For critical discussion see Recanati 2000.

32 Relatedly, Segal (2007: 6–8) argues that the arthritis argument assumes an overly strong form of *consumerism*: the thesis that when minimally competent speakers use public language terms, they not only express public language meanings, the contents of their propositional attitudes are also fixed by those meanings.

33 The example is from Burge 1979: 91.

34 The question is not how we can tell or know whether Swampman is thinking. In other words, the challenge posed by Swampman is not the traditional epistemological problem of other minds.

35 Triangulation is familiar from plane trigonometry: if one side and two angles of a triangle are known, the other two sides and angle can be calculated. For more on triangulation in Davidson's work see Glüer 2006 and N. Goldberg 2008.

36 For a similar view see Dretske 1996: 82. For further critical discussion see Fodor 1994: 117–18, and Adams and Aizawa 1997.

37 Heil (2004b: 290) thinks Swampman constitutes a counterexample to externalism, because he takes the fact that Swampman is dispositionally indistinguishable from Davidson to show that Swampman is endowed with thoughts.

38 Note that triangulation is also an integral part of Davidson's views on radical interpretation. The radical interpreter triangulates the external objects that stand at the intersection of the causal lines connecting S and herself with those objects. Such a triangular structure involving causal connections between S and the radical interpreter and between those individuals and the external object must be in place if the radical interpreter is to assign any meaning to L_O. For more details see Glüer 2006 and N. Goldberg 2008.

39 The only exception is that if knowledge of the meaning of proper names requires knowledge of their referents involving causal links to those referents, then Swampman cannot know or even have beliefs about Davidson's friends' names.

40 To say that Terkel and Twin Terkel are functionally indistinguishable is to say that they function in the same way, not that they have the same function. Teleological theories of content understand the latter as a historical notion: something has the function F just in case it was selected for F-ing. To illustrate with one of Neander's examples (1996: 121), my kidney is a kidney, not in virtue of the way it actually works, but rather in virtue of what it was selected for by natural selection. A normal kidney and a diseased kidney function very differently even though both are supposed to regulate blood pressure, excrete wastes, produce hormones, etc.

41 A two-place relation is transitive just in case Rac follows from Rab and Rbc. For instance, if a is richer than b and b is richer than c then a is richer than c.

42 See also Neander's (1996) Swampcow example.

43 Fodor (1994: 117–18) provides further considerations in support of that intuition.

44 Braddon-Michell and Jackson (1997) argue that the analogy with water and H_2O breaks down, in that particular selectional histories can be seen neither as essential properties of intentional states nor as being scientifically identified with content. One worry is that ordinary speakers typically identify content independently of selectional history. Another worry is that they do not need to care about selectional history for it to determine content in nearly the same way in which they care about the content of their beliefs and desires.

4 Varieties of narrow and wide content

1 See McLaughlin and Tye 1998b and Burge 2007a: 11. Note that since content fails to supervene on internal features in both cases, mere denial of supervenience cannot capture the differences between these two kinds of semantic externalism.

2 See also McLaughlin and Tye 1998a: 371, and 1998b: 291–95.

3 Dry Earth may seem pretty outlandish, but what conceivably happens on Dry Earth actually happened on Earth with respect to phlogiston. For a while scientists regarded phlogiston as a natural kind present in all combustible materials and released during burning, but despite appearances it turned out not to exist.

4 Häggqvist and Wikforss (2007) point out that Korman (2007) (and Ludlow 2003) constitutes a radicalization of semantic externalism. While the Twin Earth argument shows that the descriptive semantics of 'water' – what 'water' means – vary with shifts in environmental features, his view implies that the foundational semantics of 'water' – whether 'water' has a referentialist or descriptivist semantics – vary with such alterations. On their view, semantic facts of this kind should rather depend on semantic intentions or linguistic practices.

5 For a similar conclusion see McGinn 1989: 30–36, 47–48. See McLaughlin and Tye 1998b: 302–11, for critical discussion of Boghossian's Dry Earth argument.

6 Segal (2000: 32–59) offers an argument for narrow content, based on Dry Earth considerations. Basically, the semantic externalist must say either

that dry-Earthly tokens of 'water' express an empty – descriptive – concept or else no concept at all. The latter is unacceptable, because scientists clearly expressed concepts when they used the empty terms 'phlogiston' or 'ether'. Otherwise we could not make psychological sense of what they said and did. But by semantic externalist lights, dry-Earthly tokens of 'water' cannot express an empty concept either. For if they did that concept would also be expressed by Earthly tokens of 'water', and there would be a shared narrow concept. Whatever physical conditions suffice for 'water' to express the empty concept on Dry Earth are conditions that also obtain on Earth. So, although dry-Earthly tokens and Earthly tokens of 'water' have different extensions, they express the same narrow concept. For critical discussion see Korman 2007.

7 In more recent work, Burge (2010: 68–69) argues that scientists were able to think thoughts containing the empty concept **phlogiston** in virtue of bearing certain relations to other thoughts containing relevant non-empty and externally individuated concepts, e.g. **physical body**, **burning** or **mass**. **Phlogiston**-thoughts are constitutively related through inference and scientific theory to the latter thoughts. Moreover, a novice just learning phlogiston theory could be said to think **phlogiston**-thoughts through communication with experts or others in the know.

8 Some might even claim that **water** would be a natural kind concept even if H_2O ceased to exist anywhere in the universe. What matters is not whether the conditions necessary for the existence of water happen to obtain somewhere, but whether its existence is provided for by the laws of nature. Compare with mendelevium (atomic number 101), which arguably counts as a natural kind in virtue of the way in which this synthetic element is governed by the laws of nature. But if **mendelevium** is a natural kind concept, it was presumably always such a concept, even before mendelevium was created in 1955 by bombarding einsteinium with alpha particles. Note that since one cannot know the pertinent laws of nature a priori, one cannot know a priori that a given concept is a natural kind concept, thus understood.

9 Soames (2002: 36) objects that systematically implementing this strategy makes descriptivism "virtually guaranteed, a priori, to be irrefutable". For a reply to Soames see Jackson 2007.

10 See also Jackson 2003, and Burge 1982, 2007a, Stalnaker 1989, Donnellan 1993 and Farkas 2008 for discussion.

11 See also Jackson 2003: 100, and 2004: 325. Whether our descriptivist will have to buy into singular content at all depends on whether she opts for a semantics of indexical expressions which invoke such content.

12 For a related example see Kaplan (1989: 531): Castor and Pollux are twin brothers who are psychologically alike yet express distinct singular propositions when they each utter the sentence 'my brother was born before me'.

13 If Heimson and Hume are stipulated to be intrinsic duplicates, then we have a case where two such duplicates fail to share their content-bearing mental states, yet that failure is not due to variation in their external environment, i.e. they will be in those distinct states regardless of the character of their external environment. This paves the way for a weak kind of semantic externalism as defended by Searle (1983). See Newman 2005 for criticism.

14 Perry (1993: 47–50) proposes that Hume and Heimson believe distinct singular propositions under the same mode of presentation, and so although they stand in distinct belief relations, they are in the same belief state. Perry also objects (1993: 43–44) that relativized propositions fail to constitute belief content in cases where two speakers share a common belief about the same individual. Smith succumbs to no illusions and so ascribes to Hume the property of having authored the *Treatise* by uttering 'you wrote the *Treatise*' in a context in which Hume is the hearer. The shared content of Smith's and Hume's beliefs is the pair of Hume and that property. For a reply see Lewis 1979 and Recanati 2007: Chs 12, 13, for further discussion.

15 There is of course a sense in which that function amounts to assigning relative truth-conditions, in contrast to truth-conditions in a more absolute sense. More on this distinction in Section 4.3.

16 One concern about Lewis' view is reminiscent of the Perfect Earth objection to rigidified descriptivism in Section 2.3, namely that intuitively Anna can believe that water is wet without thereby having any beliefs about her instantiating certain properties. Beliefs about what the world is like need not always involve beliefs about oneself. For more details see Newman 2005: 166 and Kallestrup (forthcoming).

17 In 1996, Putnam endorsed a more thoroughgoing kind of semantic externalism.

18 See also Loar 1988 and Fodor 1987, 1991. Loar distinguished between wide, social content as individuated by features of the external environmental and narrow, psychological content as individuated by common-sense psychology. Fodor's hybrid view is more thoroughly discussed in Section 7.2.

19 The question of how mental content can have such causal or explanatory power is thoroughly dealt with in Chapter 7.

20 Here McGinn is in line with other proponents of narrow content such as Fodor (1982, 1987).

21 We shall have much more to say about that distinction in Section 4.5.

22 We shall have much more to say about to the causal-explanatory power of content in Chapter 7.

23 For more details see Davies and Humberstone 1980 and Davies 2004.

24 Intuitions may be less clear-cut in other cases. What if it transpires that we actually inhabit a mixed Earth where the watery stuff is 50 per cent H_2O and 50 per cent XYZ? Maybe 'water' then picks out a disjunctive natural kind. Compare with jade which comes as jadeite and nephrite although these chemical kinds are less heterogeneous than H_2O and XYZ are meant to be. Or maybe the answer is indeterminate.

25 Chalmers (2006, 2011) also thinks of scenarios as epistemically possible worlds, i.e. ways things might be for all the speaker knows (a priori). To say that it is epistemically possible that water is not H_2O is to say that there is an epistemically possible world which verifies that statement.

26 The 'roughly speaking' part is important. Chalmers (2002: 627) rejects the claim that narrow content is always encapsulated by definite descriptions. Narrow content is a function from (centred) worlds considered as actual to referents and truth-values, and can only be fully characterized by specifying such values at given (centred) worlds. To evaluate the epistemic content associated with Mary's use of 'water', various (centred) worlds are hypothetically accepted as actual, and then rational conclusions about the reference of 'water' are reached under that hypothesis. When examining such cases, different kinds of stuff qualify as referents of 'water' in virtue of having the watery properties (plus some causal connection to the centre of the world). Narrow content is not ineffable, but inaccuracies arise once we attempt to articulate the epistemic content of a term by means of other terms. Jackson (2004: 263–73) suggests competent speakers have implicit knowledge of narrow content.

27 See also Jackson (1998b: 68–86) who argues along similar lines that the statement that water is H_2O is associated with distinct A-intension and C-intension. Kripke (1980) was the first to argue that such theoretical identities are necessary a posteriori.

28 To use Evans' terminology (1979), 'water' is *superficially* rigid since it refers to H_2O at all counterfactual worlds, but not *deeply* rigid since its reference shifts at different possible worlds when considered as actual. For an argument that ordinary proper names are both deeply and superficially rigid see Davies 2004.

29 This assumes Chalmers' semantic or epistemic interpretation (2006) of so-called two-dimensional modal logic, roughly that terms have fixed meanings as we consider various possible worlds as actual. In contrast, Stalnaker (2001) prefers a metasemantic or contextual interpretation. For further critical discussion see Schroeter 2004, Soames 2005: Ch. 9, and Byrne and Pryor 2006.

30 For related views see Lewis 1994 and Jackson 2004. Block (1991), Stalnaker (1989, 1990) and Block and Stalnaker (1999) critique the claim that the two-dimensional apparatus can yield a notion of narrow content. Burge (2010: 77–78) argues that **the watery stuff** cannot capture the semantic, epistemic or psychological profile of **water**. For instance, one could think of some liquid as water and yet wonder or doubt whether it is watery.

31 Soames (2005: Ch. 4) provides a detailed argument against Chalmers and other 'ambitious' two-dimensionalists who in his view attempt to use something like Kaplan's distinction between propositional content and character to revive descriptivism.

32 More on this in Section 7.3.

33 After enough time has elapsed Mary will undergo some conceptual changes. In particular, because she now causally interacts with XYZ, at some point she will begin to express the concept **twin-water** when she uses 'water'. For more on slow travelling cases between Earth and Twin Earth see Section 5.4.

34 'Here' is a rigid designator that picks out the contextually salient place in all possible worlds. For instance, if I utter 'here is overcast' in Glasgow, then 'here' refers to Glasgow in all possible worlds. If I want to assess whether what I said is true at some possible world I need to determine whether in that world it is overcast in Glasgow. For more on the rigidity of indexical expressions see Kaplan 1989.

35 Evans' descriptive name 'Julius' from Section 2.1 is another case in point.

36 See also Burge 1977, Salmon 1986: Vol. I, pt 4, and Donnellan 1993.

37 For more details see Salmon 1981, 1986 and Soames 2002, forthcoming.

38 What if two distinct natural kind terms refer to the same property/natural kind yet seem to express different propositional contents? Soames (2007) proposes that natural kinds are coarse-grained properties which are both the meanings and referents of simple natural kind terms such as 'water'. In contrast, grammatically complex natural kind phrases such as 'H_2O' refer to the same coarse-grained properties, but their meanings are fine-grained, structurally complex properties. Hence, 'water' and 'H_2O' are not synonymous.

39 For more details on Hume's dictum see Stoljar (2008). See Section 2.4, fn. 22, for the intrinsic/extrinsic distinction.

40 We shall leave it open whether tanning requires exposure to such radiation, and so is really an extrinsic matter, or whether the way in which the brown-coloured pigment melanin is created is of no importance. Alternatively, take Davidson's *sunnishburn* (1987: 451–54) which is a condition of the skin detectable just by looking.

41 The following owes much to Jackson and Pettit 1993: 271, and Stalnaker 1989: 289–91.

42 Perhaps this is what Wittgenstein (1968/1953: 217) had in mind when he said that "if God had looked into our minds he would not have been able to see there whom we were speaking of".

43 For more on narrow content as intra-world narrow see Jackson and Pettit 1993: 272–73. Note that some semantic internalists aim to construct narrow content out of wide content in much the same way being a foot-shaped imprint can be formed out of being a footprint. Fodor (1991) warns against this subtraction strategy: it is like constructing a narrow bachelor by removing the unmarriedness from an existing bachelor! As we shall see in Section 7.2 Fodor takes narrow content to be what determines truth-conditions of beliefs as a function of the external environment of the believer. Others take narrow content to be the primary notion of content out of which secondary wide content can be pinned down, e.g. Chalmers 2002, 2003.

5 Self-knowledge

1 Some philosophers reserve 'a priori knowledge' for knowledge of mathematical, logical, analytic or philosophical truths, but excluding knowledge arrived at by introspection. We shall henceforth use 'a priori knowledge' more inclusively so as to encompass also introspective truths, but nothing of material importance hangs on this.

2 For critical discussion of the inner sense model of self-knowledge see Section 5.2.

3 Tye (2009: 190) rejects the claim that necessarily when our faculty of introspection functions normally, if S is in some phenomenal state, then S can know that she is in that state simply on the basis of introspection. Tye holds that the phenomenal character of an experience of red just is the colour that my experience represents, namely red. To introspect the character of my experience is therefore to attend to the redness of surfaces.

4 The following owes much to Wright 1998.

5 Whether phenomenal avowals are infallible is a vexed issue. On the one hand, Davidson (1984: 103) is careful not to understand what he dubs 'first-person authority' in terms of infallibility or incorrigibility of such self-ascriptions. There is a presumption of correctness albeit a defeasible one. On the other hand, Tye (2009: Chs 5 and 8) has recently suggested that knowledge of the phenomenal character of an experience amounts to infallible knowledge by acquaintance.

6 As Twin Earth taught us, something can seem in every way as if water without being water, but nothing can seem in every way as if a pain without being a pain – or as Kripke (1980: 152) put it, "To be in the same epistemic situation that would obtain if one had a pain *is* to have a pain".

7 Here phrased slightly differently. See also Boghossian 1994: 36, Falvey and Owens 1994: 109–10, and S. Goldberg 2007a.

8 As Falvey and Owens (1994: 109) put it, S can have introspective knowledge of content without having introspective knowledge of comparative content. For more on this distinction see Section 6.3.

9 See Burge 1996: 93, and 2003b, 504, for more details, and Casullo 2010 for critical discussion.

10 It could well be that in order to acquire certain concepts one must have had certain perceptual experiences. For instance, visual experiences of red are arguably built into the acquisition conditions of the phenomenal concept **red** – the concept of what it is like to undergo such experiences. This does not imply that all knowledge of propositions containing that concept is a posteriori. Take the proposition **nothing is both red and not red**. The question of whether such knowledge is a priori or a posteriori arises only when the knower understands that proposition, hence possesses all the constituent concepts. See Burge 1996: 94–95.

11 Wright (2003: 60–68) agrees with Burge that entitlements play an important role in accounting for basic self-knowledge. They also agree that S can have defeasible yet immediate entitlements even when she cannot provide reasons or evidence for them. On Wright's view, entitlement is a kind of non-evidential, 'unearned' warrant. But Burge would eschew Wright's claim that S can know a priori what she is thinking only if she has an entitlement to the external enabling conditions.

12 For more elaboration and critical discussion of Burge's self-verifying judgements see Section 5.3.

13 Burge (1996: 105) also argues that the inner sense model of self-knowledge cannot account for *cogito*-like thoughts, and that the fact that thoughts

and propositional attitudes lack an associated distinctive phenomenology weakens the analogy to perception of the outer world.

14 This prima facie tension between semantic externalism and self-knowledge is widely acknowledged, as in Burge 1998: 653 and Falvey and Owens 1994: 113–14.

15 Relevant alternative accounts of knowledge say that S knows that p only if S's belief that p is based on evidence that is incompatible with all relevant alternatives A to p. On Dretske's version (2003), A is relevant to p if and only if: were p false, A might hold. See also Falvey and Owens 1994: 116.

16 It is striking that Putnam (1996) was sympathetic to incompatibilism. Many semantic internalists, including Fodor 1982: 103, Searle 1983: Ch. 8, and Farkas 2008: Ch. 6, have occupied various incompatibilist positions, indeed taken incompatibilist arguments to buttress their own brands of semantic internalism.

17 But note how odd it would be for S to believe the proposition **p but I don't believe that p**. If S believes that proposition, then S believes that p and she believes that she doesn't believe that p. But if it is true that S believes that p then her belief that she doesn't believe that p is false. Her belief in that proposition is thus self-falsifying. For more on this so-called Moorean paradox and self-knowledge see Shoemaker 1995.

18 In fairness it should be noted that Burge never claimed that self-verification applies to anything other than *cogito*-like thoughts.

19 This last claim is contentious. McLaughlin and Tye (1998a: 366) maintain that we can never introspectively know what our past thoughts were.

20 Both Ludlow (1998: 309–10) and Brueckner (1998: 325) take the view that at t_2 the wide contents entertained at t_1 are obliterated, but only Brueckner concedes that S has actually forgotten something. Gibbons (1996: 295, 305) tends to agree with Boghossian (1998a) that both sets of concepts are retained, but argues that the slow switching argument misfires on either interpretation. Burge himself (1998: 356–57) denies that acquiring new concepts upon moving to a new environment obliterates old concepts deriving from an old environment. As he puts it (1998: 364), "Displacement was never part of the switching cases, at least in my understanding of them. Cohabitation was always the assumed case".

21 See also Boghossian 1992: 19–20, and Ludlow 1998 for further discussion.

22 As highlighted in Sections 3.3 and 3.4, Burge acknowledged that S can be said to believe a proposition whose constituent concepts she incompletely understands. It follows that if S has a priori knowledge of such beliefs, there will be something about their content of which she lacks knowledge.

Further, Falvey and Owens (1994: 111–13) argue that (Epistemic Transparency) fails for reasons that are orthogonal to semantic externalism. Boghossian (1994: 36) argues that referentialist brands of semantic externalism and (Epistemic Transparency) are incompatible. For discussion on this point see Kallestrup 2003. Most semantic externalists happily acknowledge the falsity of (Epistemic Transparency) – see for instance Burge 1998b, S. Goldberg 2003a and Brown 2004: Ch. 5.

23 One could imagine similar cases involving 'suspenders', 'pants', 'professor', which all have different meanings in American and British English.

24 McLaughlin and Tye (1998a: 363–64) question the underlying assumption that introspective evidence is purely qualitative. On a reliabilist account of introspection such evidence consists in the mental states that are the very occurrent thoughts which the introspective beliefs are about. That is to say, introspective access is directly to these thoughts themselves, which thus provide conclusive evidence for the corresponding introspective beliefs. We have access to the external environment by having experiences that are caused by that environment, but our access to our occurrent thoughts is unmediated by experiences that are caused by those thoughts. Our thoughts are self-presenting in that we experience our thoughts, not by having experiences of them, but by simply having them.

25 Brown (2004: 136) also contends that since slow switching is normally irrelevant, self-knowledge is normally safeguarded, but S. Goldberg (2006a: 310–11) takes that to be too concessive, because self-knowledge should not be hostage to external circumstances even in exotic cases where the alternatives are relevant.

26 To illustrate that reasoning is unpersuasive when it equivocates consider the following argument: all stars are in orbit in outer space, and Madonna is a star, so Madonna is in orbit in outer space. The mistake is easy to see when the argument is disambiguated: all celestial bodies are in orbit in outer space, and Madonna is an entertainment celebrity, so Madonna is in orbit in outer space.

27 See also Section 7.1.

28 Brown (2000) argues that the possibility of possessing concepts incompletely undermines S's ability to engage in critical reasoning, i.e. to reflectively appreciate rational relations between her propositional attitudes. Although Brown's argument is not aimed at semantic externalism, it does raise questions for Burge who in 1996 emphasizes the importance of such an ability while, as we saw in Sections 3.3 and 3.4, endorses the possibility of having beliefs with incompletely understood contents.

29 S. Goldberg (2007a: 186–87) argues that if memory fails to preserve the content of her thought in the second premise, then her memory will also fail to preserve the justification she had for the content of that thought. What justifies a proposition about twin-water does not necessarily justify (with the same strength) a proposition about water.

6 Scepticism

1 One caveat is worth highlighting. The principle of (Closure) is distinct from the following instance of modus ponens: if S knows that p then S knows that q, and S knows that p; therefore S knows that q. Those who reject (Closure) typically do not reject modus ponens.

2 Hawthorne 2005: 29. We shall henceforth assume that competently deducing q from p involves knowing that entailment. For criticism see Dretske 2005, upon which the following putative counterexample is based.

3 For a different view about introspective evidence see fn. 15 in Chapter 5.

4 For more discussion see Vahid 2003.

5 Both principles are briefly revisited in Section 6.2.

6 In Section 6.1 we opted for an amended version of this principle, but for ease of exposition we shall henceforth employ (Closure).

7 This assumes that S would be able to believe that she is not a BIV if she were a BIV. As we shall see in Section 6.3, it is doubtful whether a BIV possesses the concepts necessary to have that belief. It should also be noted in fairness that Falvey and Owens (1994) never invoked (Relevant Alternatives) in a diagnosis of the failure of the external-world-sceptical argument.

8 One might wonder how a BIV could possibly utter any words at all. Take uttering to be some mental act of rehearsing a sentence to oneself.

9 Pace Putnam (1999), neither semantic externalism nor the direct or causal theory of reference is strictly necessary for Putnam's purposes. All he needs is that reference is causally constrained, and as we saw in Section 3.2 the descriptivist or semantic internalist can allow for that by incorporating causal properties into the cluster of associated reference-determining properties, e.g. 'tree' refers to whatever typically causes sensory experiences as of tress. See also Wright 1992: 72.

10 Later Putnam (1999) explicitly took the disquotation device as a premise in his anti-sceptical proof. For more on the use of (Disquotation) in this context see Noonan 1998, Sawyer 1999, Brueckner 1999, Noonan 2000 and Johnsen 2003.

11 Brueckner (1994b: 829–30) argues that by focusing on belief rather than sensory evidence as such these modal conceptions of knowledge counter-intuitively predict that in the context of semantic externalism S can know that she is not a BIV. As he puts it, "the fact that S would express a *dif-ferent* belief by 'I am a brain in a vat' in the sceptic's counterfactual situa-tion is irrelevant to the epistemic status of the belief S actually expresses by the sentence ... the point [is] that the sensory evidence on which S bases his actual belief *could be replicated in a situation in which he is a brain in a vat*. Who cares what he would believe in such a situation?"

12 For more on dreaming scepticism see Wright 1991 and Sosa 2007: Chs 1, 2 and 5.

13 Wright (2000, 2003) and Davies (1998, 2003) argue that although McKinsey's recipe constitutes a valid form of argument, knowledge (or warrant) of the premises *fails to transmit* to the conclusion, where the transmission principle for knowledge is roughly equivalent to (Closure*) from Section 6.1. For part of what makes S know the first premise is that she already knows the conclusion. It would therefore be circular to think that S could come to know the conclusion on the basis of knowing the premises and then reason in the way she does. To illustrate the notion of transmission failure of knowledge, suppose you claim to know that God exists on the basis of the Bible saying so and the Bible being infallible. An atheist then asks you to justify your claim that the Bible is infallible when no other book is. It would be illegitimate to respond that the Bible is infallible because God wrote it. So, even if God's existence follows from the fact that the infallible Bible says so, you cannot come to know that God exists by inference from this fact, because your knowledge that the Bible is infallible depends in part on your knowledge that God exists. A pressing problem for this epistemic response is that a priori knowledge may fail to transmit across an entailment while still being closed under a priori known entailment, and the latter is all the incompatibilist needs. For more details see McKinsey 2003: 102–4, Brown 2004: Ch. 7, and Brueckner 2008: 389.

14 Here the semantic externalist owes an account of what the intrinsic properties of **water** are. Boghossian (1998a: 162, 171) suggests mere inspection of an object yields knowledge only of its intrinsic properties, and that an object's extrinsic properties cannot be known by knowing about its intrinsic properties. Bear in mind Davidson's example (1987): whether my arm is suntanned as caused by sunbathing or cosmetically tanned as caused by a sunbed cannot be determined merely by inspecting

the skin on my arm. The way my skin is intrinsically is consistent with either being the case. The only difference is causal, hence extrinsic.

15 Thus S. Goldberg (2003b: 40) thinks that since the metaphysical dependence of possessing **water** on the existence of water itself depends on the metaphysical identity between water and H_2O, the former dependence is a posteriori because the latter identity is a posteriori. But, as Gertler (2004: 46) objects, if S were chemically ignorant, she could know the former dependence without knowing the latter identity.

16 For more details see Section 4.1.

17 For more recent discussion of whether S can know a priori that she is unsure about the application conditions of her concept **water** when such determinate conditions are in place see Brueckner 2002, 2005 and Noordhof 2004, 2005.

18 For more on bullet-biting see Warfield 1995, Brown 2004: 238–39, Noordhof 2004 and Brueckner 2007b.

7: Mental causation

1 Here we rely on a two-premise version of (Closure*) from Section 6.1.

2 This term is coined by Chalmers (1996: Ch. 5).

3 See Crane 1995 for more details. We shall henceforth talk about states causing other states, and about properties causing other properties, where the latter is short for property instances causing other properties to be instantiated.

4 Yablo (2003: 321–25) argues that the following definition of causal relevance has counterexamples: a property of some cause is causally relevant to the effect if and only if the effect would not have occurred had the cause occurred without that property. He also suggests that a more complex counterfactual account fares better.

5 See also Dretske 1988: 79.

6 For ease of exposition we shall henceforth be relaxed about the differences in what causation and causal explanation relate.

7 For more details see Kallestrup 2006.

8 See for instance McGinn 1989: 133, Kim 1993b: 288, and Dretske 1993a: 187. Yablo (1997) draws intriguing connections between our two problems about mental causation, which he calls respectively the arguments 'from below' and 'from within'.

9 For more on reasons and rationality see Smith 2004.

10 In this example the object is externally individuated in virtue of appropriate causal connections between it and the external features in question.

The same is true of Davidson's sunburn example from Sections 3.1 and 4.5. But external features can individuate an object without affecting it causally. The birth of a child can make someone a great grandparent even if they never meet.

11 See also McGinn 1982, as presented in Section 4.3.

12 The term 'methodological solipsism' was coined by Putnam (1975: 136) for the assumption that 'no psychological state, properly so called, pre-supposes the existence of any individual other than the subject to whom that state is ascribed'.

13 Or take evolutionary biology where taxonomy by species is dependent on such extrinsic properties as having a certain ancestry.

14 Adams (1993: 45) argues that there is no behaviour in common between Mary and twin-Mary across contexts, hence there is no need for shared narrow states to explain any such shared behaviour. For further discussion of the modal argument see Burge 1989, Wilson 1992, Owens 1993, Peacocke 1993, Baker 1994, Barrett 1997 and Chalmers 2002.

15 It should be mentioned in fairness that Fodor (1994) later renounces narrow content thus understood.

16 Fodor's two-component view bears a resemblance to the other two such views discussed in Section 4.3.

17 Jackson and Pettit 1988: 389–91.

18 The same line of reasoning can also be found in Segal 1989 and Noonan 1991.

19 For more criticism of the dual-component conception of causal explanation see Peacocke 1993: 208–9.

20 'What caused the bull to charge at the bullfighter?' The answer 'the shaking of a red cape' is not specific enough. The redness of the cape is causally relevant but the shaking is not. As Barrett (1997: 252) remarks, many such conjunctive properties contain causally irrelevant information. Contrast with this example due to Segal and Sober (1991: 14–16): 'why did the environment cause the struck match to light?' The answer 'because the environment contained air' seems acceptable even though the oxygen is what matters. Yablo (1992: 274–77, 1997: 266–67) argues that causes must be proportional to their effects: if a putative cause is too specific, it will be screened off by a less specific cause, but if a cause is not specific enough, a more specific cause will screen it off. Being coloured is not specific enough to cause the bull's anger, and so redness will screen it off. Being crimson is too specific to cause the bull's anger, and so will be screened off by redness.

21 For more details and examples see Block 1990: 156–60, Peacocke 1993: 215–20, and Jackson 1996: 393–400.

22 Cf. Jackson and Pettit 1988: 384–88. They also argue that taking the wide contents of wide-content mental states to be essential to them prevents the semantic externalist from identifying such mental states with the physical filler states.

23 For more critical discussion see Yablo 2003.

24 For more critical discussion see Menzies 2007.

BIBLIOGRAPHY

Adams, Frederick (1993) "Fodor's Modal Argument," *Philosophical Psychology* 6: 41–56.

Adams, Fred and Aizawa, Ken (1997) "Rock Beats Scissors: Historicism Fights Back," *Analysis* 57 (4): 273–81.

Armstrong, David (1963) "Is Introspective Knowledge Incorrigible?," *Philosophical Review* 72: 417–32.

Bach, Kent (2008) "The Semantics–Pragmatics Distinction: What It Is and Why It Matters'. Manuscript. http://online.sfsu.edu/~kbach/semprag.html

Baker, Lynne Rudder (1994) "Content and Context," *Philosophical Perspectives* 8: 17–32.

Ball, Derek (2007) "Twin-Earth Externalism and Concept Possession," *Australasian Journal of Philosophy* 85: 457–72.

Bar-on, Dorit (2005) *Speaking My Mind: Expression and Self-knowledge*, Oxford: Oxford University Press.

Barrett, Jonathan (1997) "Individualism and the Cross-Contexts Test," *Pacific Philosophical Quarterly* 78: 242–60.

Block, Ned (1990) "Can the Mind Change the World?," in George S. Boolos (ed.), *Meaning and Method: Essays in Honor of Hilary Putnam*, Cambridge: Cambridge University Press, pp. 137–70.

——(1991) "What Narrow Content Is Not," in Barry M. Loewer and Georges Rey (eds), *Meaning in Mind: Fodor and His Critics*, Oxford: Blackwell, pp. 33–64.

Block, Ned and Stalnaker, Robert (1999) "Conceptual Analysis, Dualism, and the Explanatory Gap," *Philosophical Review* 108: 1–46.

Boghossian, Paul (1992) "Externalism and Inference," *Philosophical Issues* 2: 11–28.

——(1994) "The Transparency of Mental Content," *Philosophical Perspectives* 8: 33–50.

——(1998a) "Content and Self-knowledge," in Peter Ludlow and Norah Martin (eds), *Externalism and Self-knowledge*, Chicago: University of Chicago Press, pp. 149–74.

——(1998b) "What the Externalist Can Know A Priori," in Crispin Wright, Barry Smith and Cynthia Macdonald (eds), *Knowing Our Own Minds*, Oxford: Oxford University Press, pp. 271–84.

Braddon-Mitchell, David and Jackson, Frank (1997) "The Teleological Theory of Content," *Australasian Journal of Philosophy* 75: 474–89.

Braun, David (2006) "Names and Natural Kind Terms," in Ernie Lepore and Barry Smith (eds), *Oxford Handbook of the Philosophy of Language*, Oxford: Oxford University Press, pp. 490–515.

Braun, David and Sider, Theodore (2006) "Kripke's Revenge," *Philosophical Studies* 128: 669–82.

Brewer, Bill (2000) "Externalism and A Priori Knowledge of Empirical Facts," in Christopher Peacocke and Paul Boghossian (eds), *New Essays on the A Priori*, Oxford: Oxford University Press, pp. 415–33.

Brown, Jessica (1995) "The Incompatibility of Anti-individualism and Privileged Access," *Analysis* 55 (3): 149–56.

——(2000) "Critical Reasoning, Understanding, and Self-knowledge," *Philosophy and Phenomenological Research* 61: 659–77.

——(2001) "Anti-individualism and Agnosticism," *Analysis* 61 (3): 213–24.

——(2004) *Anti-individualism and Knowledge*, Cambridge, MA: MIT Press.

Brueckner, Anthony (1986) "Brains in a Vat," *Journal of Philosophy* 83: 148–67.

——(1990) "Scepticism about Knowledge of Content," *Mind* 99: 447-51.

——(1994a) "Knowledge of Content and Knowledge of the World," *Philosophical Review* 103: 327–43.

——(1994b) "The Structure of the Skeptical Argument," *Philosophy and Phenomenological Research* 54: 827–35.

——(1998) "Externalism and Memory," in Peter Ludlow and Norah Martin (eds), *Externalism and Self-knowledge*, Chicago: University of Chicago Press, pp. 319–32.

——(1999) "Semantic Answer to Scepticism," in Keith DeRose and Ted A. Warfield (eds), *Skepticism: A Contemporary Reader*, Oxford: Oxford University Press, pp. 43–60.

——(2001) "A Priori Knowledge of the World Not Easily Available," *Philosophical Studies* 104: 109–14.

——(2002) "Anti-individualism and Analyticity," *Analysis* 62: 87–91.

——(2003) "The Coherence of Scepticism about Self-knowledge," *Analysis* 63: 41–48.

——(2005) "Noordhof on McKinsey–Brown," Analysis 65: 86–88.

——(2007a) "Scepticism about Self-knowledge Redux," *Analysis* 67 (4): 311–15.

——(2007b) "Externalism and Privileged Access are Consistent," in Brian McLaughlin and Jonathan Cohen (eds), *Contemporary Debates in Philosophy of Mind*, Oxford: Blackwell, pp. 37–52.

——(2008) "Wright on the McKinsey Problem," *Philosophy and Phenomenological Research* 76: 385–91.

Burge, Tyler (1977) "Belief De Re," *Journal of Philosophy* 74: 338–62.

——(1979) "Individualism and the Mental," *Midwest Studies in Philosophy* 4: 73–121.

——(1982) "Other Bodies," in Andrew Woodfield (ed.), *Thought and Object*, London: Oxford University Press, pp. 97–120.

——(1986) "Individualism and Psychology," *Philosophical Review* 95: 3–45.

——(1988) "Individualism and Self-knowledge," *Journal of Philosophy* 85: 649–63.

——(1989) "Individuation and Causation in Psychology," *Pacific Philosophical Quarterly* 70: 303–22.

——(1993a) "Concepts, Definitions and Meaning," *Metaphilosophy* 24: 309-325.

——(1993b) "Mind–Body Causation and Explanatory Practice," in John Heil and Alfred Mele (eds), *Mental Causation*, Oxford: Oxford University Press, pp. 97–120.

——(1993c) "Content Preservation," *Philosophical Review* 102: 457–88.

——(1996) "Our Entitlement to Self-knowledge," *Proceedings of the Aristotelian Society* 96: 91–116.

——(1998) "Memory and Self-knowledge," in Peter Ludlow and Norah Martin (eds), *Externalism and Self-knowledge*, Chicago: University of Chicago Press, pp. 351–70.

——(2003a) "Social Anti-individualism, Objective Reference," *Philosophy and Phenomenological Research* 67: 682–90.

——(2003b) "Perceptual Entitlement," *Philosophy and Phenomenological Research* 67: 503–48.

——(2007a) "Introduction," in his *Foundations of Mind*, Oxford: Oxford University Press, pp. 1–31.

——(2007b) *Foundations of Mind*, Oxford: Oxford University Press.

——(2010) *Origins of Objectivity*, Oxford: Oxford University Press.

Byrne, Alex and Pryor, James (2006) "Bad Intensions," in Manuel Garcia-Carpintero and Josep Maci (eds), *Two-Dimensional Semantics: Foundations and Applications*, Oxford: Oxford University Press.

Caplan, Ben (2007) "Millian Descriptivism," *Philosophical Studies* 133: 181–98.

Cassam, Quassim (ed.) (1994) *Self-knowledge*, Oxford: Oxford University Press.

Casullo, Albert (2010) "What Is Entitlement?," *Acta Analytica* 22: 267–79.

Chalmers, David (1996) *The Conscious Mind: In Search of a Fundamental Theory*, New York: Oxford University Press.

——(2002) "The Components of Content," in David Chalmers (ed.), *Philosophy of Mind: Classical and Contemporary Readings*, Oxford: Oxford University Press, pp. 608–33.

——(2003) "The Nature of Narrow Content," *Philosophical Issues* 13: 46–66.

——(2006) "Two-Dimensional Semantics," in Ernie Lepore and Barry Smith (eds), *Oxford Handbook of the Philosophy of Language*, Oxford: Oxford University Press, pp. 574–606.

——(2011) "Propositions and Attitude Ascriptions: A Fregean Account", *Noûs* 45. DOI: 10.1111/j.1468-0068.2010.00788.x

Clark, Andy and Chalmers, David (1998) "The Extended Mind," *Analysis* 58: 7–19.

Crane, Tim (1991) "All the Difference in the World," *Philosophical Quarterly* 41: 1–25.

——(1995) "The Mental Causation Debate," *Proceedings of the Aristotelian Society, Supplementary Volume* 69: 211–36.

Crawford, Sean (1998) "In Defense of Object-Dependent Thoughts," *Proceedings of the Aristotelian Society* 98: 201–10.

Christensen, David (1993) "Skeptical Problems, Semantical Solutions," *Philosophy and Phenomenological Research* 53: 301–21

Davidson, Donald (1963) "Actions, Reasons and Causes," *Journal of Philosophy* 60: 685–700.

——(1967) "Truth and Meaning," *Synthese* 17: 304–23.

——(1970) "Events and Particulars," *Noûs* 4: 25–32.

——(1971) "Agency," in Robert Binkley, Richard Bronaugh and Ausonia Marras (eds), *Agent, Action, and Reason*, Toronto: University of Toronto Press.

——(1973) "Radical Interpretation," *Dialectica* 27: 314–28.

——(1982) "Rational Animals," *Dialectica* 36: 318–27.

——(1984) "First Person Authority," *Dialectica* 38: 101–12.

——(1987) "Knowing One's Own Mind," *Proceedings and Addresses of the American Philosophical Association* 60: 441–58.

——(1991) "Epistemology Externalized," *Dialectica* 45: 191–202.

——(1994) "Radical Interpretation Interpreted," *Philosophical Perspectives* 8: 121–28.

——(2006) "The Perils and Pleasure of Interpretation," in Ernie Lepore and Barry Smith (eds), *The Oxford Handbook of Philosophy of Language*, Oxford: Oxford University Press, pp. 1056–68.

Davies, Martin (1998) "Externalism, Architecturalism, and Epistemic Warrant," in Crispin Wright, Barry Smith and Cynthia Macdonald (eds), *Knowing Our Own Minds*, Oxford: Oxford University Press, pp. 321–61.

——(2003) "The problem of armchair knowledge," in Susana Nuccetelli (ed.), *New Essays on Semantic Externalism and Self-knowledge*, Cambridge MA: MIT Press, pp. 23–55.

——(2004) "Reference, Contingency, and the Two-Dimensional Framework," *Philosophical Studies* 118: 83–131.

Davies, Martin and Humberstone, Lloyd (1980) "Two Notions of Necessity," *Philosophical Studies* 38: 1–30.

DeRose, Keith and Warfield, Ted A. (eds) (1999) *Skepticism: A Contemporary Reader*, Oxford: Oxford University Press.

Dewitt, Michael and Hanley, Richard (eds) (2006) *The Blackwell Guide to the Philosophy of Language*, Oxford: Blackwell.

Donnellan, Keith (1993) "There Is a Word for That Kind of Thing: An Investigation of Two Thought Experiments," *Philosophical Perspectives* 7: 155–71.

Dretske, Fred (1988) *Explaining Behavior: Reasons in a World of Causes*, Cambridge, MA: MIT Press.

——(1993a) "The Nature of Thought," *Philosophical Studies* 70: 185–99.

——(1993b) "Mental Events as Structuring Causes of Behaviour," in John Heil and Alfred Mele (eds), *Mental Causation*, Oxford: Oxford University Press, pp. 121–36.

——(1995) *Naturalizing the Mind*, Cambridge, MA: MIT Press.

——(1996) "Absent Qualia," *Mind and Language* 11: 78–85.

——(2003) "Skepticism: What Perception Teaches," in Stephen Luper (ed.), *The Skeptics*, Hampshire: Ashgate, pp. 105–19.

——(2005) "The Case against Closure," in Matthias Steup and Ernest Sosa (eds) *Contemporary Debates in Epistemology*, Malden, MA: Blackwell, pp. 13–25.

Dummett, Michael (1973) *Frege: Philosophy of Language*, Cambridge, MA: Harvard University Press.

——(1978) *Truth and Other Enigmas*, London: Duckworth.

——(1981) *The Interpretation of Frege's Philosophy*, London: Duckworth.

——(1991) *The Logical Basis of Metaphysics*, Cambridge, MA: Harvard University Press.

Ebbs, Gary (2001) "Is Skepticism about Self-knowledge Coherent?," *Philosophical Studies* 105: 43–58.

——(2005) "Why Scepticism about Self-knowledge is Self-undermining'. *Analysis* 65: 237–44.

Egan, Frances (2009) "Wide Content," in Brian McLaughlin (ed.) *The Oxford Handbook of Philosophy of Mind*, New York: Oxford University Press, pp. 351–66.

Evans, Gareth (1973) "The Causal Theory of Names," *Proceedings of the Aristotelian Society, Supplementary Volume* 47: 187–208.

——(1979) "Reference and Contingency," *Monist* 62: 161–89.

——(1981) "Understanding Demonstratives," in Herman Parret and Jacques Bouveresse (eds), *Meaning and Understanding*, Berlin: Walter de Gruyter, pp. 280–303.

——(1982) *The Varieties of Reference*, Oxford: Oxford University Press.

Falvey, Kevin (2000) "The Compatibility of Anti-individualism and Privileged Access," *Analysis* 60: 137–42

Falvey, Kevin and Owens, Joseph (1994) "Externalism, Self-knowledge, and Skepticism," *Philosophical Review* 103: 107–37.

Farkas, Katalin (2003) "What Is Externalism?," *Philosophical Studies* 112 (3): 187–208.

——(2008) *The Subject's Point of View*, Oxford: Oxford University Press.

Fodor, Jerry (1982) "Cognitive Science and the Twin-Earth Problem," *Notre Dame Journal of Formal Logic* 23: 98–118.

——(1987) *Psychosemantics: The Problem of Meaning in the Philosophy of Mind*, Cambridge, MA: MIT Press.

——(1991) "A Modal Argument for Narrow Content," *Journal of Philosophy* 88: 5–26.

——(1994) *The Elm and the Expert: Mentalese and Its Semantics*, Cambridge, MA: MIT Press.

Forbes, Graeme (1990) "The Indispensability of *Sinn*," *Philosophical Review* 99 (4): 535–63.

Frege, Gottlob (1964) *The Basic Laws of Arithmetic*, partial trans. Montgomery Furth, Berkeley: University of California Press. Originally published in 1893 as *Grundgesetze der Arithmetik* (Jena: Hermann Pohle).

——(1994a) "On Sense and Reference," in Robert M. Harnish (ed.), *Basic Topics in the Philosophy of Language*, New York: Harvester Wheatsheaf, pp. 142–60. Originally published in 1892 as "Über Sinn und Bedeutung," *Zeitschrift für Philosophie und Philosophische Kritik* 100: 25–50.

——(1994b) "The Thought: A Logical Enquiry," in Robert M. Harnish (ed.), *Basic Topics in the Philosophy of Language*, New York: Harvester Wheatsheaf, pp. 517–35. Originally published in 1918 as "Der Gedanke: Eine Logische Untersuchung," in *Beiträge zur Philosophie des Deutschen Idealismus* 1: 58–77.

Garcia-Carpintero, Manuel and Macia, Josep (eds) (2006) *Two-Dimensional Semantics*, Oxford: Oxford University Press.

Geach, Peter T (1969) *God and the Soul*, London: Routledge.

Gertler, Brie (2004) "We Can't Know A Priori That H_2O Exists: But Can We Know That Water Does?," *Analysis* 64: 44–47.

——(2010) *Self-knowledge*, Abingdon: Routledge.

Gibbons, John (1996) "Externalism and Knowledge of Content," *Philosophical Review* 105 (3): 287–310.

Glüer, Kathrin (2006) "Triangulation," in Ernie Lepore and Barry Smith (eds), *The Oxford Handbook of Philosophy of Language*, Oxford: Oxford University Press, pp. 1006–19.

Goldberg, Nathaniel (2008) "Tension within Triangulation," *Southern Journal of Philosophy* 46: 363–83.

Goldberg, Sanford (2002) "Do Anti-individualistic Construals of the Attitudes Capture the Agent's Conceptions?," *Noûs* 36 (4): 597–621.

——(2003a) "What Do You Know When You Know Your Own Thoughts?' in Susana Nuccetelli (ed.), *New Essays on Semantic Externalism and Self-knowledge*, Cambridge, MA: MIT Press, pp. 241–56.

——(2003b) "On Our Alleged A Priori Knowledge That Water Exists," *Analysis* 63: 38–41.

——(2005) "The Dialectical Context of Boghossian's Memory Argument," *Canadian Journal of Philosophy* 35: 135–48.

——(2006a) "Brown on Self-knowledge and Discrimination," *Pacific Philosophical Quarterly* 87 (3): 301–14.

——(2006b) "An Anti-individualistic Semantics for 'Empty' Natural Kind Terms," *Grazer Philosophische Studien* 70: 55–76.

——(2007a) "Anti-individualism, Content Preservation, and Discursive Justification," *Noûs* 41 (2): 178–203.

——(ed.) (2007b) *Internalism and Externalism in Semantics and Epistemology*, Oxford: Oxford University Press.

Goldman, Alvin (1967) "A Causal Theory of Knowing," *Journal of Philosophy* 64: 355–72.

Häggqvist, Sören and Wikforss, Åsa (2007) "Externalism and A Posteriori Semantics," *Erkenntnis* 67: 373–86.

Hahn, Martin and Ramberg, Bjørn (eds) (2003) *Reflections and Replies: Essays on the Philosophy of Tyler Burge*, Cambridge, MA: MIT Press.

Hawthorne, John (2005) "The Case for Closure," in Matthias Steup and Ernest Sosa (eds), *Contemporary Debates in Epistemology*, Malden, MA: Blackwell, pp. 26–42.

Heck, Richard G. (1995) "The Sense of Communication," *Mind* 104 (413): 79–106.

Heil, John (1998) "Privileged Access," in Peter Ludlow and Norah Martin (eds), *Externalism and Self-knowledge*, Chicago: University of Chicago Press, pp. 129–46.

——(2004a) *Philosophy of Mind: A Contemporary Introduction*, Abingdon: Routledge.

——(2004b) "Natural Intentionality," in Richard Schantz (ed.), *The Externalist Challenge*, Berlin: Walter de Gruyter, pp. 287–96.

Huemer, Michael (2007) "Epistemic Possibility," *Synthese* 156: 119–42.

Hume, David (2000) *A Treatise of Human Nature*, ed. Norton, David F. and Norton, Mary J., New York: Oxford University Press. Originally published in 1839–40.

Jackson, Frank (1996) "Mental Causation," *Mind* 105 (419): 377–413.

——(1998a) "Reference and Description Revisited," *Philosophical Perspectives* 12: 201–18.

——(1998b) *From Metaphysics to Ethics: A Defense of Conceptual Analysis*, Oxford: Oxford University Press.

——(2003) "Narrow Content and Representation – Or Twin Earth Revisited' *Proceedings and Addresses of the American Philosophical Association* 77 (2): 55–70.

——(2004) "Why We Need A-Intensions," *Philosophical Studies* 118: 257–277.

——(2007) "Reference and Description from the Descriptivist Corner," *Philosophical Books* 48: 17–26.

Jackson, Frank and Pettit, Philip (1988) "Functionalism and Broad Content," *Mind* 97: 318–400.

——(1990) "Program Explanation: A General Perspective," *Analysis* 50 (2): 107–17.

——(1993) "Some Content Is Narrow," in John Heil and Alfred Mele (eds), *Mental Causation*, Oxford: Oxford University Press, pp. 259–82.

Johnsen, Bredo (2003) "Of Brains in Vats, Whatever Brains in Vats Might Be," *Philosophical Studies* 112 (3): 225–49.

Kallestrup, Jesper (2003) "Paradoxes about Belief," *Australasian Journal of Philosophy* 81: 107–17.

——(2006) "The Causal Exclusion Argument," *Philosophical Studies* 131 (2): 459–85.

——(2011) "Recent Work on McKinsey's Paradox," *Analysis* 71: 157–171.

——(forthcoming) "Actually-Rigidified Descriptivism Revisited," *Dialectica*, 65(3).

Kaplan, David (1978) "On the Logic of Demonstratives," *Journal of Philosophical Logic* 8: 81–98.

——(1989) "Demonstratives' in Joseph Almog, John Perry and Howard Wettstein (eds), *Themes from Kaplan*, Oxford: Oxford University Press, pp. 481–563.

Kim, Jaegwon (1993a) "Events as Property Exemplifications," in his *Supervenience and Mind: Selected Philosophical Essays*, Cambridge: Cambridge University Press, pp. 33–52.

——(1993b) "Dretske on How Reasons Explain Behavior," in his *Supervenience and Mind: Selected Philosophical Essays*, Cambridge: Cambridge University Press, pp. 285–308.

Korman, Daniel Z. (2007) "What Externalists Should Say about Dry Earth," *Journal of Philosophy* 103: 503–20.

Koslicki, Kathrin (2008) "Natural Kinds and Natural Kind Terms'. *Philosophy Compass* 3 (4): 789–802.

Kripke, Saul (1979) "A Puzzle about Belief' in *Meaning and Use*, ed. A. Margalit, Dordrecht: D. Reidel, pp. 239–83.

——(1980) *Naming and Necessity*, Cambridge, MA: Harvard University Press.

Kroon, Frederick W. (1987) "Causal Descriptivism," *Australasian Journal of Philosophy* 65: 1–17.

——(2004) "A-intensions and Communication," *Philosophical Studies* 118: 279–98.

Kvanvig, Jonathan (2006) "Closure Principles," *Philosophy Compass* 1 (3): 256–67.

Langton, Rae and Lewis, David (1998) "Defining 'Intrinsic'," *Philosophy and Phenomenological Research* 58: 333–45.

Lepore, Ernest and Ludwig, Kirk (2007) *Donald Davidson: Meaning, Truth, Language, and Reality*, New York: Oxford University Press.

Lewis, David (1972) "Psychophysical and Theoretical Identifications," *Australasian Journal of Philosophy* 50: 249–58.

——(1973) *Counterfactuals*, Oxford: Blackwell.

——(1979) "Attitudes De Dicto and De Se," *Philosophical Review* 88: 513–43.

——(1980) "Mad Pain and Martian Pain," in Ned Block (ed.), *Readings in the Philosophy of Psychology*, vol. 1, Cambridge, MA: Harvard University Press, pp. 216–22.

——(1984) "Putnam's Paradox," *Australasian Journal of Philosophy* 62: 221–36.

Lewis, David (1994) "Reduction of Mind," in Samuel Guttenplan (ed.), *A Companion to Philosophy of Mind*, Oxford: Blackwell, pp. 412–31.

——(1997) Naming the Colours," *Australasian Journal of Philosophy* 75: 325–42.

——(2002) "Tharp's Third Theorem," *Analysis* 62 (2): 95–97.

Loar, Brian (1988) "Social Content and Psychological Content," in Robert Grimm and Daniel Merrill (eds) *Thought and Content*, Tuscon: University of Arizona Press, pp. 99–110.

Ludlow, Peter (1995) "Externalism, Self-knowledge, and the Prevalence of Slow-Switching," *Analysis* 55: 45–49.

——(1997) "On the Relevance of Slow Switching," *Analysis* 57 (4): 285–286.

——(1998) "Social Externalism, Self-knowledge and Memory' in Peter Ludlow and Norah Martin (eds), *Externalism and Self-knowledge*, Chicago: University of Chicago Press, pp. 307–10.

——(2003) "Externalism, Logical Form, and Linguistic Intentions," in Alex Barber (ed.), *Epistemology of Language*, Oxford: Oxford University Press, pp. 399–414.

Ludlow, Peter and Martin, Norah (eds) (1998) *Externalism and Self-knowledge*, Chicago: University of Chicago Press.

Lycan, William (2008) *Philosophy of Language: A Contemporary Introduction*, Abingdon: Routledge.

Marti, Genoveva (1995) "The Essence of Genuine Reference," *Journal of Philosophical Logic* 24 (3): 275–89.

Mcdonald, Graham and Papineau, David (eds) (2006) *Teleosemantics*, New York: Oxford University Press.

McDowell, John (1977) "On the Sense and Reference of a Proper Name," *Mind* 86: 159–85.

——(1984) "*De Re* Senses," *Philosophical Quarterly* 34: 283–94.

——(1986) "Singular Thought and the Extent of Inner Space," in John McDowell and Philip Pettit (eds), *Subject, Thought, and Context*, Oxford: Clarendon Press, pp. 137–68.

——(1998) *Meaning, Knowledge and Reality*, Cambridge, MA: Harvard University Press.

McGinn, Colin (1977) "Charity, Interpretation, and Belief," *Journal of Philosophy* 74 (9): 521–35.

——(1982) "The Structure of Content," in Andrew Woodfield (ed.), *Thought and Object*, Oxford: Oxford University Press, pp. 206–58.

——(1989) *Mental Content*, Oxford: Blackwell.

McKinsey, Michael (1991) "Anti-individualism and Privileged Access," *Analysis* 51: 9–16.

——(2002) "Forms of Externalism and Privileged Access," *Philosophical Perspectives* 16: 199–224.

——(2003) "Transmission of Warrant and Closure of Warrant," in Susana Nuccetelli (ed.), *New Essays on Semantic Externalism and Self-knowledge*, Cambridge, MA: MIT Press, pp. 97–116.

——(2007) "Externalism and Privileged Access are Consistent," in Brian McLaughlin and Jonathan Cohen (eds), *Contemporary Debates in Philosophy of Mind*, Oxford: Blackwell, pp. 53–66.

McLaughlin, Brian and Beckermann, Ansgar and Walter, Sven (eds) (2009) *The Oxford Handbook of Philosophy of Mind*, Oxford: Oxford University Press.

McLaughlin, Brian and Cohen, Jonathan (eds) (2007) *Contemporary Debates in Philosophy of Mind*, Oxford: Blackwell.

McLaughlin, Brian and Tye, Michael (1998a) "Is Content-Externalism Compatible with Privileged Access?," *Philosophical Review* 107 (3): 349–80.

——(1998b) "Externalism, Twin Earth, and Self-knowledge," in Crispin Wright, Barry Smith and Cynthia Macdonald (eds), *Knowing Our Own Minds*, Oxford: Oxford University Press, pp. 285–320.

Mellor, Hugh. D. (1977) "Natural Kinds," *British Journal for the Philosophy of Science* 28 (4): 299–312.

Mendola, Joseph (2008) *Anti-externalism*, Oxford: Oxford University Press.

Menzies, Peter (2007) "Mental Causation on the Program Model," in Geoffrey Brennan, Robert Goodin and Michael Smith (eds), *The Common Mind: Essays in Honour of Philip Pettit*, Oxford: Oxford University Press, pp. 28–54.

Mill, John S. (1963) *System of Logic*, in *Collected Works of John Stuart Mill*, ed. J. M. Robson, Toronto: University of Toronto Press. Originally published in 1843.

Millar, Alex (2007) *Philosophy of Language*, Abingdon: Routledge.

Millikan, Ruth (1989) "Biosemantics," *Journal of Philosophy* 86: 281–97.

——(1996) "Swampkinds," *Mind and Language* 11: 103–17.

Neander, Karen (1996) Swampman Meets Swampcow, *Mind and Language* 11: 118-129.

Needham, Paul (2000) "What Is Water?," *Analysis* 60: 13–21.

Newman, Anthony (2005) "Two Grades of Internalism (Pass and Fail)," *Philosophical Studies* 122: 153–69.

Noonan, Harold W. (1991) "Object-Dependent Thoughts and Psychological Redundancy," *Analysis* 50: 1–9.

——(1993) "Object-Dependent Thoughts: A Case of Superficial Necessity but Deep Contingency," in John Heil and Alfred Mele (eds) *Mental Causation*, Oxford: Oxford University Press, pp. 283–308.

——(1998) "Reflections on Putnam, Wright and Brains in Vats," *Analysis* 58: 59–62.

——(2000) "Reply to Sawyer on Brains in Vats," *Analysis* 60 (3): 247–49.

——(2001) *Frege. A Critical Introduction*, Cambridge: Polity Press.

Noordhof, Paul (2004) "Outsmarting the McKinsey–Brown Argument?," *Analysis* 64: 48–56.

——(2005) "The Transmogrification of A Posteriori Knowledge: Reply to Brueckner," *Analysis* 65: 88–89.

Nozick, Robert (1981) *Philosophical Explanations*, Cambridge, MA: Harvard University Press.

Nuccetelli, Susana (2003a) "Knowing That One Knows What One Is Talking About," in Susana Nuccetelli (ed.), *New Essays on Semantic Externalism and Self-knowledge*, Cambridge, MA: MIT Press, pp. 169–84.

——(ed.) (2003b) *Semantic Externalism and Self-knowledge*, Cambridge, MA: MIT Press.

Owens, Joseph (1987) "In Defense of a Different Doppelganger," *Philosophical Review* 96: 521–54.

——(1993) "Content, causation, and psychophysical supervenience," *Philosophy of Science* 60 (2): 242–61.

Papineau, David (1993) *Philosophical Naturalism*, Oxford: Blackwell.

——(2005) "Naturalist Theories of Meaning," in Ernie Lepore and Barry Smith (eds), *The Oxford Handbook of Philosophy of Language*, Oxford: Oxford University Press, pp. 175–88.

Peacocke, Christopher (1981) "Demonstrative Thought and Psychological Explanation," *Synthese* 49: 187–217.

——(1993) "Externalist Explanation," *Proceedings of the Aristotelian Society* 67: 203–30.

Perry, John (1993) *The Problem of the Essential Indexical and Other Essays*, Oxford: Oxford University Press.

Pessin, Andrew and Goldberg, Sanford (eds) (1996) *The Twin Earth Chronicles*, New York: M. E. Sharp.

Prior, Elisabeth and Pargetter, Robert and Jackson, Frank (1982) "Three Theses about Dispositions," *American Philosophical Quarterly* 19: 251–57.

Pryor, James (2007) "What's Wrong with McKinsey-Style Reasoning," in Sanford Goldberg (ed.), *Internalism and Externalism in Semantics and Epistemology*, Oxford: Oxford University Press, pp. 177–200.

Putnam, Hilary (1975) "The Meaning of 'Meaning'," *Minnesota Studies in the Philosophy of Science* 7: 131–93.

——(1981) *Reason, Truth and History*, Cambridge: Cambridge University Press.

——(1990) "Is Water Necessarily H_2O?' in his *Realism with a Human Face*, Cambridge, MA: Harvard University Press, pp. 54–79.

——(1996) "Introduction," in Andrew Pessin and Sanford Goldberg (eds), *The Twin Earth Chronicles*, New York: M. E. Sharp, xv–xxii.

——(1999) "Brains in a Vat," in Keith DeRose and Ted A. Warfield (eds), *Skepticism: A Contemporary Reader*, Oxford: Oxford University Press, pp. 27–42.

Recanati, François (1993) *Direct Reference: From Language to Thought*, Oxford: Blackwell.

——(1997) "Can We Believe What We Do Not Understand?," *Mind and Language* 12: 84–100.

——(2000) "Deferential Concepts: A Response to Woodfield," *Mind and Language* 15: 452–60.

——(2007) *Perspectival Thought. A Plea for Moderate Relativism*, Oxford: Oxford University Press.

Rowlands, Mark (2003) *Externalism: Putting Mind and World Back Together Again*, Chesham: Acumen.

Russell, Bertrand (1994) "On Denoting' in Robert M. Harnish (ed.), *Basic Topics in the Philosophy of* Language, New York: Harvester Wheatsheaf, pp. 161–173. Originally published in 1905 in *Mind* 14: 479–93.

Salmon, Nathan (1981) *Reference and Essence*, Princeton: Princeton University Press.

——(1986) *Frege's Puzzle*, Cambridge, MA: Bradford Books, MIT Press.

——(2003) "Naming, Necessity, and Beyond," *Mind* 112: 475–92.

Sawyer, Sarah (1998) "Privileged Access to the World," *Australasian Journal of Philosophy* 76: 523–33.

——(1999) "My Language Disquotes," *Analysis* 59 (3): 206–11.

——(2003) "Conceptual Errors and Social Externalism," *Philosophical Quarterly* 53: 265–73.

Schantz, Richard (ed.) (2004) *The Externalist Challenge*, Berlin: Walter de Gruyter.

Schiffer, Stephen (1992) "Boghossian on Externalism and Inference," *Philosophical Issues* 2: 29–38.

Schroeter, Laura (2004) "The Rationalist Foundations of Chalmers' 2-D Semantics," *Philosophical Studies* 118: 227–55.

Searle, John R. (1958) "Proper Names," *Mind* 67: 166–73.

——(1983) *Intentionality: An Essay in the Philosophy of Mind*, Cambridge: Cambridge University Press.

Segal, Gabriel (1989) "The Return of the Individual," *Mind* 98: 39–57.

——(2000) *A Slim Book about Narrow Content*, Cambridge, MA: MIT Press.

——(2004) "Reference, Causal Powers, Externalist Intuitions, and Unicorns," in Richard Schantz (ed.), *The Externalist Challenge*. Berlin: Walter de Gruyter, pp. 329–46.

Segal, Gabriel (2007) "Cognitive Content and Propositional Attitude Attributions' in Brian McLaughlin and Jonathan Cohen (eds) *Contemporary Debates in the Philosophy of Mind*, Oxford: Blackwell.

——(2009) "Narrow Content," in Brian McLaughlin (ed.) *The Oxford Handbook of Philosophy of Mind*, New York: Oxford University Press, pp. 367–80.

Segal, Gabriel and Sober, Elliott (1991) "The Causal Efficacy of Content," *Philosophical Studies* 63: 1–30.

Shoemaker, Sydney (1995) "Moore's Paradox and Self-knowledge," *Philosophical Studies* 77: 211–28.

Smith, Michael (2004) "Humean Rationality' in Alfred Mele and Piers Rawling (eds), *The Handbook of Rationality*, New York: Oxford University Press, pp. 75-92.

Soames, Scott (1987) "Substitutivity," in Judith Thomson (ed.), *On Being and Saying*, Cambridge, MA: MIT Press, pp. 99–132.

——(1989) "Direct Reference, Propositional Attitudes and Semantic Content' *Philosophical Topics* 15: 44–87.

——(1998) "The Modal Argument: Wide Scope and Rigidified: Descriptions," *Noûs* 32: 1–22.

——(2002) *Beyond Rigidity: The Unfinished Semantic Agenda of "Naming and Necessity,"* Oxford: Oxford University Press.

——(2005) *Reference and Description: The Case against Two-Dimensionalism*, Princeton: Princeton University Press.

——(2007) "What Are Natural Kinds," *Philosophical Topics* 35 (1–2): 329–42.

Sosa, Ernest (2007) *A Virtue Epistemology: Apt Belief and Reflective Knowledge*, Oxford: Oxford University Press.

Stalnaker, Robert (1989) "On What's in the Head," *Philosophical Perspectives* 3: 287–319.

——(1990) "Narrow Content," in Anthony Anderson and Joseph Owens (eds), *Propositional Attitudes: The Role of Content in Logic, Language, and Mind*, Stanford: CSLI, pp. 131–46.

——(1997) "Reference and Necessity' in Bob Hale and Crispin Wright (eds), *A Companion to the Philosophy of Language*, Oxford; Blackwell, pp. 534–54.

——(1999) *Context and Content*, Oxford: Oxford University Press.

——(2001) "On Considering a Possible World as Actual," *Proceedings of the Aristotelian Society, Supplementary Volume* 75: 141–56.

Stanley, Jason (1997) "Names and Rigid Designation," in Bob Hale and Crispin Wright (eds), *A Companion to the Philosophy of Language*, Oxford: Blackwell Press, pp. 555–85.

Stich, Stephen (1978) "Autonomous Psychology and the Belief–Desire Thesis," *Monist* 61: 573–91.

——(1983) *From Folk Psychology to Cognitive Science*, Cambridge, MA: MIT Press.

Stoljar, Daniel (2008) "Distinctions in Distinction," in Jakob Hohwy and Jesper Kallestrup (eds), *Being Reduced: New Essays on Causation and Explanation in the Special Sciences*, Oxford: Oxford University Press, pp. 263–79.

Strawson, Peter F. (1950) "On Referring," *Mind* 59: 320–44.

Thau, Michael (2002) *Consciousness and Cognition*, New York: Oxford University Press.

Tye, Michael (2009) *Consciousness Revisited: Materialism without Phenomenal Concepts*, Cambridge, MA: MIT Press.

Vahid, Hamid (2003) "Externalism, Slow Switching and Privileged Self-knowledge," *Philosophy and Phenomenological Research* 66: 370–88.

Warfield, Ted A. (1992) "Privileged Self-knowledge and Externalism Are Compatible," *Analysis* 52 (4): 232–37.

——(1995) "Knowing the World and Knowing Our Minds," *Philosophy and Phenomenological Research* 55: 525–45.

——(1997) "Externalism, Privileged Self-knowledge, and the Irrelevance of Slow Switching," *Analysis* 57 (4): 282–84.

——(1999) "A Priori Knowledge of the World: Knowing the World by Knowing Our Minds," in Keith DeRose and Ted A. Warfield (eds), *Skepticism: A Contemporary Reader*, Oxford: Oxford University Press, pp. 76–92.

White, Stephen L. (1982) "Partial Character and the Language of Thought," *Pacific Philosophical Quarterly* 63: 347–65.

Wikforss, Åsa M. (2001) "Social Externalism and Conceptual Errors," *Philosophical Quarterly* 51: 217–31.

Williamson, Timothy (2000) *Knowledge and Its Limits*, Oxford: Oxford University Press.

Wilson, Robert A. (1992) "Individualism, Causal Powers, and Explanation,"
    Philosophical Studies 68: 103–39.

——(1995) *Cartesian Psychology and Physical Minds: Individualism and the
    Sciences of Mind*, New York: Cambridge University Press.

Wittgenstein, Ludwig (1968) *Philosophical investigations*, trans. G. E. M.
    Anscombe, New York: Macmillan. Originally published in 1953.

Wright, Crispin (1991) "Scepticism and Dreaming: Imploding the Demon,"
    Mind 100: 87–116.

——(1992) "On Putnam's Proof That We Are Not Brains-in-a-Vat," *Proceedings
    of the Aristotelian Society* 92: 67–94.

——(1998) "Self-knowledge: The Wittgensteinian Legacy," in Crispin Wright,
    Barry Smith and Cynthia Macdonald (eds), *Knowing Our Own Minds*,
    Oxford: Oxford University Press, pp. 13–46.

——(2000) "Cogency and Question-begging: Some Reflections on McKinsey's
    Paradox and Putnam's Proof," *Philosophical Issues* 10: 140–63.

——(2003) "Some Reflections on the Acquisition of Warrant by Inference," in
    Susana Nuccetelli (ed.), *New Essays on Semantic Externalism, Scepticism,
    and Self-knowledge*, Cambridge, MA: MIT Press, pp. 57–77.

Wright, Crispin, Smith, Barry and Macdonald, Cynthia (eds) (1998) *Knowing
    Our Own Minds*, Oxford: Oxford University Press.

Yablo, Stephen (1992) "Mental Causation," *Philosophical Review* 101: 245–80.

——(1997) "Wide Causation," *Philosophical Perspectives* 11: 251–81.

——(2003) "Causal Relevance," *Philosophical Issues* 13: 316–28.

Zimmerman, Aaron (2008) "Self-knowledge: Rationalism vs. Empiricism,"
    Philosophical Compass 3 (2): 325–52.

INDEX

acquaintance 66–68, 90, 96, 101–2, 104, 112, 114, 123, 241n
Adams, Frederick 211, 234n, 247n
agnosticism 181, 233n
Aizawa, Ken 234n
Armstrong, David 126–27
avowals 128–29, 241n

Baker, Lynne Rudder 247n
Ball, Derek 100, 176
Bar-on, Dorit 145–46, 156, 159
behaviour 3–5, 8, 53, 74–76, 79–80, 84–85, 90–91, 120, 123, 129–30, 152, 155, 185, 191, 206–8, 221, 225n, 247n; and action 190–91; causal explanation of 7, 9, 45, 106–8, 112, 189, 192, 198–204, 207, 210–12, 214; intentional 190–94, 197–99, 209; narrow 108, 193–99; wide 193–99, 207, 210–11

Block, Ned 205, 210, 232n, 239n, 248n
Boghossian, Paul 97–99, 122–23, 142, 177, 235n, 241–43n, 245n; and incompatibilism 7–8, 139–44; and reasoning 149–53, 155
brains-in-a-vat 8, 163–73, 176, 183, 244–45n
Braun, David 124, 229n
Brewer, Bill 8, 182
Brown, Jessica 8, 92, 156, 184, 233n, 243n, 245–46n; and incompatibilism 173, 176–77, 179–80
Brueckner, Anthony 8, 166, 183, 184, 242n; and incompatibilism 177, 179, 182; and scepticism about self-knowledge 157–59, 162, 244–46n; and brains-in-a-vat 170, 172
Burge, Tyler 6–7, 83, 92, 97, 99–100, 113–15, 123–24, 139, 143, 145–46,

148, 153, 156, 177, 180, 212, 225n, 228n, 231–36n, 239–43n, 247n; arthritis argument 69–74, 77–78, 90–91; and memory 146, 153; and psychological explanation 108–9, 192, 208; and self-knowledge 126, 132–38, 155; self-verifying judgements 140–42, 155

causal exclusion 188
causal redundancy 197–200, 211
causation 8, 9, 32, 60, 78, 82, 84, 118, 120–21, 128, 153, 163, 168, 187–88, 190, 199, 211, 214, 230n, 244–47n; and locality 8, 189, 191, 210; mental 106, 109, 185–91, 193–95, 200, 204–6, 208, 210–11, 219, 243n; structuring and triggering 209–10, 212
Chalmers, David 4, 6, 7, 9, 75, 105, 109, 116, 123, 203, 230–32n, 246–47n; and narrow content 112, 123, 238–40n; two-dimensional semantics 110–11, 228n, 238–39n
charity principle 84 Clark, Andy 9, 230n, 232n
closure principle 158, 161, 164–66, 174–75, 179, 183–84, 214, 244–46n
cognitive significance 5, 18–21, 33–35, 45, 54, 59, 78, 96, 105, 202–3
concept 2, 6, 11, 51, 65, 73–76, 78–79, 81–82, 86, 90, 107, 128–29, 132–34, 139, 143–44, 153, 155–57, 159, 170, 174–77, 179–81, 198, 200–201, 203, 208, 213, 225n, 228–29n, 232–33n, 239n, 241–44n, 246n; descriptive 65–69, 90, 99, 180, 236n; atomic 97–98, 100, 178, 200; compound/compositional

97–98, 178; indexical 112–17; natural kind 7, 67–68, 93, 98, 100, 112–17, 176–78, 180–82, 184, 200, 236n; object-dependent 93–100, 123, 176–78, 181–82, 184, 200, 236n
content 3, 5–9 13–17, 20–21, 23, 26–27, 31–32, 35, 61, 71, 74–78, 90, 93, 95–96; 103–9, 112, 121–22, 124, 130–34, 139–40, 143–49, 157–74, 187–89, 200–203, 219–21, 226n, 234–37n; assertoric 45, 56; epistemic 110–12; historical theory of 83, 90; illusions of 94–100, 179; narrow 6–8, 67, 83, 92, 105, 107–9, 111–12, 119, 121–24, 190–97, 200–201, 210–11, 238n, 240n, 247n; propositional 2, 5–6, 17–22, 33–34, 36–39, 41–42, 44, 48–50, 52, 55, 58, 62–63, 69–70, 73, 93–97, 101, 111, 116–17, 125–26, 145, 189, 202, 227–31n; representational 1–2, 6, 17, 70, 81–83, 91, 119; semantic 12, 16, 53, 59, 71, 105, 107; subjunctive 110–12; stereotypical 59, 74, 105; teleological theories of 83, 222; wide 6–8, 70, 91, 109, 122, 124, 134–35, 139–40, 143–44, 149, 165, 174, 177–78, 204–10, 240n, 248n
context 4, 26, 30, 32–33, 35, 46, 48, 57, 81, 108, 113–15, 154, 156, 170, 172, 193–94, 196–97, 202–3, 219, 237n, 244–45n, 247n; extensional 23, 218; intentional 23–24, 41, 50–51, 52, 56, 218; modal 5, 41, 44, 50–51, 56; of utterance 25, 48–49, 95, 111, 201, 203, 215, 220, 228n

counterfactuals 68, 72–77, 100, 102, 104, 109–10, 113, 123, 165, 167, 170, 193–94, 198–99, 203, 215–16, 222–23, 231n, 238n, 245–46n

Crane, Tim 5, 76–77, 187, 211, 231n, 246n

Crawford, Sean 199

critical reasoning 7, 135–38, 141, 155, 233n, 243n

Davidson, Donald 70, 84, 190; account of events 187; and radical interpretation 84–86; and self-knowledge 142, 146, 241n; Swampman 79–83, 86–91, 222, 234n

Davies, Martin 124, 174, 238n, 245n

de re/de dicto 37, 54, 71, 73, 216

Descartes, René 126, 134, 141, 155, 173; description 4, 11; 13–15, 36–41, 66, 190, 221, 231n; essential 47; other-dependent 46, 75, 233n; reference-fixing 36, 114–15; rigidified 48, 51, 55, 124, 220

descriptive names 38–39

descriptive proposition 26, 36, 38, 94, 229n

descriptivism 3–5, 10, 12–15, 21, 23, 32, 34–36, 40–41, 45, 56, 100–101, 116, 216, 224n, 226–27n, 229n, 236n, 239n; causal 231n; rigidified 50, 56, 58, 237n

direct reference 4–5, 24, 34–37, 39, 49, 51, 56–57, 93–94, 105, 124, 180, 220, 228n, 244n

disjunctive property 117

dispositional property 123, 194, 204–5

division of linguistic labour 75, 233n

Donnellan, Keith 75, 233n, 236n, 239n

doppelgänger challenge 8, 197–204

Dretske, Fred 9, 82, 86, 234n, 246n; criticism of closure principle 244n; and psychological explanation 209, 211

Dummett, Michael 4, 38, 45, 130, 226n; and descriptivism 13, 43; and communication 27, 33

Ebbs, Gary 161, 183

Egan, Frances 70

empty reference 68–69, 86–87, 90, 94, 96–98, 104, 116, 178, 182, 236n

entitlement 132, 134–37, 141, 156, 241n

epiphenomenalism 186

epistemic transparency 55, 57, 127, 130–32, 147, 149, 155, 179, 243n

essence 57, 59, 92, 201; biological 38, 47, 62, 64–65, 178; historical 88–89, 91

Evans, Gareth 95–96, 127, 131, 177, 179, 225–26n, 228n, 238–39n

explanation 54, 65, 94, 151, 154, 198, 207; causal 9, 106, 186, 188–89, 191–92, 195, 198–99, 201, 207–12, 214, 246–47n; program/process 208–9, 212; rationalizing 190; psychological 3, 108, 193, 200, 212

externalism 9, 92, 145, 156, 184, 230n, 234n; epistemological 156; historical 83, 85–86, 91–92; memory 145; natural kind 63, 69, 72, 83; semantic 2–4, 7–9, 62–63, 83, 89, 92, 99–100, 105, 107, 109, 117–18, 125, 132, 139–40, 149–50, 152–53, 155–57, 161–63, 167–68, 170, 172–78, 180–85, 189, 200, 207, 217, 221–22, 231n, 235n, 237n,

242–45n; social 73–74, 77, 83, 134, 148, 225n, 232n
extrinsic property 62, 119, 178, 189, 191, 193–94, 210, 218, 228n, 245n, 247n

Falvey, Kevin 142, 146, 160–61, 165–66, 171, 180, 183, 241–44n
Farkas, Katalin 92, 230n, 236n, 242n
Feynman, Richard 205–6
first- and second-order property 204–5, 217
Fodor, Jerry 8, 92, 191, 233–35n, 237–38n, 240n, 242n, 247n; modal argument
for narrow content 190–97, 210–12
Frege, Gottlob 3, 5, 11–12, 17–19, 24, 26, 28, 32–34, 57, 60, 63, 105, 119, 124, 224–25n, 228n; distinction between sense and reference 4, 15, 96; identity argument 15–21, 35
function 1–2, 11, 25, 72, 88, 95, 98, 103–4, 110–11, 122–23, 130, 135, 138, 196, 201, 203, 220n, 223n, 234n, 237–38n, 240n; indicator 87; teleological 82–83, 86, 91, 222n

Gertler, Brie 156, 179, 246n
Gibbons, John 142, 160–61, 177–78, 183, 242
Goldberg, Nathaniel 84, 86, 234n
Goldberg, Sanford 92, 100, 145–46, 153–54, 156, 177, 211, 231n, 241n, 243–44n, 246n

Häggqvist, Sören 179, 235n
hallucination 95, 198–99

Heil, John 139, 142, 211, 234n
Hume, David 37, 103–4, 118, 195, 237n, 240n

individualism 92, 156, 184, 211, 230n; methodological 192–93, 219
individuation 20, 60, 68, 86, 106, 153; external 7, 58, 62–63, 74, 91, 98, 100, 117–18, 122, 134, 139, 142–43, 176–77, 182, 184, 223
intension 110, 112, 123, 203, 223, 238n
internalism 9, 105, 156; semantic 4, 9, 63, 92, 101–3, 125, 156, 221, 242n; natural kind 63
inter-/intra-world narrow property 7, 120–22, 240n
intrinsic property 7, 51, 62, 74, 119–24, 178, 189, 191, 195, 204, 210, 218, 228–29n, 245n
introspection 126–27, 129–30, 143, 146–47, 158, 163, 171, 178, 182–83, 240n, 243n

Jackson, Frank 4–7, 103, 105, 116, 123–24, 226–27n, 231n, 235n, 247n; and descriptivism 4, 13, 101, 228n, 231–33n, 236n; and mental causation 205–6; and narrow content 7, 112, 238–40n, 248n; and program explanations 9, 207, 211–12, 248n

Kallestrup, Jesper 184, 225n, 229n, 237n, 243n, 246n
Kaplan, David 6, 25, 124, 202, 226n, 228n, 237n, 239n; notion of character 95, 111, 203
Kim, Jaegwon 187, 210, 246n

kind 2–3, 10–11, 13, 28, 32, 44–45,
    48, 58, 77, 90, 97, 99, 113, 119,
    123, 176–77, 179, 184, 203–4, 206,
    222; artificial 11, 70; historical 88;
    natural 3, 5, 10–11, 52, 59, 63,
    65–66, 68–70, 87–90, 99–100,
    116–17, 124, 174–75, 177–78, 182,
    190, 193, 195, 224–25n, 229n,
    231n, 233n, 235–36n, 238–39n; real
    87–89, 91; social 3
Korman, Daniel 98, 100, 235–36n
Kripke, Saul 3, 62, 114, 178, 225n,
    227–29n, 238n, 241n; modal
    argument 5, 40–45, 56–57; puzzle
    about belief 24–26, 33, 54, 77,
    225n; and rigid designation 36–40,
    105, 226n
Kroon, Frederick 13, 46, 226n, 229n,
    231n

Lepore, Ernest 84–86, 92
Lewis, David 4–7, 39, 48, 116, 124,
    228n, 231n, 239n; account of
    counterfactuals 232n; and
    descriptivism 13–14, 101, 231n;
    and egocentric thoughts 103–5,
    112, 123, 237n
Loar, Brian 77, 105, 237n
Ludlow, Peter 94, 156, 184, 235n; and
    memory 242n; and slow switching
    148–49

McDowell, John 6, 95–96, 124, 177, 179
McGinn, Colin 6, 70–71, 105–8, 111,
    123, 174–75, 235n, 238n, 246–47n
McKinsey, Michael 8, 174, 176–78,
    182–84, 245n
McLaughlin, Brian 8, 34, 57, 92, 100,
    177–78, 180, 184, 235n, 242–43n

methodological individualism
    192–93, 219
methodological solipsism 107, 193,
    195, 219, 247n
Mill, John S. 15, 34, 116, 224n, 229n
Millikan, Ruth 82, 87–88, 91
motivating reason 190–91

natural selection 6, 80, 83, 91,
    222, 234n
Noonan, Harold 8, 34, 244n;
    the redundancy argument
    198–200, 210
Noordhof, Paul 246n
normative reason 191
Nozick, Robert 165
Nuccetelli, Susana 156, 177, 184

object-dependent state/thought
    6, 93–97, 124, 177–78,
    197–200, 204
Owens, Joseph 108–9, 142, 146,
    160–61, 165, 171, 183, 192,
    241–44n, 247n

Papineau, David 82, 92
Peacocke, Christopher 108, 247–48n
Perry, John 52–53, 103, 202,
    228n, 237n
Pettit, Philip 9, 124, 207, 211–12,
    240n, 247n
phenomenal character 1–2, 9, 70,
    126, 232–33n, 240–41n
phlogiston 69, 98, 178, 235–36n
possible world 5, 37–40, 42–44,
    47–51, 56, 67, 101–4, 111–13,
    116–17, 120–23, 149, 161, 165,
    215–16, 219–23, 226n, 228n, 232n,
    238–39n; centred 103, 110, 112,

203, 238n; considered as actual/
counterfactual 110–12, 123, 203,
223, 238n; nomologically 37, 42,
65, 120, 215; metaphysically 38, 42,
65, 88–89, 91, 178, 215
pragmatics 30, 219, 225n; and
pragmatic implicature 53–54, 57,
224n
Prior, Elisabeth 124
propositional attitude 1, 4, 9, 34, 57,
71, 81, 106, 121, 127, 142, 151–52,
188, 192, 220, 234n, 242–43n
Pryor, James 8, 179, 239n
psychology 92, 129–30, 192, 195,
210–12, 237n; folk 106, 186, 197,
210; cognitive 109, 192
Putnam, Hilary 3, 7, 46, 75, 78,
83, 87–88, 92, 107, 112, 121, 123,
177, 183, 231n, 232n, 237n, 242n,
244n, 247n; and Twin Earth 5–6,
58–60, 63–65, 67, 69–70, 72,
90–91, 96, 102, 104–5, 113–16,
196, 227n, 229–30n, 232–33n;
and brains-in-a-vat 8, 163–64,
166–73, 176, 183–84

radical interpretation 6, 79, 84–85,
91, 234n
Recanati, Francois 34, 57, 124, 226n,
233n, 237n
referentialism 4–5, 15–16, 20, 22, 24,
32, 35–36, 51–53, 55–58, 94, 116–17,
220, 224n, 226n
relativized proposition 103–4, 124,
237n
relevant alternatives conception of
knowledge 37, 140, 144–48,
155–56, 160–61, 165–67, 169–70,
183, 215, 217, 220, 242–44n

rigid designation 5–6, 35, 37–40,
42–45, 47–51, 55–57, 101–3, 109,
115–17, 203, 205–6, 220–21,
226–27n, 229n, 237–39n; de facto
38–39, 56, 220; de jure 39, 220;
different from direct reference
37–39
rigidification 45–48, 220–21, 229n,
237n
role/filler property 204–5, 217, 248n
Russell, Bertrand 4, 13, 131

Salmon, Nathan 5, 34, 57, 92, 124,
225n, 227–29n, 239n
Sawyer, Sarah 177, 181, 232n, 244n
scepticism 125–26, 159–60, 163,
170–72, 183–84, 214–17, 245n;
about the external world 8, 125,
162–66, 171–73, 183, 244n; about
self-knowledge/content 8, 125,
157–63, 172, 183, 244n
Schiffer, Stephen 152–53
Searle, John 4, 13–14, 231n, 237n,
242n
Segal, Gabriel 5, 77–78, 92, 124, 212,
231n, 234n, 247n; and narrow
content 202–3, 235n
self-knowledge 7–8, 125–28, 130,
132–34, 138, 145–48, 154–56, 159,
163, 172, 174–75, 181, 221, 240–
43n; incompatible with semantic
externalism 7, 125, 132, 139, 143,
149, 155–57, 161, 184, 217
semantic deference 6, 31, 46, 73,
75–76, 78, 91, 99, 148, 221, 228n,
233n
semantics 7, 11, 20, 34, 53, 105, 114,
116, 123–24, 156, 219–20, 236n;
descriptive 13, 96, 235n;

descriptivist 98, 235n;
   foundational 13, 57, 96, 235n;
   referentialist 7, 226n, 235n; teleo-
   6, 82–83, 88, 91–92, 222; two-
   dimensional 124, 223, 239n
semantic value 11–12, 15
Shoemaker, Sydney 242n
singular proposition 53–55, 57,
   93–94, 124, 202, 220, 229n,
   233n, 237n
Soames, Scott 5, 57, 226–29n,
   236n, 239n
Stalnaker, Robert 7, 13, 109, 119,
   124, 226n, 231–32n, 236n,
   239–40n
Stich, Stephen 192
supervenience 7, 60–64, 70–71,
   73–74, 80, 83, 93, 106–7, 109,
   119–20, 123, 191–92, 195–96, 204,
   221–22, 230n, 235n

Swampman 6, 79–89, 91, 167–68,
   177, 222, 234

triangulation 81–82, 86,
   91–92, 234n
Tye, Michael 8–9, 76, 100,
   177–78, 180, 184, 232–33n,
   235n, 240–43n

underdetermination 78, 159–61,
   166, 223n

Warfield, Ted 147–48, 172, 184, 246n
Wikforss, Åsa 179, 232n, 235n
Williamson, Timothy 9, 206–7, 211–12
Wilson, Robert 92, 211, 247n
Wright, Crispin 156, 169–70,
   172–73, 183–84, 241n, 244–45n

Yablo, Stephen 231n, 246–48n